The College of Law
of England and Wales
14 Store Street
Bloomsbury
London
WC1E 7DE

FOR REFERENCE ONLY

The College of Law, Bloomsbury
S08951

Trade Mark Law and Sharing Names

Trade Mark Law and Sharing Names

Exploring Use of the Same Mark by Multiple Undertakings

Edited by

Ilanah Simon Fhima

Lecturer and Co-Director of the Institute of Brand and Innovation Law, University College London, UK

Edward Elgar
Cheltenham, UK • Northampton, MA, USA

© The editor and contributors severally 2009

All rights reserved. No part of this publication may be reproduced, stored in a retrieval system or transmitted in any form or by any means, electronic, mechanical or photocopying, recording, or otherwise without the prior permission of the publisher.

Published by
Edward Elgar Publishing Limited
The Lypiatts
15 Lansdown Road
Cheltenham
Glos GL50 2JA
UK

Edward Elgar Publishing, Inc.
William Pratt House
9 Dewey Court
Northampton
Massachusetts 01060
USA

A catalogue record for this book
is available from the British Library

Library of Congress Control Number: 2008943828

Mixed Sources
Product group from well-managed
forests and other controlled sources
www.fsc.org Cert no. SA-COC-1565
© 1996 Forest Stewardship Council

FSC

ISBN 978 1 84720 279 6

Typeset by Cambrian Typesetters, Camberley, Surrey
Printed and bound in Great Britain by MPG Books Ltd, Bodmin, Cornwall

Contents

List of contributors	vii
Table of cases	xi

PART I OVERVIEW

1	Introduction *Ilanah Simon Fhima*	3
2	An economic perspective on shared name issues in trade mark law *Andrew Griffiths*	13

PART II REGISTRABILITY ISSUES

3	The rise and fall of honest concurrent use *Phillip Johnson*	31
4	Coexistence in Community trade mark disputes: when is it recognized and what are its implications? *Arnaud Folliard-Monguiral*	51
5	The approach of the UK-IPO to co-ownership of registered trade marks: nanny leaves the Registry, but not completely *Edward Smith*	71
6	The business end of collective and certification marks *Dev Gangjee*	79

PART III SHARED NAME LITIGATION

7	Same name, different goods – death of the principle of specialty *Ilanah Simon Fhima*	101
8	Is there an own-name defence in the common law tort of passing-off? The implications of *Asprey*, *Reed* and *Newman v Adlem* *Christopher Wadlow*	129
9	The own-name defence in relation to registered trade mark law *Ashley Roughton*	141

v

PART IV SHARED NAME TRANSACTIONS

10	Co-branding *Spyros Maniatis and Stefan Schwarzkopf*	155
11	Splitting trade marks and the competition laws *Thomas Hays*	171
12	Aspects of sublicensing *Neil Wilkof*	185

Index 199

Contributors

Dr Dev Gangjee is a graduate of the National Law School of India (BA, LLB) and the University of Oxford (BCL, DPhil), where he was a Rhodes Scholar. Dev is presently a Lecturer at the London School of Economics, where he teaches Intellectual Property, as well as the Law of Obligations. He has a primary research interest in Intellectual Property and was an invited researcher at the Institute of Intellectual Property, Tokyo. His publications include articles and reports on IP, with an emphasis on geographical indications and trade mark law. He has also acted as an expert in IP litigation, as well as on governmental advisory panels.

Andrew Griffiths is a Solicitor and Reader in Law at the University of Manchester. His teaching and research interests include Trade Mark Law, Company Law and Law-and-Economics. He is the author of *Contracting with Companies* (Hart Publishing, 2005).

Dr Thomas Hays, BA, JD, LLM, has a PhD from Cambridge University in England where he specialized in intellectual property law. He is a member of the Centre for Intellectual Property Law at the Molengraaff Institute for Private Law Research in Utrecht, The Netherlands. He is licensed as an attorney in the United States and a solicitor in England and Wales. He practises law with Taylor Vinters Solicitors in Cambridge, England.

Phillip Johnson is a barrister practising at 7 New Square. He was a legal adviser to the UK Intellectual Property Office from 2003 to 2007, during which time he worked on the implementation of various Directives and Treaties, as well as most changes made to domestic intellectual property legislation. He also worked on a number of trade mark cases before the Court of Justice, including *Gillette*, *Adam Opel* and *Bovemij*.

He is a visiting Senior Fellow at Queen Mary Intellectual Property Research Institute, University of London and lectures on their professional courses. He is the review editor of the *Journal of Intellectual Property Law and Practice* and a contributing editor on private international law for *Jowitt's Dictionary of English Law* (Sweet & Maxwell, London, forthcoming). He is also the author of *Ambush Marketing: A Practical Guide to Protecting the Brand of a Sporting Event* (Sweet & Maxwell, London, 2007).

Dr Spyros Maniatis is Professor in Intellectual Property at Queen Mary, University of London. From September 2008 he is taking over the position of Director of Queen Mary's Centre of Commercial Law Studies. His teaching and research focus on trade mark and unfair competition law. His interests also cover the history, politics, and economics of intellectual property and innovation.

Spyros has published work on the justifications and history of trade mark and unfair competition laws, the economics of intellectual property, and contemporary issues in trade mark law. He is currently working on the second edition of *Trade Marks in Europe: A Practical Jurisprudence* (Sweet & Maxwell, London, 2006). He is also co-author of *Trade Marks, Trade Names and Unfair Competition, World Law and Practice* (with Garrigues and Olsen) (Sweet & Maxwell, London, 1996 and updates) and *Domain Names, Global Practice and Procedure* (with Olsen, Wood, and Zographos) (Sweet & Maxwell, London, 2000 and updates). He is a member of the Athens Bar.

Arnaud Folliard-Monguiral is admitted to the Bar of Paris and is qualified as a Trade Mark & Design Professional Representative. He joined the Office for Harmonization in the Internal Market (OHIM) in 2000. He is a member of the Industrial Property Litigation Unit (IPLU). As such, he is appointed agent of the OHIM in proceedings before the Court of First Instance and the European Court of Justice.

Arnaud writes a monthly review of Community Trade Mark related case law for the French IP review 'Propriété Industrielle'. Arnaud is also the author of a number of articles, the latest of which is dedicated to the case law of the Community courts (in the *Journal of Intellectual Property Law and Practice*, April 2007).

Ashley Roughton is a barrister practising at Hogarth Chambers, where he specializes in intellectual property and data protection law. He is the co-author of *The Modern Law of Trade Marks* and *The Modern Law of Patents*, both of which are published by LexisNexis, London. Ashley is contributing editor of the third edition of *Intellectual Property in Europe*, published by Sweet & Maxwell, and edits the intellectual property section of *The Civil Court Practice* ('the Green Book'). He is also a council member of the International Association for the Protection of Industrial Property and a committee member of The Competition Law Association.

Before becoming a barrister in 1992, Ashley was an engineer with Mercedes Benz. He took his PhD at Cambridge and BSc at King's College, London. He also has an MSc in economics from City University.

Stefan Schwarzkopf is Lecturer in Marketing in the School of Business and

Management at Queen Mary, University of London. Previously, he studied modern history, history of science, and human biology at the University of Jena (Germany). After graduating in modern history, he worked in the market research department at Leo Burnett advertising agency in Frankfurt. His main research interests are in the relevance of political culture and political concepts for the study of marketing. He is currently finishing his PhD thesis at Birkbeck College on the politics and cultures of advertising in early twentieth-century Britain. His latest article in *Contemporary British History* looks at the cross-links between the cultures of the Cold War and the advertising industry in the United Kingdom. He has published on various aspects of cultural transfer through marketing and advertising between America and Europe. New research projects include a study of the Austro-American 'consumer guru' Ernest Dichter and the complexity of the co-evolution of American and European marketing and consumer cultures in the twentieth century.

Dr Ilanah Simon Fhima is a lecturer at University College, London, where she is also co-director of the Institute of Brand and Innovation Law. Ilanah completed her PhD on trade mark dilution in Europe and the United States as a Herchel Smith Research Scholar at the Intellectual Property Research Institute of Queen Mary, University of London. She has published in the UK and the United States. Ilanah is deputy editor of the European Trade Mark Reports and serves on the editorial board of the European Intellectual Property Review. She is also co-founder and a contributor to the IPKat intellectual property weblog (www.ipkat.com).

Ilanah's research focuses on intellectual property law, and trade mark law in particular. She is especially interested in infringement issues and the influence of European law on intellectual property law and has considerable research experience in comparative trade mark law.

Edward Smith is a hearing officer and is responsible for trade marks training at the UK-IPO. He holds a Masters Degree in Intellectual Property Law from the University of Glamorgan. He has a specific interest in unconventional trade marks and the blurring of traditional boundaries between IP rights in respect of which such marks in particular can give rise. He has had a number of articles and case commentaries published in the academic press, including pieces on the *Dyson* and *Limoncello* cases.

In the past Edward has served as Secretary to the Standing Advisory Committee on Industrial Property (then called SACIP, now renamed SABIP).

Professor Christopher Wadlow holds a Chair in Law at the Norwich Law School, University of East Anglia. He formerly practised intellectual property law at the London offices of international law firm Simmons & Simmons, and is the author of *The Law of Passing-off: Unfair Competition by Misrepresentation* (3rd edn, Sweet & Maxwell, London, 2004).

Neil Wilkof is a partner and head of the intellectual property and information technology department of the law firm of Herzog Fox & Neeman, Tel-Aviv, Israel. He is the author of the first edition and is co-author with Daniel Burkitt of the second edition of *Trade Mark Licensing* (Sweet & Maxwell) and is a co-editor of *Intellectual Property in the Global Marketplace* (John Wiley). He serves as an adjunct lecturer at the University of Haifa, Tel-Aviv University and the Interdisciplinary Center Herzliya.

Table of cases

UNITED KINGDOM

ACEC [1965] RPC 369, 373 (Reg) **45**

Ad-Lib Club v Granville [1971] FSR 1 **45**

Addley Bourne v Swan (1903) 20 RPC 105, 117-20 **33**

Allen & Hansburys Limited's (Salbutamol) Patent [1987] RPC 327 **197**

Andrew (John) v Kuehnrich (1913) 30 RPC 677 **17**

Annabel's (Berkeley Square) Ltd v G Shock (t/a Annabel's Escort Agency) [1972] FSR 261 **107**

Aristoc v Rysta [1945] AC 68, HL **16**

Asprey & Garrard Ltd v WRA (Guns) Ltd and Asprey [2001] EWCA Civ 1499; [2002] ETMR 47, reversing [2002] FSR 30 **129–139, 150**

Bali Trade Mark (No 2) [1978] FSR 193, 221 **45**

Barclays Bank plc v RBS Advanta [1997] ETMR 199; [1996] RPC 307; (1996) 15 Tr LR 262; The Times 8 Feb 1996 **145, 146**

Baywatch Production Co Inc v The Home Video Channel [1997] FSR 22 **122**

Bristol Myers Squibb v Paranova [1996] ETMR 1 **25**

British Lead Mills Ltd's Application [1958] 17 RPC 425 **73**

British Sugar plc v James Robertson & Sons Ltd [1996] RPC 281, [1997] ETMR 118 **115**

Burgess v Burgess (1853) 3 de GM&G 896; (1853) 43 ER 90, CA **129**

Cable & Wireless plc v British Telecommunications plc [1998] FSR 383 **146**

Chocosuisse Union des Fabricants Suisse de Chocolat v Cadbury [1999] ETMR 1020 **81**

Clark v Freeman (1848) 11 Beav 112 (50 ER 759) **34**

Codas TM [2001] RPC 14 (Reg) **46, 48**

Commissioners of Inland Revenue v Muller & Co's Margarine [1901] AC 217 **20**

Consorzio del Prosciutto di Parma v Marks & Spencer plc and others [1991] RPC 351, 368, CA **149**

Continental Shelf 128 Ltd v Hebrew University of Jerusalem, sub nom Continental Shelf 128 Ltd's Trade Mark Application, Einstein Trade Mark [2007] RPC 23 **71–72, 73**

Dent v Turpin (1861) 1 J & H 139 (70 ER 1003), 144 ER 1005 **33, 34, 35**

Dewhurst & Sons' Application [1896] 2 Ch 137 **40**

Edelsten v Edelsten (1863) 1 De G J & S 185 (46 ER 72) **32**

Electrix App [1957] RPC 369 **44**

Emperor of Austria v Day and Kossuth (1861) 3 DE G F & J 217 (45 ER 861) **34**
Erven Warnick BV v J Townsend & Sons (Hull) Ltd [1980] RPC 31 **108**
Esure Insurance Ltd v Direct Line Insurance plc [2007] EWHC 1557 (Ch), 29 Jun 2007, unrep **119, 123**
European Limited v Economist Newspaper Limited [1996] EMLR 394; [1996] FSR 431 **146**
Fiorelli Trade Mark [2007] RPC 18 **74**
Focus Business (2004) O-023-04 (Reg) **48**
Fortuna-Werke [1957] RPC 84 (Reg) **45**
GE Trade Marks [1972] 1 WLR 729 **32, 33, 44**
Glaxo Group v Dowelhurst [2000] FSR 529 **16**
Granada [1979] RPC 303 (Reg) **43, 44**
Habib Bank Ltd v Habib Bank AG Zurich [1981] 1 WLR 1265 **34**
Harrods Ltd v Harodian School Ltd [1996] RPC 697 **109**
Harrods Ltd v Harrods (Buenos Aires) Ltd and another [1997] FSR 420, ChD; [1999] FSR 187, CA **188**
Henderson and another v Radio Corporation Pty Ltd [1969] RPC 218 **105, 106, 108**
Hodson, Tessie & Co's TM (1881) [1902] 86 LTNS 188 **36, 39**
Holt [1957] RPC 289, 294 **45**
Hyde & Co's TM (1878) [1884] 54 LJ Ch 395 **37**

Inland Revenue Commissioners v Muller & Co's Margarine Limited [1901] AC 217, HL(E) **149**
Intel Corp Inc v CPM United Kingdom Ltd [2007] ETMR 59 **124, 126**
Irvine and anor v Talksport Ltd [2002] 1 WLR 2355 **110**
Jackson v Napper (1886) 35 Ch D 162 **38**
James & Sons v Wafer Razor (1932) 49 RPC 597 **34**
Jelly's Case (1878) 51 LJ Ch 639 **35, 38**
John Fitton & Co's Application (1949) 66 RPC 110, 112 **43**
L'Oreal SA and ors v Bellure SA and ors [2008] ETMR 1 **111**
Leather Cloth Company v The American Leather Cloth Company (1863) 4 De G J & S 137 (46 ER 868); (1865) 11 HLC 523 (11 ER 1435) **34**
Legal Aid Trade Mark Application, Re, H Ct 2000, No 00817, unrep but noted **85**
Lego System Aktieselskab and another v Lego M Lemelstrich Ltd [198] FSR 155 **108, 109**
Lehmann & Co's App (1918) 35 RPC 92, 99 **42**
Leonardt, Re (1878) Sebastian's Digest 610 **39**
Lyndon's TM (1886) 32 Ch D 109 **38**
Lyngstad v Anabas Products Ltd [1977] FSR 62 **108**
McCulloch v Lewis A May (Produce Distributors) Ltd (1948) 65 RPC 58 **104, 105, 106, 108, 110, 112**
Maeder (1916) 33 RPC 77 **42**

Major Bros v Franklin [1908] 1 KB 712 **16**
Mitchell, Re (1878) Sebastian's Digest 611 **39**
Nestlé SA's Trade Mark Application [2005] RPC 5 **75**
Newman (I N) Ltd v Adlem [2006] FSR 16 **129–139**
Nicholson's Application (1931) 48 RPC 227, CA **17**
Origins Natural Resources Inc v Origin Clothing Ltd [1995] FSR 280 **34**
Parker-Knoll v Knoll International [1962] RPC 265 (HL(E)) **129, 130, 133, 135, 151**
Parkington's Application (1946) 63 RPC 171 **44**
Pebble Beach Co v Lombard Brands Ltd [2003] ETMR 21 **125**
Peddie (1944) 61 PRC 31, 36-7 **44**
Perry v Truefitt (1842) 6 Beav 66 (49 ER 749) **33**
Pirie and Sons (1933) 50 RPC 147 **42, 43, 44, 73**
Portogram (1952) 69 RPC 241 (Reg) **44**
Powell, Re and Pratt, Re (1878) Sebastian's Digest 589 **37**
Primark v Lollypop Clothing [2001] ETMR 334 **16**
R v Ghosh [1982] 1 QB 105, CA **146**
Reckitt and Colman Products Ltd v Borden Inc (JIF Lemon case) [1989] 1 WLR 491 **108**
Reed Executive plc and Reed Solutions plc v Reed Business Information Ltd and others [2004] EWCA Civ 159; [2004] ETMR 56; [2004] Info TLR 55; [2004] RPC 40; [2004] Masons CLR 29; (2004) 148 SJLB 298; The Times 9 Mar 2004, CA **47, 73, 129–139, 147, 148**
REEF TM [2002] RPC 19 **42**
Road Tech v UNISON (Roadrunner case) [1996] FSR 805 **48**
Rodgers (Joseph) & Sons Ltd v W N Rodgers & Co (1924) RPC 277 **129, 132, 133, 138, 150**
Royal Brunei Airlines Sendirian Berhad v Philip Tan Kok Ming [1995] 2 AC 378, [1995] 3 WLR 64, [1995] 3 All ER 97, [1995] BCC 899, (1995) 92(27) LSG 33, (1995) 145 NLJ 888, [1995] 139 SJLB 146, (1995) 70 P & CR D12, The Times 29 May 1995, The Independent 22 June 1995, HL(E) **148**
Saunders v Sun Life Assurance Company of Canada [1894] 1 Ch 537 **151**
Scandecor Development AB v Scandecor Marketing AB [1998] FSR 500; (1998) 95(12) LSG 28; The Times 9 Mar 1998; [2001] ETMR 74, [2002] FSR 7 **16, 17, 72, 146, 193, 194**
Sea Island Cotton [1989] RPC 87 **86**
SDS Biotech UK Limited v Power Agrichemicals Limited [1995] FSR 797 **149**
Singer Manufacturing v Loog (1880) 18 Ch D 395, 412 **33**
Sir Robert McAlpine Limited v Alfred McAlpine plc [2004] EWHC 630; [2004] RPC 711 **151**
Southorn v Reynolds (1865) 12 LT 75 **33, 34, 35**
Spa Esprit Pte v Esprit International (2004) Ltd 07987-00 **49**

Star Industries v Yap Kwee Kor [1976] FSR 256, PC **45**
Stilton [1967] RPC 173 **82**
Stringfellow v McCain Foods (GB) Ltd and another [1984] RPC 501 **108, 109**
Sutherland v V2 Music [2002] EMLR 28 **45**
Tattinger SA and others v Allbev Ltd and another [1993] FSR 641 **111**
Tavener Rutledge v Trexapalm Ltd [1977] RPC 275 **106**
The European Ltd v The Economist Newspaper Ltd [1998] FSR 283 **74**
Thornloe v Hill [1894] Ch 569 **17**
Turton v Turton (1889) 42 Ch D 128, CA **129**
Unidoor v Marks and Spencer [1988] RPC 275 **23**
Vergeras, Re (1881) 3 June unreported **38**
Vodafone Group plc v Orange Personal Communications Services Limited [1997] EMLR 84; [1997-98] Info TLR 8; [1997] FSR 34; The Times 31 Aug 1996 **146**
Walkden Aerate Waters Co (1877) [1884] 54 LJ Ch 394 **36, 38, 39**
'White Rose' (1885) LR 30 Ch D 505 **40**
Wombles Limited v Wombles Skips Ltd [1977] RPC 99 **105, 106**
World Wide Fund for Nature (formerly World Wildlife Fund) v World Wrestling Federation Entertainment Inc [2004] FSR 161, CA **187**
Worthington TM (1880) 14 Ch D 8 **38**

Trade Marks Registry

Customer First BL 0/048/06, 14 Feb 2006, unrep **90**
Fenchurch Environmental Group Ltd v Ad Tech Holdings Ltd, sub nom Bactiguard Trade Mark BL O/236/05, 25 Aug 2005 **77**
Legal Aid BL 0/056/00, 27 Jan 2000 **85**
MADARA ROCK BL 0/215.05, 29 Jul 2005 **97**
Omega SA (Omega AG) (Omega Ltd) Application BL O/554/01, 10 Dec 2001 **77**
Star Pads BL O/156/03 11 June 2003 **90**
Thomas Plant (Birmingham) Ltd v Rousselon Freres et Cie concerning use of the mark Babatier BL O/288/07, 28 Sep 2007 **77**
Wheels 'R' Us Ltd v Geoffrey Inc BL 0/296/06, 19 Oct 2006 **123**
WiFi/WISI BL 0/290/06 16 Oct 2006 **90**

EUROPEAN UNION

European Court of Justice (ECJ)

Adam Opel AG v Autec AG (OPEL BLITZ) [2007] ETMR 33 **67**
Adidas-Salomon v Fitnessworld Case C-408/01 [2004] FSR 21; [2003] ETMR 91 **26, 95, 122, 123, 124**
Alcan Inc v OHIM (BSS) Case C-192/03 P [2004] ECR I-8993 **68**
Arsenal Football Club plc v Matthew Reed Case C-206/01 [2003] Ch 454; [2003] 3 WLR

450; [2003] All ER (EC) 1; [2002] ECR I-10273; [2003] 1 CMLR 345; [2003] CEC 3; [2003] ETMR 227; [2003] RPC 144; (2002) 152 NLJ 1808; The Times 18 Nov 2002   **3, 13, 83, 143, 144**

BAT Cigaretten-Fabriken GmbH v Commission Case 35/83 [1985] ECR 363, [1985] 2 CMLR 470 **180**

BMW Case C-63/97 (1) Bayerische Motorenwerke Aktiengesellschaft (BMW) and (2) BMW Nederland Besloten Vennootschap v Ronald Karel Deenik [1999] All ER (EC) 235; [1999] ECR I-905; [1999] 1 CMLR 1099; [1999] CEC 159; [1999] ETMR 339   **146, 147**

Boehringer Ingelheim v Swingward Case C-143/00 [2002] ETMR 898; [2002] 2 CMLR 26; [2004] ETMR 65, CA; [2004] 3 CMLR 4   **25, 26, 157**

British Leyland v EC Commission Case 226/84 [1986] ECR 3263, [1987] 1 CMLR 185   **181**

Canon Kabushiki Kaisha v Metro-Goldwyn-Mayer Inc Case C-39/97 [1999] RPC 117   **90, 114, 116, 117, 118, 119, 126**

Celine Sarl v Celine SA [2007] ETMR 1320   **148**

Centrafarm v American Home Products Case 3/78 [1978] ECR 1823, [1979] 1 CMLR 326   **177**

CNL-Sucal v Hag (HAG II) Case C-10/89 [1990] ECR I-3711, [1990] 3 CMLR 571   **16, 177, 179, 182**

Consten and Grundig-Verkaufs v EEC Commission Case 58/64 [1966] ECR 299, [1966] CMLR 418   **171, 174, 180**

Davidoff v Gofkid Case C-292/00 [2003] ETMR 534   **26, 122, 123, 124, 125**

Deutsche Grammophon v Metro-SB-Grossmarkte Case 78/70 [1971] ECR 487, [1971] CMLR 631   **174, 180**

Elizabeth Emanuel Case C-259/04 **78**

EMI Records v CBS United Kingdom Case 51/75 [1976] ECR 811, [1976] 2 CMLR 235   **182**

General Motors v Yplon Case C-375/97 [1999] ECR I-5421, [1999] ETMR 950   **26, 95, 96, 123**

Gerolsteiner Brunnen Gesellschaft mit beschränkter Haftung & Co v Putsch Gesellschaft mit beschränkter Haftung Case C-100/02[2004] ECR I-691; [2004] ETMR 559; [2004] RPC 761   **146, 147**

Gilette Company and Gilette Group Finland Osakeyhtiö v LA-Laboratories Limited Osakeyhtiö Case C-228/03 [2005] All ER (EC) 940; [2005] ECR I-2337; [2005] 2 CMLR 1540; [2005] CEC 734; [2005] ETMR825; [2005] FSR 808   **147**

HAG I see Van Zuylen Frères v Hag AG (192/73) [1974] E.C.R. 731 (HAG 1)   **9, 176, 177, 182**

HAG II see CNL-Sucal v Hag (HAG II)

Hoffmann-la Roche & Co AG and Hoffmann-la Roche AG v Centrafarm Vertriebsgesellschaft Pharmazeutischer Erzeugnisse mbH Case 102/77 [1978] ECR 1139; [1978] 3 CMLR 217   **3, 15**

Ideal Stamdard: IHT International Heiztechnik, GmbH, Uwe Danziger v Ideal Standard GmbH Case C-9/93 [1994] ECR I-2789, [1994] 3 CMLR 857   **178, 179**

Levi Strauss & Co v Casucci Spa Case C-145/2005   **61, 64–69**

Lloyd Schuhfabrik Meyer & Co GmbH v Klijsen Handel BV Case C-342/97 [2000] FSR 77   **90**

LTJ Diffusion SA v Sadas Vertbaudet SA Case C-291/00 [2003] ETMR 83   **90**

Michael Holterhoff v Ulrich Freiesleben Case C-2/00 [2002] All ER (EC) 665; [2002] I ECR 4187; [2002] ETMR 917; [2002] FSR 802   **144**

Nederlandsche Banden-Industrie Michelin v EC Commission Case 322/81 [1983] ECR 3461, [1985] 1 CMLR 282   **182**

Nokia Corp v Joachim Wärdell (NOKIA) Case C-316/05 [2007] ETMR 20   **67**

Parke Davis & Co v Probel, Reese, Beintema-Interpharm and Centrfarm Case 24/67 [1968] ECR 55, [1968] CMLR 47   **174**

Pharmon v Hoechst AG Case 19/84 [1985] ECR 2281, [1985] 3 CMLR 775   **177**

Postkantoor Case C-363/99   **75**

Premier Brands UK Ltd v Typhoon Europe Ltd and another [2000] ETMR 1071   **125**

Sabèl BV v Puma AG Case C-251/95 [1998] RPC 199; [1998] ETMR 1   **90, 92, 115, 122**

Sirena, SrL v EDA, SrL Case 40/70 [1971] ECR 69, [1971] CMLR 260   **176, 182**

Société des Produits Nestlé SA v Mars UK Ltd Case C-353/03 [2006] All ER (EC) 348; [2005] 1 ECR 6135; [2005] 3 CMLR 259; [2006] CEC 3, [2005] ETMR 1128; [2006] FSR 4; The Times 20 Jul 2005   **144**

Société des Produits Nestlé SA v OHIM (QUICKY/QUICK, QUICKIES) Case C-193/06 P, not yet pub   **63**

Terrapin (Overseas) Ltd v Terranova Industrie CA Kapferer & Co Case 119/75 [1976] ECR 1039, [1976] 2 CMLR 482   **177**

United Brands Co and United Brands Continental BV v EC Commission Case 27/76 [1978] ECR 207, [1978] 1 CMLR 429   **174**

Van Zuylen Frères v Hag AG (192/73) [1974] E.C.R. 731 (HAG I)   **9, 176, 177, 182**

Vedial v OHIM Case C-106/03 P [2004] ECR I-9573, [2005] ETMR 23; [2008] EWCA Civ 842   **119**

Windsurfing International Inc v EC Commission Case 193/83 [1986] ECR 611, [1986] 3 CMLR 489   **174, 176**

Zino Davidoff v A & G Imports and Levi Strauss v Tesco Stores and Levi Strauss v Costco UK Joined Cases C-414-416/99 [2002] ETMR 109   **19**

Court of First Instance (CFI)

Alcan Inc v OHIM (BSS) Case T-237/01 [2003] ECR II-411   **68**

Assembled Investments (Proprietary) Ltd v OHIM; Waterford

Wedgwood plc intervening (WATERFORD STELLENBOSCH), Case T-105/05, 12 June 2007 **117**

Budějovický Budvar, národní podnik v OHIM; Anheuser-Busch Inc intervening (BUDWEISER), Joined Cases T-53-56, 58 & 59/04, 12 June 2007, unrep **118**

Budějovický Budvar, národní podnik v OHIM; Anheuser-Busch Inc intervening (BUD) Joined Cases T-60-64/04, 12 June 2007, unrep **118**

Castellblanch SA/OHIM (CRISTAL CASTELLBLANCH) Case T-29/04, not yet pub **56**

DEF/TEC Defense Technology GmbH/OHIM (FIRST DEFENSE AEROSOL PEPPER PROJECTOR/DEFENSE & FIRST DEFENSE) Case T-6/05, not yet published **59**

Durferrit GmbH v OHIM (nutride/tufftride) Case T-224/01 [2003] ECR II-1589 **62**

Faber Chinica Srl v OHIM (FABER/NABER) Case T-211/03, 20 Apr 2005, not yet pub **62, 63**

GfK AG v OHIM (CRISTAL CASTELLBLANCH) Case T-135/04, 24 Nov 2005 **63**

Grupo Sada, pa SA v OHIM (GRUPO SADA/SADIA) Case T-31/03, judgment of 11 May 2005 **55, 56**

Japan Tobacco Inc v OHIM (CAMELO/CAMEL) Case T-128/06, unpublished **58**

José Alejandro SL v OHIM (BUDMEN/BUD) Case T-129/01 [2003] ECR II- 2251 **545**

L'Oréal SA v OHIM (FLEXI AIR/FLEX) Case T-112/03, 16 Mar 2005, not yet pub **62**

Madaus AG v OHIM (ECHINAID/ECHINACIN) Case T-202/04 [2006] ECR II-1115 **62**

Mast-Jägermeister AG v OHIM (VENADO) Joined Cases T-81, 82 & 103/03 14 Dec 2006, not yet pub **63**

Mülhens v OHIM; Minoronzoni intervening (TOSCA BLU) Case T-150/04, 11 Jul 207, unrep **117**

PepsiCo, Inc v OHIM (RUFFLES/RIFFELS) Case T-269/02 [2006] ETMR 94 **53, 54**

Sadas SA v OHIM (ARTHUR ET FELICIE) Case T-346/04 [2006] ETMR 27 **53, 55, 56**

Sergio Rossi SpA v OHIM; Sissi Rossi intervening (SISSI ROSSI) Case T-169/03 [2005] ECR II-685 **117**

Société des produits Nestlé SA v OHIM (QUICKY/QUICK, QUICKIES) Case T-74/04 22 Feb 2006, not yet pub **63**

TeleTech Holdings Inc v HIM (TELETECH GLOBAL VENTURES/TELETECH INTERNATIONAL) Case T-288/03, 1 Mar 2005 **54, 56**

Tetra Pak Int'l SA v EC Commission Case T-83/91 [1994] ECR II-755 **174, 181**

Vincenzo Fusco v OHIM (ENZO FUSCO/ANTONIO FUSCO) Case T-185/03 **54**

Council Decisions

IMA, AG and others v Windsurfing International Inc and others Dec

83/400/EEC [1983] OJ L-229/1, [1984] 1 CMLR 1 **174, 176**
Pennys 78/193/EEC [1978] OJ L60/19, [1978] 2 CMLR 100 **181**

OHIM Decisions

First Board of Appeal
BLU ARC/ARC, 8 June 2005, R 764/2004-1 **55**
GOLDSHIELD/SHIELD, 12 Sep 2000, R 415/1999-1 **52**
Grana Biraghi/GRANA PADANO R 153/2002-1, 16 June 2003 **98**
GRENFELL/GREENFIELD 30 Sep 2003 R 60/2003-1 **54**
MANGO R 308/2003-1, 12 Mar 2004 **57, 58**
NIKE/NIKE, 30 Sep 2002 R 16/2000-1 **51**
OHM/OHM 11 Jan 2007 R 92/2006-1 **54**
OPIUM/OPIUM 17 Nov 2004, R 237/2004-1 and R 299/2004-1 **126**
RUFFLES MAX/RIFFELS 29 Apr 2003, R 477/2002-1 **55**
SOL DE AYALA/AYALA, 22 Nov 2006, R 718/2006-1 **53**
VICHY/VICHY CATALAN R 24/2003-1, 12 Jul 2004 **60**
Wi-Fi/WISI R 864/2005-1, 26 Oct 2006 **91**
Wi-Fi/WISI R 1365/2005-1, 26 Oct 2006 **91**
Wi-Fi/WISI R 243/2006-1, 28 Feb 2007 **91**

Second Board of Appeal
BUD/BUD 14 June 2006 R 234/2005-2 **98**
BUD/BUD 28 June 2006 R 241/2005-2 **98**
BUDWEISER/BUDWEISER BUDVAR et al 11 Jul 2005, R 509/2004-2 **98**
BUDWEISER/BUDWEISER BUDVAR et al 11 Jul 2005, R 514/2004-2 **98**
BUDWEISER/BUDWEISER BUDVAR et al 20 Mar 2007, R 299/2006-2 **98**
CAMELO/CAMEL 22 Feb 2006, R 669/2003-2 **58**
COMPAIR/COMPAIR R 590/1999-2, 30 Jul 2002 **59**
Geronimo Stilton/STILTON 26 Jul 2006, R 982/2002-2 **97**
HELLO!/HALLO, 5 Aug 2004 R 132/2002-2 **54**
LIFESPASPA et al 19 June 2007, R 1136/2006-2 **126**
MARIE CLAIRE/MARIE CLAIRE R 530/2004-2 **56**
MARIE CLAIRE/MARIE CLAIRE et al 6 Mar 2006, R 530/2004-2 **126**
MX HONDA/HONDA 8 July 2003 R 691/2002-2 **54**
OMEGA/OMEGA R 330/2002-2, 10 Dec 2004 **60**
POLO/FARTONS POLO 18 May 2004 R 503/2003-2 **54**
RED STAR/BLUE STAR **62**
TUDAPETROL/Hands Logo R 214/2004-2, 13 Mar 2006 **95, 96**
UTS/UPS R 518/2002-2, 30 Aug 2004 **60**

Third Board of Appeal
BROOK & CROSSFIELD/BROOKFIELD 5 Mar 2003 R 860/2000-3 **54**

DEER HEAD R 213/2001-3, 4 Jun 2003 **61**
GARO/GIRA 24 Apr 2002, R 907/2001-3 **55, 56**
IKZ R 359/1999-3, 3 Mar 2000 **87**
MAGIC/MAGIC BOX 27 Feb 2002 R 851/2000-3 **54**
MEMBER OF THE SOCIETY OF FINANCIAL ADVISERS R 865/1999-3, 12 Mar 2001 **87**
TORTI/TOSTI 23 Jan 2002 R 566/2001-3 **54**

Fourth Board of Appeal
FLEXI AIR/FLEX 15 Jan 2003, R 396/2001-4 **61, 62**
LEE/LEE COOPER, 16 June 2004, R 952/2002-4 **55**
LORAC/LIERAC, 15 Jan 2007 R 27/2006-4 **54**
Mermonde/DER GRÜNE PUNKT (The Green Dot) 10 Jan 2006, R 345/2003-4 **91, 92, 93, 94**
NO LIMITS/LIMMIT 8 Jan 2002 R 360/2000-4 **54**
REGENT ASSOCIATES/MASTER CARD, 25 Feb 2004, R 264/2002-4 **52**
SER/SER (FIG.Mark), CADENA S.E.R) 17 Jan 2006, R 0404/2004-4 **126**
YAGER/YAGA 14 Mar 2006, R 125/2005-4 **59**

Opposition Division
CBF/CBI No 2510/2002, 26 Aug 2002 **91**
Culatello di Zibello No 981/2001, 19 Apr 2001 **91**
DIN/Din-Lock No 464/2002, 28 Feb 2002 **91**
Mayocéan Mermonde/DER GRÜNE PUNKT 740/2003, 31 Mar 2003 **92**
NF/MF No 1702/2005, 23 May 2005 **85, 914**

International Cases

Australia
Bi-Lo App (1988) AIPC 90-466, Australian Registry **44**

Canada
Novopharm Ltd v Eli Lilly and Co; Apotex Inc v Eli Lilly and Co 80 CPR (3d) 321, 1998 CPR LEXIS 95 (SC Canada 1998) **195**

United States of America
American Speech-Language-Hearing Association v National Hearing Aid Society 224 USPQ 798, 806-808 (TTAB 1984) **86–87**
Carey v United States 326 F 2d 975 (Ct Cl 1964) **195, 196**
Cyrix Corporation v SGS-Thomson Microelectronics Inc et al 77 F 3d 1381 (Fed Cir 1996) **196**
E I Du Pont de Nemours and Co v Shell Oil Company 498 A 2d 1108; 227 USPQ 233 (SC Del 1985); Del Ct Chancery, 6 Jun 1984, unreported, 9 Delaware Journal of Corporate Law) **196**
Florida v Real Juices Inc 330 F Supp 428, 171 USPQ 66 (MD, Fla 1971) **80**
Good Humor Corporation of America v Bluebird Ice Cream Charlotte Russe Inc 1 Supp 850 (EDNY 1932) **188**
Hazeltine Research Corporation v

Freed-Eisenmann Radio Corporation 3 F 2d 172 (EDNY 1924)   **188**

Idaho Potato Commission v M & M Produce Farm and Sales 335 F 3d 130 (2d Cir 2003), cert den 541 US 1027 (2004)   **86**

Institut National des Appellations d'Origine v Brown-Forman 47 USPQ 2d 1875 (TTAB 1998)   **81**

LA Gear Inc v ES Originals Inc 859 F Supp 1294, 1299-1300 (CD Cal 1994)   **186**

Lisle v Edwards 771 F 2d 693 (Fed Cir 1985)   **195**

Midwest Plastic Fabricators Inc v Underwriters Laboratories Inc 906 F 2d 1568, 15 USPQ 2d 1359 (Fed Cir 1990)   **81**

Nabisco Inc and Nabisco Brands Company v PF Brands Inc and Pepperidge Farm Inc 191 F 3d 208, 219 (CA2, 1999)   **127**

Oberlin v Marlin Am. Corp 596 F 2d 1322, 1327 (7th Cir 1979)   **186, 187**

Original Appalachian Artworks Inc v S Diamond Associates Inc 911 F 2d 1548 (11th Cir 1990)   **188**

Rhone-Polenc Agro SA v DeKalb Genetics Corporation 284 F 3d 1323   **189**

Tea Board of India v The Republic of Tea, Inc 80 USPQ 2d 1881 (TTAB 2006)   **91**

Weight Watchers of Quebec v Weight Watchers International 188 USPQ 17, 21 (EDNY 1975)   **188**

PART I

Overview

1. Introduction

Ilanah Simon Fhima

1. WHY A BOOK ON SHARING NAMES?

In using the term 'sharing names', this book refers to situations where trade mark owners (and, in some circumstances, those who hold rights protected by the law of passing off) find themselves in a situation where another trader is concurrently using a mark which is identical or very similar to that held by the trade mark owner. This can happen voluntarily, for example, when a trade mark owner decides to license his mark to another trader in respect of part of his business but continues to use the mark for the rest of his business. It may also happen involuntarily, for example, when another trader starts using a very similar mark without the owner's authorization in an infringement-type situation.

The sharing of names may seem like a rather abstract theme for a book. However, it is hoped that this volume will persuade readers that this subject is of great practical importance. The range of topics covered in the chapters shows that it has a place in every aspect of trade mark law, from registrability to infringement to transactions involving trade marks. In all of these areas, traders are either asking the authorities to give legal recognition to the ways in which they are voluntarily sharing their trade marks, or to stop other traders from sharing their marks without their authorization.

Perhaps more importantly, the ability of traders to share names and the traders' inability to stop others from sharing their names raises questions about the theoretical underpinnings of the trade mark system as a whole. The European Court of Justice has told us that the essential function of a trade mark is 'to guarantee the identity of origin of the marked goods or services to the consumer or end user by enabling him, without any possibility of confusion, to distinguish the goods or services from others which have another origin'.[1]

---

[1] This definition was originally used in *Hoffmann-la Roche & Co AG and Hoffmann-la Roche AG v Centrafarm Vertriebsgesellshaft Pharmazeutischer Erzeugnisse mbH* 102/77 [1978] ECR 1139, para. 7 but returned to prominence with a similar statement from the ECJ in *Arsenal Football Club plc v Matthew Reed* C-206/01 [2003] ETMR 19, paras 48–50. See further, I. Simon, 'How Does Essential Function Doctrine Drive European Trade Mark Law?' 36 IIC 401 (2005).

In other words, to function effectively as a trade mark, a mark must identify the goods of *one* undertaking and enable consumers to tell *that* owner's goods or services apart from the goods or services of other undertakings. Once the law refuses to stop other traders from making use of the mark, it potentially puts that function in jeopardy. More worryingly, if courts and registries recognize voluntary agreements that parties have made to share names, they may be allowing the private interests of the parties in sharing the name to override the public interest in avoiding consumer confusion by preventing confusingly similar marks from being used and keeping such marks off the Trade Mark Register. However, there is a balance to be struck. While we want to preserve the ability of trade marks to act in accordance with their essential function, we also need to take into account the needs of competitors to use certain marks, and our desire to maintain a market economy where transactions involving trade marks are possible. The chapters within this book examine how this balance has been made in the key areas where name sharing takes place and evaluate whether it has been made correctly.

2. THE BOOK IN OUTLINE

2.1 Overview

As well as this introduction which includes an overview of the legal issues, in this section Andrew Griffiths considers the economic effects of name sharing. Bearing in mind the potential conflict between the essential function of a trade mark and name sharing, Griffiths begins by outlining how the ECJ has defined the essential function, and the economic benefits which arise out of trade marks performing that function, *viz*, the ability of the mark to carve out an identity for the products bearing that mark, and therefore to act as a focus for goodwill to accrue around. He concludes by distinguishing between the economic effects of voluntary and involuntary name sharing.

Griffiths argues that voluntary name sharing is consistent with the essential function, and is also economically efficient since it enables the trade mark owner to maintain control over its goodwill, while at the same time realizing the benefits of modern production and marketing methods. However, involuntary name sharing may be harmful, particularly if consumers are confused as to origin, since such use of the mark will damage its ability to fulfil its essential function, and, as a result, will impair the owner's ability to realize the economic benefits of his/her investment in the mark. Even where there is no origin confusion, he argues that the mark may be damaged in other ways where the name sharing is involuntary.

2.2 Registrability Issues

This part of the book considers the various ways in which name sharing can come up at the registration stage. These include the response of trade mark registries when faced with situations when parties have agreed to share trade marks, and when the applicant for registration has made previous, innocent use of the mark. Finally, there are some marks, the very nature of which requires them to be shared.

Phillip Johnson considers the beginnings, development and ultimate death of honest concurrent user provision. This was an English provision that, in its heyday, enabled the registrar of trade marks to register a trade mark, even though it might infringe an earlier trade mark, where the applicant had been making honest use of it prior to applying for registration. Johnson argues that the rule has its origins in provisions designed to implement the trade mark registration system in the face of the multiple users of the same marks prior to registration who all wanted to gain registration of identical marks when registration became a possibility. However, over time, the provision evolved, and became a means for existing users to gain registration where the use had been honest, even though the use of such marks could cause confusion amongst consumers. In other words, it forced registered owners to share their marks with other users, even though this was capable of harming the ability of their marks to act as an unequivocal guarantee of origin.

However, there was no such provision in the European Trade Mark Directive (Directive 89/104), and although the UK did retain an honest concurrent user provision on implementing the Directive, it was far weaker and, under the influence of case law, weakened even further to the extent of effective non-existence. The provision was removed completely in October 2007 when the UK made extensive changes to the way in which it examines potentially opposing trade marks. Nevertheless, Johnson notes that the concept of the honest concurrent user could make a comeback in the light of the potential for coincidental choices of the same trade mark in a European Union made up of 27 Member States.

Arnaud Folliard-Monguiral examines the role that coexistence plays in the Office for Harmonization in the Internal Market (OHIM)'s decision-making on the registrability of marks. He identifies two areas where coexistence may be relevant: in disproving likelihood of confusion (because the two marks have coexisted on a particular market without evidence of consumer confusion) and in reducing an earlier mark's level of distinctiveness to the point that its scope of protection against confusion is reduced.

Folliard-Monguiral concludes that the impact of coexistence on the first situation is relatively minimal. Although OHIM is prepared to concede that coexistence may be of persuasive value in demonstrating a lack of confusion, coexistence will never be decisive of the point. In some circumstances an earlier user may have been prepared to tolerate a degree of confusion caused by coexistence because of the cost or difficulty of taking action. Furthermore, in contrast to the position of the UK Intellectual Property Office, described in the next chapter by Edward Smith, OHIM does not feel itself obliged to take coexistence agreements between the two parties into account when establishing confusion.

However, coexistence plays more of a role in the second scenario identified by Folliard-Monguiral. It is the position in Europe that confusion is more likely when the earlier mark has an enhanced level of distinctiveness. Such distinctiveness will be lower when other traders are using similar marks on the market and so, where the earlier mark is coexisting with similar marks of third parties, the scope of protection of the earlier mark may be reduced. However, he regrets that, as yet, there is no clear guidance on the correct approach where the earlier mark's distinctiveness is diminished by third-party use which postdates the registration of the earlier mark.

Edward Smith details how the UK Intellectual Property Office, and more specifically, its Trade Marks Registry, has adopted a more liberal approach to trade mark registration where there are possible conflicts between marks. As such, it is not overly concerned with the confusion that may occur when trade marks which overlap are shared. Whereas the Registry previously viewed itself as tasked with an overriding duty to protect consumers from the confusion that could be caused by conflicting trade marks, that is no longer the case. Instead, the Registry takes its lead from the rather permissive Trade Marks Act 1994, and tolerates multiple ownership of marks without the need for rigorous quality control by the first registered trade mark owner. Smith gives examples of how this can be seen through the Registry's practice, and the decisions of its officers. In particular, the Registry does not interfere with private agreements to share marks. It is prepared to take a charitable view of situations where potentially conflicting marks have coexisted without evidence of confusion and it adopts a light touch to the need for quality control by the proprietor in assessing whether there has been use of a mark for the purposes of avoiding revocation.

Smith acknowledges that this can lead to a conflict with the essential function of a trade mark, but notes that the Registry does not see itself as the guardian of the essential function, and, by extension, of consumers. Instead, it favours an approach based on consent between otherwise potentially conflicting users of the trade mark system where this is possible.

Dev Gangjee discusses certification and collective marks, and their place in the trade mark system. These marks are of particular interest because the parties involved have voluntarily agreed to share the name in question. After analysing their nature, and the conditions for obtaining them, Gangjee considers the way in which they have been treated in infringement actions, and the way in which their unique nature has influenced the way of the scope of their protection as compared to 'conventional' trade marks.

Gangjee sets collective and certification marks in the context of the wider trade mark system. They do not do the ordinary job of a trade mark, which is to indicate the origin of the goods of a *single* undertaking. However, he notes that most consumers are not overly concerned with the physical origin of their products (and indeed, a trade mark will no longer give them this information). Instead, they view trade marks as a proxy for a message about quality. He asks whether reliance on conventional trade marks is the best way for consumers to obtain their messages about quality, or if there is instead a greater scope for the use of certification marks.

2.3 Shared Name Litigation

This section of the book considers the role of name sharing in *inter partes* disputes, with chapters on infringement and the defences

In Chapter 7 I examine the diminishing role of the specialty rule under both passing off and registered trade mark law. Under the specialty rule, trade mark protection was limited to the prevention of uses of marks on identical, or perhaps very similar, goods or services. This meant that an earlier user of a mark could be forced to share that mark when the later use was on dissimilar goods, even if the later use caused confusion, took advantage of the earlier mark's reputation or otherwise damaged the earlier mark or its reputation. In recent years though, the role of the specialty rule has been drastically reduced under the law of both registered and unregistered trade mark law by two trends: (i) a widening conception of confusion and (ii) the willingness in Europe (and indeed further afield) to recognize dilution, which historically has not required a link between the parties goods, as an actionable harm.

However, I argue that, although great strides have been made in abolishing the specialty rule, and consequently, reducing the number of name-sharing situations, specialty has managed to work its way back into the system. Under passing off, all actions require a showing of misrepresentation and, although the courts have accepted that the parties' goods or services do not need to be in the same field of activity for misrepresentation to be shown, they have held fast to the idea that a shared field of activity will make confusion more likely. If anything, the creeping resurgence of specialty is even more pernicious in registered trade mark law. In fact, specialty never really went away in confusion-based infringement, since there has always been a need for the parties' goods or services to be similar (although the courts have been quite willing to take a wide approach to establishing that similarity). Most surprising though is that under the dilution head of infringement, there have been concerted efforts, particularly by courts in the UK to argue that dilution is more likely when the parties' goods are closer together. This is at odds with the original definition of dilution and has culminated in a reference to the ECJ.

Christopher Wadlow considers whether there is an own name defence under the law of passing off in the UK. Allowing a trader to use his (or her) own name involves forcing the earlier user to share the name with the eponymous second-comer. However, for reasons of fairness, and in recognition of the fact that one cannot choose one's own personal name, we might want to allow the second user to use his own name. The difficulty is that the second use of a name may cause confusion with the goods or services of the earlier user, even if the second user did not intend to bring such confusion about. Registered trade mark law is, to some extent at least, prepared to tolerate this confusion. However, as Wadlow demonstrates, passing off favours the prevention of deception.

Wadlow comes to the startling conclusion that there probably is *not* an own name defence to passing off. He argues that to be classed as a defence, the mechanism that protects the use of one's own name would have to be extraneous to the requirements for proving that passing off has occurred. After considering the three relatively recent cases on the issue, he finds that although there is sympathy from some quarters for the ability of traders to use their own names, ultimately, what the so-called defence boiled down to is a consideration of whether the use causes deception, rather than mere confusion. If deception is made out, there will be passing off, even if the selection of the mark in question was motivated by the second user's desire to use his own name, rather than an intention to cause deception. To make matters worse, he points out that 'there is no known example in a reported case of the defence ever succeeding on the facts'.

Ashley Roughton considers the scope of the own name defence under registered trade mark law, contrasting it with the position under passing off. He considers why a trader should be forced to share his mark with another in these circumstances, concluding that there are good policy reasons why we should recognize an own name defence. However, he finds that the European system's recognition of an own name defence has been undercut by the approach of the courts to defining the 'honest practices' proviso. Most of the European trade mark defences (including the own name defence) require the defendant's behaviour to have been in accordance with honest practices in industrial or commercial matters. However, Roughton argues that what is considered dishonest, according to the courts, is the same as the constituent elements of infringement, meaning that anyone who is before the courts for infringement will automatically fall foul of the proviso and will be left without a defence. This is more than is needed to protect trade mark owners, and leaves those who want to use their own names in an unfortunate position.

Roughton contrasts the situation under registered trade mark law with that under the law of passing off. The analysis is, in a sense, simpler under passing off as there is no real consideration of the needs of consumers, or even other traders. Consequently, there is no real defence under the common law action, with the question limited to a consideration of whether the defendant has passed his goods off as those of another. If he has, then his activities are actionable, if not (for example, if the name and/or address of the claimant are not the thing that engenders the goodwill) then they are not.

2.4 Shared Name Transactions

This section of the book discusses the permissibility and advisability of various consensual means of sharing names.

Spyros Maniatis and Stefan Schwarzkopf discuss the practice of co-branding, adopting both a marketing and legal approach. They define the phenomenon and identify the types of co-branding. They also outline advantages and possible disadvantages of the practice from the perspective of branding theory. They then examine the legal steps that should be taken in drafting a co-branding agreement, proposing a test for enabling, monitoring, and evaluating a co-branding scheme.

While co-branding is an example of voluntary name sharing, one thing to emerge from Maniatis and Schwarzkopf's chapter is that the trade practice nevertheless involves a risk for the parties' brands, and by extension their trade marks. While one may exercise the utmost care in selecting one's co-branding partner, there is always the risk that your partner's reputation may change for the worse. By causing your trade mark to share a platform with your partner's any harm to your partner's trade mark could cause harm to yours as well through that association. This is proof once again that, once trade marks are shared, the role of the trade mark as an unequivocal indicator of the undertaking that is responsible for the quality of the product is jeopardized.

Thomas Hays considers the competition law aspects of sharing names, in particular whether splitting the ownership of a trade mark, so that a mark which was originally used by one entity is now used by two, will lead to a competition law violation. Europe initially took an exceptionally dim view of such splits, as is apparent from the Court of Justice's development of the common origin doctrine in *HAG I*. Under this doctrine, a trade mark owner could not partition the European market by splitting the ownership of a mark which was once in common ownership in order to use the now differently owned trade mark rights to oppose the sale of the goods in different national markets. However, the circumstances of the most prominent common origin doctrine case, *HAG I*, were unfortunate, for rather than being a deliberate attempt to circumvent the competition laws, the split in ownership had been imposed on the original owner when one of the marks had been sequestered as enemy property at the end of the Second World War. The two companies had operated completely separately for decades and to treat both marks as essentially the same, and any attempt to enforce one against the other as anti-competitive, meant that the Court was favouring the need to complete the single market over the ability of trade marks to function as accurate indications of origin. Nevertheless, Hays sees some potential value to the common origin doctrine in situations where the split is voluntary, since if the original owner has received a reward from the division of his mark, it is arguable that he and his successors should not be allowed to obtain a 'second bite of the cherry' by differentially enforcing the two marks in different Member States of the EU.

Hays also discusses the contemporary position under Articles 81 and 82 of the EC Treaty. A single trade mark can be divided up territorially, leading to a reduction in intrabrand competition and the development of market-sharing cartels. Such activities are prohibited under Article 81. Breaches of Article 82 are more difficult to demonstrate, since a necessary ingredient is that the would-be defendant must have a dominant position on the market in question. A single branded product is generally not a market in and of itself. Instead, a branded product generally competes with a number of similar products sold under different brands. However, if such dominance is found, in contrast to Article 81, splitting the trade mark could *alleviate* market dominance, as introducing additional users of the trade mark into the market would increase intrabrand competition. Thus, it seems impossible to draw the simple conclusion that the sharing out of a trade mark is either 'good' or 'bad' for competition law. However, what will be harmful to competition law is when trade marks are divided in a way designed to partition the EU market and hinder market integration.

Finally, Neil Wilkof writes about the practice of sublicensing trade marks. He begins by analysing the conceptual basis of sublicensing. He then considers why parties may wish to enter a trade mark sublicensing agreement before going on to consider whether there is a need for the original licensor to impose quality control conditions on the sublicensee. He concludes by considering the position of sublicensees if the underlying licence is terminated.

Sublicensing poses particular issues for the sharing of names, since the original licensor/owner of the trade mark will, under a sublicensing agreement, not only be sharing his mark with his originally selected licensee, but will also be sharing the mark with the licensee's own licensee. As Wilkof points out, this arrangement leads to particular issues regarding quality control by the trade mark's ultimate owner. One of the recognized functions of a trade mark is to act as a 'guarantee' of consistent quality of the goods sold under the trade mark. Where a trade mark is licensed, it is possible for the licensee to sell goods of a different quality to those of the licensor. To this end, some jurisdictions have imposed a requirement that the licensor exercises quality control over the licensee's use of the mark. If there is also a sublicensing agreement, there is an even greater risk of differential quality, and so Wilkof argues that the licensor must maintain quality control over the sublicensee, either directly, or through the licensee. Even in the UK, where the quality control principle has been rejected, it is arguable that this applies because there will be a *de facto* message of consistent quality where there is only an exclusive licensee. As Wilkof points out, this reasoning may not apply in sublicensing situations if both the licensee and the sublicensee are active on the relevant market.

3. CONCLUSION

The chapters in this book demonstrate the central, though sometimes silent role that name sharing has in the trade mark system. Moreover, it is submitted that it reveals divergent trends in respect of voluntary and involuntary name sharing.

Involuntary name sharing is considered to be bad, both from an economic point of view and from the point of view of preserving the essential function of a mark, and protecting consumers from confusion. Moreover, the courts and legislators have shown themselves increasingly willing to prevent involuntary name sharing. This can be seen most clearly in the way in which the rights of trade mark owners have trumped those of defendants in own name situations in both passing off and registered trade marks, but also from the widening of the definition of infringement in both causes of action and from the removal of the honest concurrent user provision in UK registered trade mark law.

However, voluntary name sharing appears to be more positive from an economic and legal standpoint, particularly because those who share their names can often impose conditions which mean that they can ensure that all goods sold under their marks are of comparable quality, removing at least to some extent the fear about name sharing harming the mark's essential function. This positive reception of voluntary name sharing can been seen through the trade practices of sublicensing and co-branding, and through the approaches of courts and registries under competition law, and also in the extent to which they are willing to recognize coexistence agreements and forms of trade marks which can, by their nature, only be shared. Perhaps surprisingly, the exception to this trend appears to be OHIM. There voluntary name sharing in the shape of coexistence agreements appears to be of little value, whereas the presence of unauthorized third-party users of a mark may diminish its distinctiveness to the point where the scope of its protection is reduced.

2. An economic perspective on shared name issues in trade mark law

Andrew Griffiths

1. INTRODUCTION

In the European Trade Mark Directive ('the EC Directive')[1], a trade mark is defined as a sign that is 'capable of distinguishing the goods or services of one undertaking from those of other undertakings'.[2] The European Court of Justice ('the ECJ') has stated that the essential function of a trade mark is to 'guarantee the identity of origin of the marked goods or services to the consumer or end user by enabling him, without any possibility of confusion, to distinguish the goods or services from others which have another origin'.[3] It might be inferred from this that a trade mark must relate exclusively to one particular undertaking and that every undertaking should therefore use a separate trade mark to identify the goods it produces or the services it provides. However, this oversimplifies the basis of the differentiation that trade marks achieve and their economic role.

This book explores a number of scenarios in which two or more undertakings use the same trade mark to identify their output when it is marketed and

---

[1] First Council Directive of 21 December 1988 to approximate the laws of the Member States relating to trade marks; 89/104/EEC. The EC Directive has substantially harmonized Trade Mark Law throughout the European Union and was implemented in the United Kingdom by the Trade Marks Act 1994 ('the 1994 Act').

[2] The EC Directive, art. 2. See also the 1994 Act, s. 1(1) and the Agreement on Trade-related Aspects of Intellectual Property Rights 1994 ('the TRIPs Agreement'), art. 15.1. The term 'undertaking' is a general term used in European directives to refer to a firm or business organization regardless of its legal form. It thus includes the partnership and other kinds of unincorporated entity, but in practice most undertakings are companies.

[3] See, for example, *Arsenal FC* v. *Matthew Reed* C-206/01 [2003] ETMR 227 at para. 48. For an analysis of the history and development of this statement, see I. Simon, 'How Does Essential Function Drive Trade Mark Law?' 36 IIC 401 (2005). See also the tenth recital to the EC Directive, which states that the function of the legal protection obtained from a registered trade mark 'is in particular to guarantee the trade mark as an indication of origin'.

this chapter will consider such instances of 'name sharing' from an economic perspective.[4] Name sharing can be either 'voluntary' or 'involuntary'. In the former, undertakings use the same trade mark pursuant to a consensual arrangement of some kind. Voluntary name sharing includes hierarchical arrangements in which one undertaking retains ultimate control over the use of the trade mark and collaborative arrangements in which two or more undertakings exercise ultimate control jointly. Involuntary name sharing occurs where two or more undertakings use the same trade mark coincidentally or in other circumstances where there is no consensual arrangement. It includes both the use of the same name for the same kind of goods or services and the use of the same name for different goods or services.[5] The latter practice has become much more of a problem as the identities that undertakings seek to establish through names and other trade marks have become much broader and corporate in nature rather than being focused on a specific product.[6]

This chapter will proceed as follows. Section 2 will examine the legal meaning of the term 'origin' in the ECJ's statement of the essential function of a trade mark. This will show how the key factor is that one undertaking (or at least one group of undertakings acting as a single entity through a consensual arrangement of some kind) must have ultimate control over the use of a trade mark as a means of identifying and differentiating products for marketing. From this perspective, voluntary name sharing in its various guises is consistent with the ECJ's statement, whereas involuntary name sharing threatens to undermine the trade mark's essential function.

Section 3 will then examine the economic benefits that can result from a trade mark's performance of its essential function. This section will show how these benefits derive from a trade mark's capacity to establish an identity for products that can acquire a reputation and provide a focus for goodwill. This capacity depends on one undertaking (or a collaborating group of undertakings) having exclusive control of the trade mark as a means of conferring an identity on products, and is therefore a result of its performance of its essential function as elaborated in Section 2.

---

[4] For convenience, this chapter will use the term 'name sharing' to apply to any situation in which two or more undertakings use the same trade mark unless the context requires otherwise. Also, this chapter will focus on the shared use of the same trade mark rather than the use of trade marks that are merely similar to each other.

[5] A trade mark is registered on the basis that it is being used or that its owner has a *bona fide* intention of using it for the goods or services designated in the registration. The internationally recognized Nice Classification divides goods and services into 45 categories for this purpose.

[6] See C. Lury, *Brands: the Logos of the Global Economy* (Routledge, Oxford, 2004) at p. 28 on how corporate branding has come to eclipse product branding since the 1980s.

Section 4 will consider the economic implications of voluntary and involuntary name sharing. It will argue that the former is generally not a problem and in fact enhances the economic role of a trade mark through facilitating the adaptation of arrangements for the production and distribution of goods and the delivery of services and the evolution of more efficient structures for these. Involuntary name sharing, can however, impair or even undermine the economic role of the trade mark, although its impact depends on whether or not consumers are actually misled about the 'origin' of products. If they are not, then the costs and benefits are more closely balanced

2. THE MEANING OF 'ORIGIN' IN TRADE MARK LAW

Trade mark law has presented the function of a trade mark as being to indicate the 'source', 'origin' or 'trade origin' of a product and to enable consumers or end users to distinguish products on this basis 'without any possibility of confusion'.[7] The ECJ has provided an elaboration of this 'essential function', which reveals the combination of exclusive control and flexibility of structure that underlies a trade mark's economic role:

> This guarantee of origin [provided by a registered trade mark] means that the consumer or ultimate user can be certain that a trade-marked product which is sold to him has not been subject at a previous stage of marketing to interference by a third person, without the authorisation of the proprietor of the trade mark, such as to affect the original condition of the product.[8]

This shows that the proprietor (or 'owner') of a trade mark must authorize the use of the trade mark for marketing goods or services under it and must do so at the point at which the 'condition' in which they are to be marketed is determined.

The key factor that makes products those 'of' one undertaking and gives them a specific 'origin' is that one undertaking (or a collaborating group of undertakings) has had ultimate control over their 'condition' at the point of marketing and sanctions their presentation to consumers under the trade mark. The owner does not therefore have to make the goods or deliver the services itself, but it must somehow sanction and endorse them as its goods or services. In effect, a trade mark indicates that one undertaking has accepted commercial responsibility, this 'economic guarantee' reflecting its power to control their

---

[7] See above at n. 3.
[8] *Hoffmann-la-Roche* v. *Centrafarm* C-102/77 [1978] 3 CMLR 217 at para. 7.

condition and its exclusive right to authorize the use of the trade mark.[9] If its owner has not authorized the marketing of goods or services under a trade mark, then these goods or services do not have the 'origin' that it indicates and using the trade mark to identify them makes a false statement about their 'origin'. It does not matter if the products in question are the same in every material respect to products that the trade mark's owner has authorized to be sold under it.[10]

A trade mark can therefore be viewed as the 'aegis' or 'banner' of an undertaking.[11] It provides a means of conferring a distinctive marketing identity on products,[12] which is under the exclusive control of one undertaking and which roughly corresponds to the marketing concept of a 'brand'.[13] Moreover, the

---

[9] Advocate General Jacobs described the precise way in which a trade mark operates as a 'guarantee' of quality in his Opinion to the ECJ in the *Hag II* case: 'The guarantee of quality offered by a trade mark is not of course absolute, for the manufacturer is at liberty to vary the quality; however, he does so at his own risk and he – not his competitors – will suffer the consequences if he allows the quality to decline. Thus, although trade marks do not provide any form of legal guarantee of quality . . . they do in economic terms provide such a guarantee, which is acted upon daily by consumers': *SA Cnl-Sucal* v. *Hag* C-10/89 (*'Hag II'*) [1990] 3 CMLR 571 at 583. See also the judgment of Lord Nicholls in *Scandecor Development* v. *Scandecor Marketing*: '. . . in relying on a trade mark consumers rely, not on any legal guarantee of quality, but on the proprietor of a trade mark having an economic interest in maintaining the value of his mark. It is normally contrary to a proprietor's self-interest to allow the quality of goods sold under his banner to decline': [2001] ETMR 800 at para. 19.

[10] *Major Bros.* v. *Franklin* [1908] 1 KB 712; *Primark* v. *Lollypop Clothing* [2001] ETMR 334.

[11] Lord Nicholls endorsed these terms in *Scandecor Development* v. *Scandecor Marketing* [2001] ETMR 800 at para. 19. He drew them respectively from the judgment of Lord Wright in *Aristoc* v. *Rysta* [1945] AC 68 (HL) at 101–02 and the judgment of Laddie J in *Glaxo Group* v. *Dowelhurst* [2000] FSR 529 at 540–1.

[12] There is a crucial difference between using a trade mark in order to confer an identity upon products so that the firm in control of the identity has commercial responsibility for them and using a trade mark as a means of identification or reference to indicate that certain products have a particular marketing identity that has been duly conferred upon them. Whereas the former use should be exclusive to the firm that controls the trade mark, the latter need not be since it is being used to give factual information about a characteristic of the products in the same way as a descriptive term. This difference is relevant to the analysis of the legal protection that trade marks require.

[13] A firm might use one trade mark alone for such an identity or it might use it in combination with other signs and devices, which might or might not be registrable as trade marks. There is no legal definition of the term 'brand' and the precise nature of the relationship between a trade mark and a brand is a matter of speculation: see, for example, J. Davis, 'The Value of Trade Marks: Economic Assets and Cultural Icons', in Y. Gendreau (ed.), *Intellectual Property: Bridging Aesthetics and Economics* (Editions Themis, Montreal, 2006).

identity of the controlling undertaking and the way in which it arranges for the designated products to reach the market can change over time without altering the fact that the designated products continue to have the common identity signified by the trade mark. Lord Nicholls noted this flexibility in the *Scandecor* case:

> A trade mark is not usually to be understood as a representation regarding the identity of the source, namely, who is in control of the business in which the mark is being used. Rather, with the changes in trade, a trade mark can 'fairly be held to be' only a representation that the goods were manufactured in the course of the business using the mark, without any representation as to 'the persons by whom that business was being carried on' . . . This approach accords with business reality and customers' everyday expectations. Customers realise that there is always the prospect that, unbeknown to them, the management of a business may change. To confine the use of a trade mark to the original owner of a business would be to give the concept of a business origin or business source an unrealistically narrow and impractical meaning.[14]

This flexibility means that a trade mark can function as a discrete component in the organization of production and can facilitate the evolution of more efficient structures.[15]

The owner of a trade mark is free to determine the basis on which it is willing to bring certain products under this banner and exclude others and a trade mark can come to signify something in addition to 'origin'. An undertaking can, for example, choose to use a particular trade mark in order to indicate the quality or some other characteristic of its products.[16] It can use different trade marks to differentiate its products on this basis and in effect have more than one banner at its disposal, each of which represents a distinct 'origin'.[17] This is a useful capacity where product differentiation is a key factor in competition. An undertaking can thus use trade marks to signify the various banners or identities that it controls, to distinguish them from each other and, according to its wishes, to mask or highlight the fact that they are connected to each other.

---

[14] *Ibid.* at paras. 21 and 22, citing the judgment of Romer LJ in *Thorneloe v. Hill* [1894] Ch. 569.

[15] It has enabled, for example, manufacturing firms to restructure their operations through outsourcing and sub-contracting and to cease to have any direct involvement in manufacturing. This has been depicted as the evolution of 'weightless' firms whose activities are limited to developing and managing the images of their brands: see generally N. Klein, *No Logo* (Flamingo, London, 2000).

[16] Any information about the characteristics of products must not mislead consumers: the 1994 Act, ss. 3(3) & 4646(1)(d).

[17] See, for example, *(John) Andrew v. Kuehnrich* (1913) 30 RPC 677 at 695 and *Nicholson's Application* (1931) 48 RPC 227 (CA).

Arrangements for voluntary name sharing are therefore consistent with the essential function of a trade mark provided that they are based upon the trade mark owner's ultimate power of control over its use. Such arrangements illustrate the flexibility of the trade mark as a structuring device and the range of structures to which it can contribute. The owner exercises its power of control through entering into such an arrangement and through those terms of the arrangement that govern the right of other undertakings to use the trade mark. Further, as noted already, the owner (or effective controller) of a trade mark need not be a single undertaking, but can be a collaborating group of undertakings. In such a case, the voluntary arrangement defines a collaborating group of separate legal entities as the 'undertaking' with the exclusive power of control and provides how it is to act in this respect.[18]

The fact that a trade mark can be shared through voluntary arrangements shows the artificiality of the banner or identity that a trade mark signifies. However, this would still be the case even if the right to use a particular trade mark were to be restricted to one particular undertaking to use only on its own output since an undertaking is essentially artificial. In the case of a company, its separate legal personality, which gives it an independent and indefinite identity, can mask extensive changes in its ownership, management and other personnel. A trade mark simply provides a further mask for a product or range of products giving them a distinctive identity that creates an illusion of stability and continuity over time, but which in reality can screen a complex and fluctuating set of business arrangements. Such a mask creates an illusory identity that can obscure not only extensive changes in personnel, but also changes in the legal structures through which the personnel operate.

Voluntary name sharing merely increases the range of legal arrangements that can be used to organize the production and distribution of goods and services and the scope for adapting and reorganizing these arrangements. The evolution of such arrangements can be related to the idea that a firm or undertaking is not a simple alternative to the market as a forum for transactions, but lies towards one end of a spectrum of possibilities including long-term relational contracts.[19] From this perspective, the flexible notion of 'origin' in trade mark law means that the goodwill focused upon a trade mark can accommodate the full range of organizational possibilities.

Where name sharing is involuntary, this can be inconsistent with the trade mark's performance of its essential function, especially when used for the

---

[18] See above at n. 2 on the meaning of 'undertaking'.
[19] See generally I. Macneil, 'Contracts: Adjustments of Long-Term Economic Relations under Classical, Neoclassical and Relational Contract Law' 72 *Northwestern University LR* 854 (1978) and O. Williamson, *The Economic Institutions of Capitalism* (The Free Press, New York, 1985).

same kind of product, since the same trade mark is used for products that, by definition, do not have the same 'origin'. However, such name sharing might not in practice mislead consumers about 'origin'. There is much less likelihood of confusion where the same trade mark is used for different kind of products, though this can still occur. And even where the products are the same, there might be other features of the products or their presentation that prevent this from occurring, such as where an undertaking always uses one trade mark in combination with another.[20]

Involuntary name sharing can also arise in the context of parallel imports of trade marked goods. The owner of a trade mark has the right to authorize its use for the first marketing of goods within the European Economic Area ('EEA'), which means that goods only acquire their 'origin' at this point.[21] However, to give effect to the fundamental principle of the free movement of goods, it has been established that importers of goods that have already been marketed within the EEA also have the right, in certain circumstances and subject to certain conditions, to sell the goods under a trade mark despite having interfered with the 'condition' of the goods in a way that should normally be the prerogative of the trade mark's owner.[22] Such use of a trade mark is therefore misleading about the 'origin' of the goods in the trade mark sense of the word and amounts to involuntary name sharing.

3. THE ECONOMIC ROLE OF A TRADE MARK

The economic role of a trade mark is based on the exclusive control that its owner enjoys both over its use as a banner or means of identification and over the condition of the goods or services marketed under it. Although any sign that can be represented graphically can be used as a trade mark,[23] a trade mark is likely to be something that consumers readily notice and can easily remember. Signs such as brand names, devices and logos should be much more effective in this respect than full corporate names or registration numbers.[24] A trade

---

[20] See above at n. 13.
[21] EC Directive, art. 7; 1994 Act, s. 12. See generally *Zino Davidoff* v. *A & G Imports* and *Levi Strauss* v. *Tesco Stores* and *Levi Strauss* v. *Costco UK* Joined Cases C-414/99 to C-416/99 [2002] ETMR 109.
[22] See generally T. Hays, *Parallel Importation under European Union Law* (Sweet & Maxwell, London, 2004).
[23] The EC Direcitve, art. 2; the 1994 Act, s. 1(1).
[24] This presentation over-simplifies the role of some trade marks. An undertaking may use more than one trade mark to identify products as having a particular origin and these trade marks may have differing levels of prominence in signifying an identity based on origin. In particular, logos and unconventional trade marks such as shapes and colours are likely to be used in combination with a word mark or device mark.

mark can then help consumers to choose among competing products on the basis of their 'origin' and to acquire information on this basis whether from their own experience or from other sources. It can function as both a product identifier and a reference point for consumers. However, its value in performing this function depends on the significance that consumers actually attach to the fact that products have a specific 'origin'.

A recognizable and memorable identity based on 'origin' is something that can acquire a reputation in the minds of consumers provided that they expect products with the same identity to be consistent in quality and any other characteristics that they regard as important. Such an identity provides a focus for 'goodwill'.[25] A number of explanations have been suggested as to why consumers might prefer products that have a particular identity based on their 'origin' and appear willing to pay premium prices for trade marked products. In broad terms, this should reflect a reduction in transaction costs, an increase in utility or a combination of these effects. These effects can both be linked to the exclusive control that a trade mark's owner enjoys over its use and the condition of the products sold under it. Voluntary name sharing should not therefore impair either of these effects, but involuntary name sharing could threaten them both.

Neo-classical economic analysis of trade mark law has explained the appeal of trade marks as reflecting a reduction in transaction costs,[26] in particular 'search costs'.[27] These are the costs that consumers face when they lack perfect information about the quality or other significant characteristics of a product and this information is hard to acquire prior to purchase through inspection or other low-cost means. The costs of such uncertainty include the risk of disappointment and the risk that a party with superior information has

---

[25] In a classic statement about 'goodwill', Lord Macnaghten referred to it as 'the benefit and advantage of the good name, reputation, and connection of a business' and 'the attractive force that brings in custom', indicating that it 'must emanate from a particular centre or source': *Commissioners of Inland Revenue* v. *Muller & Co.'s Margarine* [1901] AC 217 at 223–4. Where products have a distinctive identity reflecting their connection to one undertaking, the identity and the trade mark that signifies it can provide such a centre or source.

[26] Transaction costs are the various incidental costs incurred by parties in making a bargain and include 'search costs', 'bargain costs' and 'enforcement costs': see R. Cooter and T. Ulen, *Law and Economics* (Pearson Addison Wesley, London, 2004) at pp. 91–5 and A. Ogus, *Regulation: Legal Form and Economic Theory* (Clarendon Press, Oxford, 1994), p. 17.

[27] See W. Landes and R. Posner, 'Trademark Law: An Economic Perspective' 30 *Journal of Law & Economics* 265 (1987) above, N. Economides, 'The Economics of Trademarks' 78 *Trademark Reporter* 523 (1988) and W. Landes and R. Posner, *The Economic Structure of Intellectual Property Law* (The Belknap Press, Cambridge, MA, 2003).

an incentive to exploit this for its own benefit. One device that can help reduce these costs is having a reputation for meeting the expectations of other parties, since this can be of benefit to the party enjoying it as well as to others.[28] In effect, once a party acquires a reputation for behaving well, it has an incentive not to lose it. There is an economic logic in trusting a party with a good reputation and in finding reassurance in such a reputation. The greater the investment needed to acquire and maintain a good reputation, the greater the reassurance it should provide. This incentive gives a good reputation a 'self-enforcing' aspect.[29]

A trade mark provides a basis for acquiring a good reputation and moreover one that need not always be linked to the same undertaking. It signifies an identity, and this identity has the capacity to acquire a reputation as long as there is, at any given time, one undertaking (or one collaborating group of undertakings) with the exclusive power to determine the products that are to be marketed with the identity and to control their condition at the point of marketing. This exclusive power means that the undertaking has the ability to ensure that the condition of the products maintains or improves the reputation of the identity and, since it exclusively enjoys the benefit of earning a good reputation, it has an incentive to do this. A trade mark therefore achieves an alignment between having an interest in maintaining a reputation and having the power to do so.

However, it seems unlikely that a trade mark's capacity for reducing search costs provides the sole explanation of its power to attract consumers to the products it identifies. It is, for example, hard to reconcile this theory with the fact that in practice undertakings are willing to invest substantial time and resources in choosing their trade marks since this suggests that some signs are capable of attaining a much greater value than others for reasons other than the reputation they earn.[30] Also, other legal devices such as better consumer protection regulation have mitigated the problems associated with lack of perfect information and reduced the role that trade marks can play here. In any event, the neo-classical explanation rests on a set of assumptions about the operation of market forces, and consumer demand is treated as something fixed and beyond influence.[31] If consumers are in fact viewed as indecisive

---

[28] See, for example, B. Klein, and K.B. Leffler, 'The Role of Market Forces in Assuring Contractual Performance' 89 *Journal of Political Economy* 615–41 (1981) and S. Tadelis, 'What's in a Name? Reputation as a Tradeable Asset' 89 *American Economic Review* 548–63 (1999).

[29] Landes and Posner, 'Trademark Law' n. 27 above at p. 270.

[30] See generally S.L. Carter, 'The Trouble with Trademark' 99 *Yale LJ* 759 (1990).

[31] See generally Cooter and Ulen, *Law and Economics*, n. 26 above, ch. 2, 'A Review of Microeconomic Theory'.

and open to persuasion, then the barrier they must overcome before entering market transactions can be viewed in terms of 'persuasion costs' as well as 'search costs', with trade marks having a role to play in the process of persuasion.[32]

Insofar as the role of trade marks goes beyond that of reducing transaction costs of some kind, it must involve the provision of some kind of utility to consumers in addition to that they derive from the functional attributes of the product. It is possible to argue, for example, that even if they do no more than help to establish a superficial differentiation of products that are essentially the same in functional terms, this represents an additional benefit because consumers value such differentiation and derive utility from it.[33] It is also arguable that some trade marks provide a means of conferring emotional or psychological attributes upon the products they identify, with some consumers appearing to attach much greater value to such 'non-material' attributes than to functional ones. Whilst some trade marks might have an intrinsic appeal to consumers that operates in this way, the main basis of any such capacity is the identity that the trade mark signifies and the reputation that it has acquired in the minds of consumers.

A reputation with this capacity involves much more than a reputation for meeting the expectations of consumers as to the quality and other functional characteristics of the marked products. It can be developed through advertising and other promotional exercises to engage with and influence the expectations of consumers and create an attractive image for the identity. Themes used in advertisements, marketing devices such as sponsorship and endorsement and the declaration of a set of 'values' for the identity can all contribute to the shaping of such an image.[34] The role of a trade mark becomes more than one of signifying the identity: it provides consumers and other end users with a means of signifying their association with the identity and the reputation and

---

[32] See, for example, B. Beebe, 'Search and Persuasion in Trademark Law' 103 *Michigan Law Review* 2020 (2005).

[33] For a sceptical consideration of such differentiation through 'gold-plating', see R. Sennett, *The Culture of the New Capitalism* (Yale University Press, New Haven, CT, 2006), at pp. 142–51. The neo-classical explanation was put forward as a response to criticisms of the trade mark system as facilitating artificial and unnecessary product differentiation and tending to reinforce the monopolistic power of large corporations: see, for example, R. Brown, 'Advertising and the Public Interest: Legal Protection of Trade Symbols' 57 *Yale LJ* 1165 (1948).

[34] Some trade marks have been portrayed evolving from a mere sign, through being the symbol of an attractive reputation and image, to being a 'myth' that encompasses broader cultural themes and values as well: see T.D. Drescher, 'The Transformation and Evolution of Trademarks: From Signals to Symbols to Myth' 82 *Trademark Reporter* 301 (1992).

image it has acquired.[35] Such association might give some consumers a sense of community or a means of self-expression.[36] And consumers have come to regard products bearing certain trade marks as symbols of prestige and social status.[37]

Trade marks signifying such identities perform a transformational role inasmuch as they provide the means of conferring the additional non-material attributes on the marked products, which goes far beyond the relatively passive role of providing consumers with information or reassurance about their attributes. In practice, the appeal of a particular trade mark might represent a combination of a capacity to reduce transaction costs and a capacity to confer benefits. And the kind of reputation that can provide substantial emotional and psychological utility to consumers is likely to be founded on a reputation for meeting consumers' expectations on matters such as quality.

4. NAME SHARING AND THE ECONOMIC ROLE OF TRADE MARKS

When analysing the sharing of a trade mark, it is important to recall that its owner has an interest in maintaining or increasing its value and in ensuring that its appeal to consumers is not diminished. It is the alignment of this interest with the ultimate power of determining which products can legitimately be marketed under the trade mark and of controlling their condition that enables it to provide a focus for goodwill and to reduce transaction costs. The owner is likely to exercise this power to advance its interest and maximize the benefit that it derives from the trade mark. This means striking an optimal balance between any return it can generate from name sharing and the costs that this might entail, which include the risk of reducing the trade mark's appeal to consumers. The potential returns from name sharing include reducing the costs of production and increasing the scale or range of marked products that can be marketed to consumers.

---

[35] On the practice of using trade marks as a feature of products that end users can display, see the comments of Whitford J in *Unidoor v. Marks and Spencer* [1988] RPC 275 at 278–9.
[36] See, for example, J.B. Swann, 'Trademarks and Marketing' 91 *Trademark Reporter* 787, 796–7 (2001), and D.A. Aaker and E. Joachimsthaler, *Brand Leadership: The Next Level of the Brand Revolution* (The Free Press, New York, 2000) pp. 48–9.
[37] See, for example, G.S. Becker and K.M. Murphy, with E. Glaeser, 'Social Markets and the Escalation of Quality: The World of Veblen Revisited', in G.S. Becker and K.M. Murphy (eds.), *Social Economics: Market Behaviour in a Social Environment* (The Belknap Press, Cambridge, MA, 2000).

For any particular trade mark, a number of factors are relevant to this balancing exercise. One is the basis of the trade mark's appeal to consumers and the relative importance of its capacity to reduce transaction costs. As has been seen, such a capacity depends on the marked products having a reputation for meeting consumers' expectations in terms of their quality and other characteristics regarded as important and consistently matching up to this reputation. A trade mark's owner therefore has an incentive to ensure that name sharing does not damage this reputation. This means that any arrangements for this should include effective mechanisms that enable the owner to detect, respond to and remedy any problems concerning the condition of products sold under the mark or other relevant factors. Subject to there being satisfactory safeguards, voluntary name sharing confirms the versatility of the trade mark as a structuring device and demonstrates how it can facilitate the evolution of more efficient structures for the production and distribution of goods and the provision of services.

The discrete and versatile nature of the trade mark as a focus for goodwill has facilitated the evolution of flexible structures for organizing the production and distribution of goods and the delivery of services such as subcontracting and franchising. Such structures are based on voluntary name sharing. It has already been seen how they can be viewed as an extension of the concept of an undertaking beyond a single legal entity to include a wider range of organizational possibilities.[38] As well as being consistent with the legal notion of 'origin', such arrangements need not impair the goodwill focused on the trade mark. The economic rationale of such voluntary name sharing is that it achieves greater productive efficiency.[39] In a franchise, for example, relatively small undertakings, which are relatively close to consumers and have the incentive to meet their expectations, provide goods or services, but can take advantage of the goodwill enjoyed by the organization as a whole.

The gains in productive efficiency from name sharing, however, have to be weighed against the need to maintain or improve the trade mark's reputation and value. Insofar as this means exercising effective control over the quality and condition of the goods or services that are to share the identity, this will set a practical limit on the range of organizational possibilities. However, where this is not the case, the range of possibilities expands to include looser forms of arrangement based on licensing, although the undertaking's right of

---

[38] See above at n. 15.
[39] According to this standard, social welfare can be improved through producing a given output with a lower-cost combination of inputs or through producing more output with the same combination of inputs: see Cooter and Ulen, *Law and Economics*, n. 26 at 16.

control still forms the basis of such an arrangement. Thus, where the appeal of a trade mark is largely due to its capacity to confer non-material attributes of various kinds on products, its owner might have much less of an incentive to maintain vigilance on matters such as quality and to be able to exercise practical control over those it licenses to use the trade mark. In theory at least, any reduction in vigilance would reflect the preferences of consumers.

As regards involuntary name sharing, the impact of this depends on whether it is likely to mislead consumers about 'origin'. If so, this may undermine the trade mark's capacity to act as a focus of goodwill. This can be damaging even where the same trade mark is used for different kinds of product since goodwill is something that can be exploited across a range of markets and used to reduce the costs of entering a new market. The scale of the problem increases with the number of parties that are using the same trade mark without mutual consent. Whilst all such parties have an interest in maintaining or improving the trade mark's reputation, they have less of an incentive to invest resources in doing so in the absence of a consensual arrangement since they would not benefit exclusively from it, but would have to share the return with the other sharers.

In effect, involuntary name sharing that misleads consumers about 'origin' weakens the alignment of interest that enables a reputation to provide reassurance. The problem is analogous to that of 'shirking'. This problem arises where parties provide a collective input and receive a collective reward, but their individual contributions cannot be detected, thereby weakening the alignment between input and reward.[40] There is therefore a case for preventing or minimizing involuntary name sharing that has this effect. Where it is permitted to further another policy goal, it should be strictly regulated to minimize the impact on the trade mark's goodwill. This applies to the right of parallel importers of goods already marketed within the EEA to use a trade mark despite interfering with the condition of the goods in a way that would normally be the prerogative of the trade mark's owner.[41] This right is equivalent to a compulsory licence and should be restricted and subjected to conditions that as far as possible achieve the same outcome as if the name sharing had been voluntary.[42]

---

[40] See A. Alchian and D. Demsetz, 'Production, Information Costs and Economic Organization' 62 *American Economic Review* 777 (1972).

[41] See above at n. 21.

[42] On the conditions that a parallel importer must satisfy, see the ECJ's judgment on this in *Bristol-Myers Squibb* v. *Paranova* [1996] ETMR 1 and *Boehringer Ingelheim* v. *Swingward* C-143/00 [2002] ETMR 898. There is still uncertainty about some of these conditions and thus the precise scope of the 'free movement' defence:

Even where it does not mislead consumers about 'origin', involuntary name sharing can still have an adverse impact. It can reduce the scope for exploiting a trade mark in new markets; it can reduce a trade mark's capacity to differentiate products;[43] it can damage a trade mark's appeal, insofar as this goes beyond having the kind of reputation that provides reassurance about quality and other characteristics; and, where the trade mark has the kind of appeal to consumers that can be exploited without misleading them about 'origin', it can amount to unfair free-riding on the investment that has given it this appeal. All of these potential adverse effects of involuntary name sharing can be related to the designated effects that can amount to trade mark infringement under the additional protection that the EC Directive has conferred on trade marks with a 'reputation'.[44]

However, it is hard to make an economic case for entitling trade mark owners to prohibit involuntary name sharing that does not mislead consumers about origin unless the adverse impact on the trade mark's owner reduces the net overall benefits attributable to the trade mark. In other words, account should be taken not only of any losses to the owner that would be avoided, but also of the benefits to other parties that would be lost. Some traders might, for example, derive benefit from using signs identical to trade marks because they have an intrinsic appeal to consumers or an eye-catching quality or provide a convenient and effective means of conveying non-origin information to consumers. And where certain consumers are attracted to a sign registered as a trade mark for reasons other than its signification of a specific origin, then entitling the trade mark's owner to prohibit involuntary name sharing would give it a monopoly over this object of desire and deprive these consumers of the benefits of competition.[45]

5. CONCLUSION

Voluntary name sharing is consistent with a trade mark's performance of its

---

see the subsequent judgment of the Court of Appeal in the *Boehringer Ingelheim* litigation [2004] ETMR 65, the questions that the Court of Appeal has put to the ECJ [2004] 3 CMLR 4.

[43] See Beebe, 'Search and Persuasion', n. 32 above.

[44] EC Directive, art. 5.2; 1994 Act, s. 10(3). A 'reputation' in this context means that the trade mark must have achieved a minimum level of recognition with relevant consumers: *General Motors* v. *Yplon* C-375/97 [1999] ETMR 950. On the scope of this additional protection, see the ECJ's judgments in *Davidoff* v. *Gofkid* C-292/00 [2003] ETMR 534 and *Adidas-Salomon* v. *Fitnessworld* C-408/01 [2004] ETMR 129.

[45] See generally S.L. Dogan and M.A. Lemley, 'The Merchandising Right: Fragile Theory or Fait Accompli?' 54 *Emory LJ* 461 (2005).

essential function of indicating 'origin' in accordance with the ECJ's statement. It should not, therefore, impair or undermine a trade mark's capacity to provide the economic benefits that can result from the performance of this function. These benefits include those traditionally associated with goodwill, such as the reduction of search costs, and those that reflect the role of brands in modern marketing such as the conferring of emotional and psychological attributes on products. Whilst indiscriminate name sharing could damage a trade mark's capacity to generate these benefits, the interest of trade mark owners in maintaining this capacity should minimize this danger where name sharing is voluntary and thus has to be based on their consent.

Involuntary name sharing is more problematic. Where the same trade mark is used for the same kind of goods or services, this must impair the trade mark's capacity to perform its essential function and differentiate products according to their 'origin'. This in turn is likely to reduce or undermine the trade mark's capacity to generate the economic benefits that can result from this function, though the impact would depend on the scale of the name sharing. In practice, however, use of the same trade mark might not mislead consumers about 'origin'. Even so, such involuntary name sharing can reduce some of the benefits that a trade mark can generate for its owner, although these must be weighed against the benefits to the other parties involved.

PART II

Registrability issues

3. The rise and fall of honest concurrent use

Phillip Johnson

1. INTRODUCTION

Over a hundred and thirty years ago trade mark registration began in the United Kingdom with the Trade Marks Registration Act 1875[1] and soon afterwards the problem caused by two people wanting to register an interest in the same mark arose. It therefore became necessary to address how these two people, who both had an interest in the mark, could 'share' the use of the mark without undermining the integrity of the trade mark itself, something which even prior to registration had been acknowledged as having the purpose of denoting the origin of the goods.[2] The solution eventually adopted was the creation of the concept of the 'honest concurrent user' which provided a mechanism for two or more traders to register the same mark for the same goods (or services); once registered, concurrent users could sue third- party users, but not each other. This chapter begins by looking at the proposition by Lord Diplock that the rule began under the common law, but then moves on to suggest the more likely origins of the rule. The chapter concludes by looking at the rule's evolution and eventually its slow death[3] following the enactment of the Trade Marks Act 1994.

---

[1] 38 & 39 Vict. c. 91.
[2] See the definition of trade mark in section 1 of the Merchandise Marks Act 1862 (25 & 26 Vic. c. 88).
[3] In the United Kingdom at least; the rule is still going strong in other Commonwealth jurisdictions: see section 44(3) of the Trade Marks Act 1995 (Aus) and section 26 of the Trade Marks Act 2002 (NZ). In Canada there is provision relating to honest concurrent user (section 21 of the Trade Marks Act 1985), but it is different in nature in that concurrent use is permitted, although concurrent marks may not be registered.

2. BASED ON COMMON LAW RULES . . .

In *GE Trade Marks*[4] Lord Diplock explained how he believed honest concurrent use came into being:

> . . . the interest of the public in not being deceived about the origin of goods had and has to be accommodated with the vested right of property of traders in trade marks which they have honestly adopted and which by public use have attracted a valuable goodwill. In the early 19th century trade was still largely local; marks which were identical or which closely resembled one another might have been innocently adopted by traders in different localities. In these their respective products were not sold in competition with one another and accordingly no question of deception of the public could then arise. With the rapid improvement of communications, however, in the first half of the 19th century markets expanded; products of two traders who used similar marks upon their goods could thus come to be on sale to the same potential purchasers with the consequent risk of their being misled as to the origin of the goods . . . To meet this kind of situation the doctrine of honest concurrent user was evolved.

Lord Diplock therefore traced the origins of the honest concurrent user back to the protection of common law trade marks.[5] Of course, the exact nature of the rights in a trade mark under the 'common law' was very uncertain; prior to registration in 1875 there were two actions: a common law action for deceit;[6] and an action in equity for passing off.[7] However, the scope and rules for these two different causes of action[8] criss-crossed for most of the

---

[4] [1972] 1 WLR 729, 743; also see Gardiner, Comment (1973) 36 MLR 300.
[5] *Ibid.*, 742.
[6] This required fraud on the part of the defendant: see *Edelsten v Edelsten* (1863) 1 De G J & S 185 (46 ER 72).
[7] From 1863 it was possible to bring an action against anyone who fraudulently marks a good under the Merchandise Marks Act 1862 (25 & 26 Vict. c. 88); although, ironically, the requirements of the Act eventually gave a boost to foreign (in particular, German) industry: see D. Higgins '"Made in Britain"? National Trade Marks and Merchandise Marks: the British experience from the late 19th Century to the 1920s' (2002) 5 *J of Ind Hist* 50.
[8] It should also be remembered that prior to the Judicature Acts 1873 and 1875 (36 & 37 Vict. c. 66) and (38 & 9 Vict. c. 77) an action for passing off was commenced in the Court of Chancery and an action for deceit in the Court of the Common Pleas or the Court of the King's Bench (as an action between two subjects, and not between the King and his subject, it should have always been started in Common Pleas, but by way of certain procedural fictions (most notable the Bill of Middlesex) it was possible to bring an action before the King's Bench. These fictions were abolished by the Process in Courts of Law at Westminster Act 1832 (2 & 3 Will. 4 c. 39) section 4, but the jurisdiction of the King's Bench was maintained in relation to cases where this fiction had been used).

nineteenth century and so it is difficult to find any coherent conception of a 'common law mark' from which the honest concurrent user could spring.[9]

Notwithstanding the lack of certainty over the nature of the cause of action, in contrast to patents or copyright, the common law mark was thought to grant no monopoly;[10] and so it was possible for more than one trader to have a separate and distinct right[11] to use the same mark. Each such trader could pursue third parties who were improperly using the mark. It was the existence of these concurrent common law rights, Lord Diplock suggests, that led to the Court of Chancery creating the doctrine of honest concurrent use. His provenance for this proposition is two cases from the 1860s. The first, *Dent v Turpin*[12] determined that two users of a mark (which had derived from a common predecessor) had a separate right to obtain an injunction against a third person using the mark.[13] The second case, *Southorn v Reynolds*,[14] relied on *Dent* and came to a similar conclusion on very similar facts. Neither of these cases, however, was a dispute between 'concurrent users' and so it is difficult to see how they can provide support for a common law honest concurrent user.[15]

It was only during the 1860s[16] that the first signs that a trade mark might

---

[9] For a general discussion see F. Schechter, *The Historical Foundations of the Law Relating to Trade-Mark Law* (2nd edn, Lawbook Exchange, Clark, NJ, 2002), Chapter 6; *Addley Bourne v Swan* (1903) 20 RPC 105, 117–20; L. Bently and B. Sherman, *The Making of Modern Intellectual Property Law* (Cambridge University Press, Cambridge, 1999), pp. 166–72; and C. Wadlow, *The Law of Passing-Off: Unfair Competition by Misrepresentation* (3rd edn, Sweet & Maxwell, London, 2004), pp. 16–36.

[10] To that effect see *Singer Manufacturing v Loog* (1880) 18 Ch D 395, 412 (James LJ, 'I am of [the] opinion that there is no such thing as a monopoly or a property in the nature of a copyright, or in the nature of a patent, in the use of any name'). *Cf* Lord Diplock, *GE Trade Marks*, *supra*, p. 742. Whether it granted a property right is far more complicated – see below.

[11] See *Dent v Turpin* (1861) 2 J & H 139 (70 ER 1003), 144 (ER 1005).

[12] (1861) 2 J & H 139 (70 ER 1003).

[13] This rule was formalized by the proviso to section 39 of the Trade Marks Act 1905.

[14] (1865) 12 LT 75.

[15] Indeed, in a treatise of the day these cases were discussed in respect of multiplication of marks by way of assignment and not anything to do with concurrent use – see F. Adams, *A Treatise on the Law of Trade-marks* (Butterworths, London, 1876), pp. 92–3.

[16] Before that time most courts would agree with the views of Lord Langdale MR in *Perry v Truefitt* (1842) 6 Beav 66 (49 ER 749) who said 'it does not seem to me a man can acquire property in [a] mark' (at 73 or ER 752). For a discussion of the debates in the nineteenth century over the proprietary nature of trade marks see Schechter n. 9, 150–60 and L. Bently 'From Communication to Thing: Historical Aspects of the Conceptualisation of Trade Marks as Property' in G. Dinwoodie and M. Janis (eds.), *Trademark Law and Theory: A Handbook of Contemporary Research* (Edward Elgar, Cheltenham, 2008).

be attributed a proprietary nature[17] appeared. The recognition of concurrent rights only becomes important once exclusivity attaches to a mark; otherwise infringement is no different from other actions where multiple persons have a joint, but severable, interest. The Court of Chancery in *Dent* and in *Southorn* was not, therefore, protecting an exclusive proprietary right, but restraining a person from misrepresenting his or her goods as those of another. Or, put another way, it was not recognizing concurrent rights in a mark, but rather allowing two marks to be simultaneously used where there was no misrepresentation.

There are three further reasons why honest concurrent use should not be traced back to the common law. The first is that passing off does not contain a defence of honest concurrent use; instead such use just goes to the issue of whether or not there was a misrepresentation.[18] Thus the distinctiveness of the mark might be destroyed by conduct which began as downright dishonest, nevertheless no action for passing off will succeed if the claimant does not act in time (i.e. whilst the dishonest statement is still a misrepresentation).[19] The second is that the doctrine of honest concurrent use applied only to the registration of a mark, and the courts have never allowed it to be raised as a defence to infringement.[20] Therefore, if concurrent use were traced back to infringement cases, which occurred before the introduction of registration, it would lead to concurrent use's very nature needing to be re-invented. Finally, when registration was introduced, distinct and separate provision was made to cover the situation where the goodwill of one person passes to two different succes-

---

[17] This was more or less the result of Westbury LC overturning previous thinking in the *Leather Cloth Company v The American Leather Cloth Company* (1863) 4 De G J & S 137 (46 ER 868) (at 142 or ER 870) confirmed by the House of Lords at (1865) 11 HLC 523 (11 ER 1435). It is probable that this issue became important following *Emperor of Austria v Day and Kossuth* (1861) 3 De G F & J 217 (45 ER 861) when it was reaffirmed that the Court of Chancery could only ever grant an injunction to prevent damage to proprietary interests. Prior to that decision this requirement was largely ignored by the courts; although see *Clark v Freeman* (1848) 11 Beav 112 (50 ER 759).

[18] *Habib Bank Ltd v Habib Bank AG Zurich* [1981] 1 WLR 1265 at 1275 *per* Oliver LJ.

[19] See C. Wadlow, *The Law of Passing-Off: Unfair Competition by Misrepresentation*, n. 9, p. 780.

[20] See *Origins Natural Resources Inc v Origin Clothing Ltd* [1995] FSR 280; although an infringement case could be stayed pending the outcome of an application for registration based on honest concurrent use: *James & Sons v Wafer Razor* (1932) 49 RPC 597; further section 7 of the Trade Marks Act 1938 (section 41 of 1905 Act) provided protection for those persons who started using a trade mark before the first registered proprietor.

sors.[21] Accordingly, had the owners of the marks in *Dent* and *Southorn* sought to register the marks, they would not have done so as honest concurrent users but rather as successors. The beginning of the rule must accordingly be traced to a time when the registration of marks was underway.

3. ITS REAL BEGINNINGS – THE 'THREE MARK RULE'

When registration was first introduced on 13 August 1875 it granted the first person to register a trade mark the exclusive right to use it.[22] It made no provision for situations where there had been more than one user of the mark prior to that date; although it did allow two identical marks to be registered with the special leave of the court.[23] It was soon apparent to the registrar of trade marks that a strict rule allowing only the first person to register a mark to have any rights in it would lead to an injustice[24] where more than one trader had been using the mark prior to August 1875; but if every prior user of a mark could register it this would lead to a confusing multitude of rights. Indeed, the 1875 Act, as originally passed, included another sting in its tail: it only allowed trade mark infringement proceedings to be commenced if the mark was registered.

Unsurprisingly, this led to a deluge of registrations, particularly by the cotton merchants at the Manchester Office.[25] However, once it became clear many of these registrations would be rejected the sting became particularly painful. This problem, unlike that of multiple marks, was remedied almost

---

[21] This was initially dealt with (indirectly) by rule 29 of the Trade Marks Rules under the 1875–6 Act (in Sebastian n. 27 at 224 *et seq.*) and later expressly under section 23 of Trade Marks Act 1905.

[22] Section 3 of the Trade Marks Registration Act 1875; for the first five years registration was *prima facie* evidence of the right, but after that period expired it became conclusive evidence. It should be noted that the way the Act was drafted did not confer the right, but simply provided a statutory evidential presumption relating to a pre-existing common law right.

[23] Section 6 of the 1875 Act; the registrar was precluded from registering such marks until 1919 (Trade Marks Act 1919 section 12 and Second Schedule).

[24] In *Jelly's Case* (1878) 51 LJ Ch 639 n. (1), Jessel MR gives a good example 'Look at the monstrous injustice that would be done if a man who had a trade-mark for, perhaps, forty years, should lose it, because another man who had it for four years happened to register it first' (at 640).

[25] This deluge had still had not cleared by the end of the decade where some 44,000 applications were caught in a backlog: see Note (1879) *Solicitors' Journal* 819 (16 August 1879). The merchants complained bitterly about the 1875 Act and even sent a deputation to London to ask that a commission of inquiry be set up: see Legal News (1876) *Solicitors' Journal* 402 (18 March 1876).

straight away. The Trade Marks Registration Amendment Act 1876[26] provided that where an application to register a mark which had been used prior to August 1875[27] had been refused by the registrar, a certificate of refusal had to be issued.[28] A person who had such a certificate was left with the same rights in the mark as he or she had prior to the 1875 Act.[29] This left a residual category of traders who retained only common law protection. It did not, however, answer the question of how many traders were allowed on the register before certificates of refusal should be issued for further similar marks. To address this issue, following the Lord Chancellor's advice, the registrar introduced the 'three mark rule'.

It was the Master of the Rolls[30] who first mentioned the rule in *In re Walkden Aerate Waters Co*:[31]

> The Registrar came to me to ask how many [identical trade marks] he was to register. He said that the Lord Chancellor had stated three . . . If this mark is registered, then there will be the full number of three, because then there would be no trade mark at all . . . the Lord Chancellor has intimated his opinion that where there are more than three it ceases to be a distinctive trade mark.[32]

It can be seen that the three mark rule was originally, and continued to be,[33] a rough and ready way to determine when a mark became 'common to the trade' (or in modern terms, generic).[34] Such a mark could not be registered and if

---

[26] 39 & 40 Vict. c. 33.

[27] In relation to the textile trade this date was modified to 1 January 1878 in pursuance of an Order in Council of 12 December 1877 (a copy of which is in L. Sebastian, *The Law of Trade Marks and Their Registration, and Matters Connected Therewith* (Stevens & Son, London, 1878) at 233b-4).

[28] Section 2.

[29] Section 1 of the Trade Marks Registration Amendment Act 1876 amended section 1 of the 1875 to this effect; this was replaced by section 77 of the Patents, Designs and Trade Marks Act 1883 (46 & 47 Vict. c. 57).

[30] The Master of the Rolls was responsible for the supervision of the trade mark register.

[31] (1877) [1884] 54 LJ Ch 394. Surprisingly for the son of a merchant, Jessel MR opens his judgment by showing his contempt for *trade*: 'The poverty of invention of the people *in the middle class* has never, to my mind, been more strikingly, exemplified than since I have had the supervision of the registration of trade marks.' [emphasis added].

[32] *Ibid.* at 395.

[33] This rule was codified as section 74(3) of the 1883 Act.

[34] To be common to the trade it was necessary for more than three persons to use the mark prior to 13 August 1875; those persons would, however, have to be making substantial use of the mark: *In re Hodson, Tessier & Co* (1881) [1902] 86 LTNS 188.

registered was liable to be removed from the register.[35] There appears to have been no rationale for selecting three as the magic number and there was no requirement of geographical diversity, only of *bona fide* use.[36] So if the first three traders who registered the mark all operated in London (and not beyond) a fourth trader in Aberdeen would not be permitted to register the mark[37] notwithstanding the fact that registering that fourth mark would have had a smaller effect on the ability of the previous users of the mark to distinguish their goods than the second or third registration did. Yet the arbitrary figure of three remained in place.

This presented particular problems to the Manchester cotton merchants.[38] The use of cotton marks was somewhat different from the use of other marks in that merchants (essentially the middle men dealing with the export market) would sell identical wares under different marks to different traders. This enabled each such trader to sell identical goods under a different mark in the same market without directly competing with each other.[39] The effect of this was that each merchant used tens (or even hundreds) of different marks, which in turn created significant duplication of marks (or at least similarity between marks). Although this duplication was usually inadvertent, it made it difficult for individual cotton marks to be distinctive and so many long-standing marks could not be registered.[40] This in combination with the problems with the restriction on word marks[41] meant that, in contrast to other traders, those in the cotton industry were badly affected by the introduction of registration,[42] so

---

[35] *Hyde & Co's TM* (1878) [1884] 54 LJ Ch 395; it was still possible to register a mark which was common to the trade as a constituent of another mark, but the common part must be disclaimed: section 74(2) of the 1883 Act. This led to practice of developing a complex web of additions with disclaimers, which were eventually swept away by the Trade Marks Act 1905.

[36] *Re Powell and Re Pratt* (1878) Sebastian's Digest 589.

[37] Indeed, he might apply to rectify the register to remove the first three marks so that nobody owned an interest in the mark.

[38] For a history of the cotton marks see D. Higgins and G. Tweedale 'The Trade Mark Question and the Lancashire Cotton Textile Industry, 1870–1914' (1996) 27(2) *Textile History* 207.

[39] *Ibid.*, 212.

[40] *Ibid.*, 211.

[41] Under the 1875 Act a word could only be registered in combination with a device (section 10); the 1883 Act permitted a 'fancy words or words not in common usage' (section 64(1)) to be registered; the restriction was maintained in a modified form by the 1905 Act (section 9); before finally being more or less swept away by the 1919 Act (section 7). This restriction was particularly problematic for cotton marks because cotton merchants typically used (non-fancy) words as marks.

[42] This was acknowledged by the *Report of the Committee to Inquire into the Duties, Organisation, and Arrangements of the Patent Office* (1888) C 5350 (Herschell Committee) at viii.

much so that they had a preference to be excluded from the 1875 Act altogether wishing to rely on other legislation.[43]

Some special rules were introduced for cotton marks, most notably applications for cotton marks were examined by a Committee of Experts who could either indicate that a mark was registerable or that it was not. Those which were not registered were included in a register of 'refusals';[44] being on that register gave owners of old marks (which were in terms of the Act 'common to the trade') the same right to sue as they would have had but for the introduction of registration. However, these special rules for the Manchester cotton traders did not last very long in the main, and were abolished in 1883; nevertheless the register of refusals and the fight to have a proper Manchester Office[45] continued much longer. These matters are outside the scope of this piece and must be left for another day.

The problems with multiple users were far broader than simply those faced by the Manchester traders. Nevertheless it was soon possible to identify a 'concurrent user' as one of the three persons who was already a trade mark proprietor by reason of having lawfully acquired and used the mark[46] (although the term 'concurrent user' was yet to be coined). Initially, the rule applied to both new marks (post-August 1875) and old marks (pre-August 1875) and *Walkden* itself related to the registration of a new mark where two old marks were already on the register (similarly in *Re Vergeras*[47] registration of two new marks was permitted where one old mark had previously been registered). However, the Court of Appeal took against the registration of new marks where they were similar to old marks;[48] and in *Jackson v Napper*[49] Stirling J states the three mark rule only in terms of 'old marks'.[50] His decision could be seen as the result of an implicit overruling of *Walkden* by the Court of Appeal's stance on registering new marks, although it was not put in those terms.

---

[43] Higgins and Tweedale n. 38, 211 (in particular the Merchandise Marks Act 1862).
[44] See rule 59 in Sebastian n. 27 at 237; this is distinct from the certificate of refusal mentioned above.
[45] There was strong (and successful) lobbying for a Manchester Office during the passage of the 1905 Act and the Trade Marks Act 1938 still included some special provision: see section 39.
[46] *Jelly's Case, supra,* 640.
[47] (1881) 3 June (unreported), but described in L. Sebastian, *The Law of Trade Marks and Their Registration, and Matters Connected Therewith* (4th edn, Stevens 1899) at 313.
[48] See *Worthington TM* (1880) 14 Ch D 8 and *Lyndon's TM* (1886) 32 Ch D 109.
[49] (1886) 35 Ch D 162.
[50] *Ibid.*, 169.

This confusion over whether new marks fell within the three mark rule caused the commentators to diverge in their analysis. Whilst Lewis Sebastian suggests that the rule continued to apply to new marks,[51] Sir Duncan Kerly categorically states that it did not so apply.[52] Instead he suggests that the rule was likely to be important predominately in relation to the rectification of the register in relation to existing marks (for example, when they were shown to be common to the trade).[53] Indeed, this seems to have been the view of the Herschell Committee when it recommended the retention of the rule. Thus, the Committee recommended that the rule should be modified so that it covered the scenario where two new users started using a mark at different times, but it is unclear which started first.[54] This recommendation was not implemented in the Patents, Designs and Trade Marks Act 1888[55] and it had to wait until 1905.

4. CONSENT VERSUS THE PUBLIC INTEREST

When the 'three mark rule' was first adopted, a subsequent concurrent user could only register the second (or third mark) if the owner of the first (and second) mark consented to the registration; the Master of the Rolls stated his requirements in *Walkden*:

> I require [the other proprietor's] consent to be obtained, for the marks are substantially the same, and I have no doubt that I should grant an injunction to restrain the company from using their mark if I found that any mistake had occurred amongst the customers.[56]

Initially, therefore, the three mark rule simply reinforced the proprietary nature of the right[57] in the mark by requiring consent of the proprietor;[58] and

---

[51] Sebastian, n. 47 at 313.
[52] D. Kerly, *The Law of Trade-Marks, Trade-Name, and Merchandise Marks* (1st edn, Sweet & Maxwell, London, 1894), 179 (although he erroneously says that it has *never* been applied to new marks).
[53] P. 179.
[54] Herschell Committee recommendation 31 (p. xiii) and comptroller's evidence, Q3164 to 3169 (p. 186).
[55] 51 & 52 Vict. c. 50.
[56] In *Hodson, Tessie and Co's TM* (1881) [1902] 86 LTR 188 the court indicated that the test for concurrent user was whether, on the date the 1875 Act came into effect, the registered proprietor could have obtained an injunction to prevent the applicant from using the mark (at 189).
[57] The 1875 Act did not grant a proprietor right as such (see n. 22).
[58] Also see *Re Leonardt* (1878) Sebastian's Digest 610 and *Re Mitchell* (1878) Sebastian's Digest 611.

if the public was confused by two marks being on the register that was not a relevant concern. Consequently, for a short time, the courts were letting the proprietary nature of the trade mark trump its identified functions of guaranteeing origin and stopping traders misrepresenting their goods.[59] However, before long the courts became concerned about customers becoming confused or deceived by two different marks being used simultaneously and so the importance of obtaining consent diminished.[60] And at the close of the century, in *Dewhurst & Sons' Application*,[61] the court adopted a rationale that would remain the cornerstone of the honest concurrent user:

> Let us, then, consider what the position of the register will be, and how far the interests of the public will be protected if this mark is registered. As to the consents, I do not say that they are immaterial. They are valuable as affording some evidence that there will not be deception . . .[62]

This new consideration meant that registration based on the three mark rule was no longer something that could be left to the concurrent users to agree amongst themselves, but instead it was necessary to consider the effect the registration would have on a customer's ability to know which goods came from which proprietor (put another way, recognizing that even where there is concurrent use a trade mark is intended to inform the customer about the origin of the goods). In any event, the three mark rule introduced many elements of what was to become the honest concurrent user, but during its lifetime it was little more than a transitional provision to protect those who started using a mark before registration was introduced in August 1875. This was how the law stood prior to the Trade Marks Act 1905.[63]

---

[59] In some ways, section 5(5) of the Trade Marks Act 1994 brings it round full circle.

[60] In *'White Rose'* (1885) LR 30 Ch. D 505 the court was reluctant to allow two similar marks to be on the register at the same time as it might cause confusion to the public, but the court permitted it as the second user was an 'old mark' (that is, pre-1875).

[61] [1896] 2 Ch. 137.

[62] *Ibid.*, 148.

[63] 5 Edw. 7. c. 15; this Act was introduced as a Private Members Bill by John Fletcher Moulton. He had previously introduced Bills in an attempt to consolidate trade mark law in 1899 (Bill No. 287), in 1901 (Bill No. 79), in 1902 (Bill No. 128), in 1903 (Bill No. 174) and in 1904 (Bill No. 53). Honest concurrent use first appeared in the 1903 Bill and remained unchanged in the 1904 Bill and the Bill that became the 1905 Act.

5. THE INTRODUCTION OF THE HONEST CONCURRENT USER

The 1905 Act made substantial changes to trade mark law including superseding the old 'three mark rule' by giving the court power to permit the registration of a mark in the case of honest concurrent user or of other special circumstances.[64] It was acknowledged by the Bill's promoter to be a new power,[65] but its links to the 'three mark rule' are clear. Yet by making this change it was also making a fundamental shift in the purpose and effect of the rule; changing it from being a transitional arrangement, which came into being as a necessary consequence of registration, into a rule which had potentially indefinite application. The necessity and reason for this change was questioned privately by the Lord Chief Justice[66] (amongst others) although not by the Select Committee itself;[67] yet it was finally enacted as section 21 of the 1905 Act:

> In case of honest concurrent user or of other special circumstances which, in the opinion of the Court, make it proper so to do, the Court may permit the registration of the same trade mark, or of nearly identical trade marks, for the same goods or description of goods by more than one proprietor subject to such conditions . . . as it may think it right to impose.

The power was originally limited to the court and so the registrar was unable to register a mark even where there was indisputable honest concurrent use. Thus, it was only on appeal from the registrar that honest concurrent use came into play. The 1905 Act also included a provision which was closely related to honest concurrent use. This was found in the proviso to section 41 of the 1905 Act,[68] which prohibited the proprietor of a registered trade mark

---

[64] Section 21 of the 1905 Act (special circumstances are briefly discussed below).

[65] *Report and Special Report from the Select Committee on the Trade Marks Bill* (7 July 1905), '[Chairman:] Is there such a power now? – [Fletcher Moulton] No, there is not really a power, but the courts have nibbled at it. They have no statutory power, and I think it ought to be given to them.' (para. 129).

[66] *Memorandum of Lord Chief Justice* (Alverstone CJ) on Trade Marks Bill 10 June 1905, '[Section 21] raises a very difficult question I think concurrent rights should scarcely ever be allowed for registered marks...' (National Archive BT 209/945).

[67] Aside from the comment set out in n. 65, the only other comments were by Fletcher Moulton suggesting that 'perfectly honest, independent concurrent user of the same Trade Mark was not uncommon' (Select Committee Report, para. 4); the comptroller, when asked if he had any comments on the clause, simply answered 'No' (*ibid.*, para. 373).

[68] Subsequently re-enacted as section 7 of the 1938 Act.

from interfering with another person's use of a trade mark where that use began before the first person's application for registration was made. It also precluded a person who registered the mark first, but who started use second, from opposing an application to register the mark under section 21. Section 41 was a necessary incident of the new rule that, absent fraud and limited other circumstances, a registration became conclusive after seven years[69] and it remained the alternative for honest concurrent users.

The prohibition on the registrar registering a mark on the grounds of honest concurrent use meant that during the users first decade there were no reported cases. The first such case was *Maeder*,[70] where the court held that section 21 removes the disability imposed on the registration authority where two marks are identical or similar.[71] The court went on to acknowledge the purpose of the provision: to allow registration of similar marks, even where there may be confusion, provided the second user has acquired an interest through long concurrent use.[72] Thus, fairness to the honest concurrent user required the function of a trade mark (in particular, indicating origin) to be subordinated.

After *Maeder*, the number of applications under section 21 grew, but when the Trade Marks Act 1919[73] gave the registrar the power to register a mark under that section the number of concurrent user registrations substantially increased and a registry practice developed.[74] Even though the number of reported cases swelled, it was only when the House of Lords provided definitive guidance in *Pirie and Sons*[75] that the law started to take shape. Their Lordships agreed with the suggestion in *Maeder* that a mark could be registered by an honest concurrent user even where it was confusingly similar to the earlier mark,[76] and they went on to set out the matters which should be taken into account when deciding whether to allow such registration.

---

[69] D. Kerly and F. Underhay, *The Trade Marks Act 1905* (Sweet & Maxwell, London, 1906), 91.

[70] (1916) 33 RPC 77.

[71] *Ibid.*, 81; also see section 19 of the 1905 Act.

[72] *Ibid.*, 82. The fact that registration could proceed notwithstanding deception or confusion was confirmed again in *Lehmann & Co's App* (1918) 35 RPC 92, 99.

[73] The Second Schedule included an amendment to section 21 to allow the registrar to exercise the same power as the court. This amendment was introduced by the Solicitor-General during Committee Stage in the House of Commons.

[74] See, for example, *Notes of Official Rulings* (1929) 46 RPC App A (i).

[75] (1933) 50 RPC 147. The case also included an interesting discussion of whether or not the House of Lords could hear an appeal relating to trade mark registration. It also reaffirmed the great respect that should be accorded to the decision of the registrar (it was the *REEF TM* [2002] RPC 19 of its day).

[76] *Ibid.*, 158.

These were refined by the registrar in *John Fitton & Co*[77] to a simple list of five factors:

(a) the extent of use in time and quantity and the area of the trade;
(b) the degree of confusion likely to ensure from the resemblance of the marks which is to a large extent indicative of the measure of public inconvenience;
(c) the honesty of the concurrent use;
(d) whether any instances of confusion have in fact been proved; and
(e) the relative inconvenience which would be caused if the mark were registered, subject if necessary to any conditions and limitations.

The five factors remained central in determining whether a mark could be registered by a concurrent user and, to some extent, made it clear how honest concurrent use should be reconciled with any customer confusion caused by two conflicting marks in the marketplace.

6. THE HIGH POINT FOR THE HONEST CONCURRENT USER

The effect of section 5 of the Trade Marks Act 1905 was restated[78] as section 12(2) of the Trade Marks Act 1938[79] and the honest concurrent user entered its heyday.[80] Although the principles for registration of such a user did not change in substance from those in *Pirie* they evolved. But the honesty of the user remained of prime concern. Where a mark's use was honest, the fact the concurrent user knew of the other mark was less important. As the registrar once noted 'if [the concurrent use] is not honest it is as nothing'[81] and where an application is clearly dishonest then it will fail. This occurred in

---

[77] *John Fitton & Co's Application* (1949) 66 RPC 110, 112 (Reg) (the factors as expressed above have been slightly simplified).
[78] The *Report of the Departmental Committee on the Law and Practice Relating to Trade Marks* (1934) Cmd 4568 (Goschen Committee) supported the retention of the honest concurrent user.
[79] The Trade Marks Act 1938 was a consolidation of the Trade Marks Act 1905, the Trade Marks Act 1919 and the Trade Marks (Amendment) Act 1937.
[80] Although there were reviews of trade mark law between 1938 and 1994 they supported the retention of the honest concurrent use provision: see in particular, *Report of the Committee to Examine British Trade Mark Law and Practice* (1974) Cmnd 5601 (Mathys Committee), pp. 39–41.
[81] *Granada* [1979] RPC 303, 313.

Parkington's Application[82] where, with knowledge of the earlier mark, the concurrent user secretly adopted the mark and put it to commercial use: conduct the court could not condone as honest.[83] Normally, however, honesty could be inferred from a statutory declaration to the effect that the use was honest[84] and it fell to the proprietor of the earlier mark to challenge the declaration. As Lord Diplock suggested in *GE Trade Mark*[85]

> Under [the doctrine of honest concurrent use] a trade mark remained entitled to protection in cases where the use of it had not originally been deceptive but a risk of deception had subsequently arisen as a result of events which did not involve any dishonesty or other wrongful conduct upon the part of the proprietor of the mark. If, however, his own wrongful conduct had played a part in making the use of the mark deceptive, the Court of Chancery would not grant him an injunction against infringement.[86]

The period of use required to become a concurrent 'user' was never fixed as it depended on the facts of each case. This was because what was important was not the duration of use as such, but the second comer providing evidence that the use had been sufficient for real commercial value and goodwill to be generated. In the words of Handworth MR in *Pirie's Application*,[87] the court had to always weigh 'whether or not the use has been of such a length of time as would justify it being called a user . . . . It would be impossible to say that in all cases a particular span of time must be accomplished before it can be treated as justifying a user within' the honest concurrent user provision. For example, the registrar noted in *Peddie*[88] that he knew of no reported case where a period of use as short as two and half years was sufficient for concurrent use, but he then went on to register the concurrent mark with such short use.[89] In contrast, a period of a few months, no matter the monetary expenditure on the mark, has been said never to be sufficient.[90] Concurrent use,

---

[82] (1946) 63 RPC 171.
[83] *Ibid.*, 183.
[84] See *Electrix App* [1957] RPC 369; the court looked to see whether the conduct of the applicant was sufficient to 'cleanse' its earlier dishonesty.
[85] [1972] 1 WLR 729.
[86] *Ibid.*, 743. This statement related to the so-called common law right, but it was meant to have continuing application.
[87] (1932) 49 RPC 195.
[88] (1944) 61 RPC 31, 36–7.
[89] In one case a person was allowed to withdraw an application and apply again to extend the period of use: see *Portogram* (1952) 69 RPC 241 (Reg); the period of use ends on the date of the application: *Granada* [1979] RPC 303, 315 (Reg).
[90] *Bi-Lo App* (1988) AIPC 90-466 (a decision of the Australian Registry on section 34(1) of the Trade Marks Act 1955 (now section 44(3) of the Trade Marks Act 1995)).

however, did not need to be continuous[91] although long-term non-use[92] or abandonment[93] would not be tolerated.

Alongside honest concurrent use it was possible to allow registration in 'special circumstances'. This included any circumstances 'which justify taking the case out of the ordinary rules so that justice may be done to the applicant';[94] they could even relate to matters arising before the earlier mark was registered or used.[95] Special circumstances, which relied so greatly on the discretion of the registrar or court, were often pleaded as an alternative to concurrent user, in case something about the use enabled a mark to still be registered. However, unlike honest concurrent use, the power to register in special circumstances was not maintained after the implementation of the Trade Marks Directive.[96]

7. THE NEAR DEATH EXPERIENCE FOR THE HONEST CONCURRENT USER: THE TRADE MARKS BILL

The Trade Marks Directive brought about a fundamental shift in the trade mark law of the United Kingdom and put the proprietor of a registered mark in a much stronger position than he or she had ever been under the 1938 Act. The Directive requires that a trade mark *shall* not be registered if it is identical or similar to an earlier mark;[97] unless the proprietor of the earlier mark

---

[91] *Holt* [1957] RPC 289, 294 (although this case was decided on the grounds of being a special circumstance).

[92] For example non-use for 21 years was held to be too long: *Fortuna-Werke* [1957] RPC 84 (Reg).

[93] *Ibid.,* abandonment occurs when a person stops affecting his or her mark to goods; it must be remembered that the goodwill in a business can be abandoned and this might affect any action under the law of passing off: *Star Industries v Yap Kwee Kor* [1976] FSR 256, PC (business closed down and good will disposed of, cannot sue for passing off); *Ad-Lib Club v Granville* [1971] FSR 1 (reputation survived four years after business closed. No intention to abandon goodwill); also see *Sutherland v V2 Music* [2002] EMLR 28. However, unlike goodwill, 'concurrent use' cannot 'diminish' by lack of use, but residual reputation can be a special circumstance allowing registration.

[94] *Bali Trade Mark (No. 2)* [1978] FSR 193, 221, *per* Fox J; for example, the registration of a mark in the United Kingdom where the mark was the ordinary mark of a foreign company was held to be such a special circumstance: *ACEC* [1965] RPC 369, 373 (Reg).

[95] *Holt* [1957] RPC 289, 294.

[96] Council Directive No. 89/104/EEC of 21 December 1988 to approximate the laws of the Member States relating to trade marks.

[97] Article 4(1).

consents.[98] There is no room for a mark which is confusingly similar to an earlier mark to be registered in any other circumstance.

This new regime meant that the Trade Marks Bill, as introduced in Parliament, included no provision relating to the honest concurrent user. During the Committee stage in the House of Lords, an amendment was proposed to retain it in a similar form to that in the 1938 Act. The Government asked to consider the amendment, but indicated that it took the view that maintaining the honest concurrent user was incompatible with the strict regime of the Directive.[99]

After considering the matter further, the Government moved an amendment, which became section 7 of the 1994 Act, during the third reading of the Bill. However, unlike the amendment proposed during Committee, it did not provide a special ground for allowing registration where there is an earlier conflicting mark – such a result being contrary to the Directive. Instead it provided a procedural mechanism. This mechanism meant that where the registrar concluded that a mark should not be accepted due to a conflicting earlier trade mark, he could still accept the application[100] if the applicant could show that he or she is an honest concurrent user.[101] But it was not possible for the registrar[102] to impose any terms or conditions under the limited procedural mechanism and so its utility was greatly reduced.

Once such an application was accepted by the registrar it was published.[103] Thereafter, notice of opposition could be given to the registrar by any person, including the proprietor of the earlier trade mark,[104] on the basis of the earlier (conflicting) trade mark. If the registrar upheld those objections, the application would be refused whether or not there was honest concurrent use of the later mark. The Government never expressed why it believed section 7 of the Trade Marks Act 1994 was compatible with the Directive. However, it is likely that it viewed the provision as purely procedural and, in accordance with recital (5) of the Directive, something left to Member States.[105]

---

[98] Article 4(5).
[99] *Hansard* (HL) (Committee Stage), Lord Strathclyde, 13 January 1994, Col. 19.
[100] Under section 37(5) of the 1994 Act.
[101] The definition of an 'honest concurrent user' under the 1938 Act was retained: see section 7(3) of the 1994 Act.
[102] The applicant could agree to impose limitations on himself or herself: section 13 of the 1994 Act.
[103] Section 38(1) of the 1994 Act.
[104] Section 38(2) of the 1994 Act; the effect of this provision was amended by article 2 of the Trade Marks (Relative Grounds) Order 2007 (SI 2007/1976) and now only the proprietor of the earlier trade mark (or earlier right), and no one else, can oppose registration on the basis of the earlier mark.
[105] This appears to be the view of the registry: see *Codas TM* [2001] RPC 14, 247.

The procedural device required a process where the registrar examined an application for registration on relative grounds and determined whether there were any conflicting earlier trade marks. This sort of examination had been conducted by the registrar from the very beginning of trade mark registration. However, by the time the Trade Marks Bill was before Parliament it was clear that the Community Trade Mark Office[106] would not be examining Community trade mark applications on relative grounds. Instead, the proprietor of an earlier mark would have to oppose an application for registration in opposition proceedings.[107]

Parliament's intention was to retain examination of domestic trade mark applications, but it acknowledged that in time it might be worth ending examination on relative grounds and to bring domestic practice in line with that at the Community Trade Mark Office. Accordingly, what became section 8 (power to require that relative grounds be raised in opposition proceedings) was included in the Act. This section gives the Secretary of State power[108] to make an order[109] to change the law so that relative grounds can only be raised in opposition proceedings and then only by the proprietor of the earlier mark. Or, put another way, the registrar would accept an application even where there is an earlier conflicting mark, and the proprietor of the earlier mark would have to oppose the registration after it was published. A necessary incident of ending examination on relative grounds would be turning off the procedural mechanism introduced by section 7: there is no need to compel the registrar to accept an application of an honest concurrent user where the registrar has to accept the application of a conflicting mark in any event. Therefore, the honest concurrent user provision ceases to have effect automatically once an order is made under section 8.[110] The retention of honest concurrent user in section 7 therefore gave it a reprieve for at least ten years.[111]

8. THE DEATH OF THE HONEST CONCURRENT USER

The preservation of honest concurrent user by the 1994 Act was, as it turns out,

---

[106] The Office for the Harmonization of the Internal Market, which processes Community trade mark and Community design applications.

[107] In *Reed Executive v Reed Business* (2004) RPC 40, Jacob LJ noted that the nature of the Community trade mark, and the need for coexistence, may require something like honest concurrent use to be adopted across the Community (at 800).

[108] After the end of the period of ten years from when Community trade mark applications may first be filed: see section 7(5) of the 1994 Act.

[109] By way of statutory instrument.

[110] Section 7(5) of the 1994 Act.

[111] See n. 108, *supra*.

of little effect. Soon after the Act came into force, the user was dealt a crippling blow by Walker J in the *Roadrunner Case*[112] when he held that where the proprietor of an earlier trade mark objects to registration of an identical concurrent user the registrar is required to reject the application.[113] In contrast, where the concurrent mark was only similar the registrar does not have to reject the application outright, but instead should consider the concurrent use as a factor in determining whether there was confusion.[114] In many ways, however, this is not honest concurrent use in the traditional sense; instead it is using the term to support a factual finding of no confusion. And where there is no confusion between the mark registered and trade mark in suit there is no ground to refuse the mark under the 1994 Act. This interpretation of honest concurrent use means that it never had any real effect again because all it did was get an application to publication.[115]

This limited scope for the honest concurrent user meant that there were very few decisions relying on section 7 of the 1994 Act, probably because concurrent users were faced with two alternatives. The first was to seek the consent of the registered proprietor of the earlier trade mark; if consent is given then the mark can be registered in any event[116] and if consent was refused then the earlier proprietor was on notice of the application and might well object. Alternatively, the second-comer could push on and try and argue honest concurrent user before the registrar, which could ultimately be undermined by an opposition based on the proprietor of the earlier mark objecting after publication.

In 2006, the Patent Office launched a consultation on ending examination on relative grounds.[117] In essence this was asking whether the Secretary of State should make an order under section 8 of the 1994 Act. Later in 2006, the Office issued a draft of the legislative changes required to implement that policy.[118] The ending of examination on relative grounds occurred on 1

---

[112] *Road Tech v UNISON* [1996] FSR 805.
[113] *Ibid.*, 813.
[114] *Codas TM* [2001] RPC 14, 248 (Reg); this supports the statement of Lord Strathclyde when introducing the amendment: *Hansard* (HL), 14 March 1994, Col. 71.
[115] See *Focus Business* (2004) O-023-04 (Reg), p. 6; Also see *Codas TM, supra* 'the fact that honest concurrent use has been shown at the examination stage cannot overcome the objection' in opposition proceedings (at 247).
[116] In accordance with section 5(5) of the 1994 Act.
[117] UK Patent Office, *Relative Grounds of Refusal – The Way Forward* (2006). This was the third consultation in this area previously there were: the UK Patent Office, *The Future of Relative Grounds Examination: A Pre-Consultation* (2005) and UK Patent Office, *Future of Official Examination on Relative Grounds* (2001).
[118] UK Patent Office, *Consultation on the proposed legislative changes to relative grounds for refusal* (2006).

October 2007 when the Trade Marks (Relative Grounds) Order 2007[119] came into force and so the honest concurrent user was finally laid to rest.[120]

9. CONCLUSION

The honest concurrent user was the surprising offspring of a glorified transitional provision; it began as an unwanted child, little used by the profession. Once the registrar, rather than just the court, was able to register the mark of an honest concurrent user it rose to prominence. Ultimately, despite it being central to trade mark law, it stumbled during the process of harmonization, ultimately falling when the United Kingdom followed the practice of the Community Trade Mark Office and abandoned examination on relative grounds. Yet there have always been traders who have shared a trade mark in the same marketplace. The British regime acknowledged that this sharing may not be welcomed by either trader and so provided a mechanism whereby both honest sharers could protect their interests provided it did not confuse their customers. As the Community expands, one wonders whether the honest concurrent users should make some form of a comeback. The reasons identified for permitting names to be shared in this way in the domestic context apply with even more veracity to the Community. One never knows when the concept might come back in some form or another to enable the involuntary honest sharing of trade marks to begin again.

---

[119] SI 2007/1976.
[120] In Singapore a similar approach to honest concurrent use under the 1994 Act continues. See section 9 of the Trade Marks Act 1998 (No. 46 of 1998) and the registrar there has adopted a similar practice (see for example *Spa Esprit Pte v Esprit International* (2004) ldtm 07987-00); and in relation to some other Commonwealth countries see n. 3.

4. Coexistence in Community trade mark disputes: when is it recognized and what are its implications?

Arnaud Folliard-Monguiral*

1. INTRODUCTION: COEXISTENCE OR ACQUIESCENCE?

In trade mark law, as in diplomacy, coexistence may provide a pragmatic alternative solution to a conflict by favouring a principle of mutual tolerance. That a name is shared by two trade mark holders may thus, under certain conditions, render those marks compatible.

It is accepted that in *inter partes* proceedings before the Office for Harmonization in the Internal Market (OHIM), coexistence of the conflicting trade marks in the same territory may be a relevant criterion when assessing whether there is likelihood of confusion in a given market. However, the argument taken from the coexistence of the marks must be distinguished from acquiescence within the meaning of Article 53 of Council Regulation 40/94 on the Community trade mark (CTMR). A claim for acquiescence constitutes an exception which can only be invoked before OHIM as a defensive argument in an action for invalidity and not in opposition proceedings, not least because Article 53 requires that the mark in regards to which the use was acquiesced for more than five years be registered.[1]

The impact of coexistence is two-fold. First, coexistence between the two marks involved in the opposition or invalidity proceedings may be persuasive of the non-existence of a conflict between the marks in the relevant public's perception. Secondly, where many similar marks (other than the two marks involved in the opposition or invalidity proceedings) are used by competitors, such coexistence may affect the scope of protection of the earlier right relied on in the *inter partes* proceedings.

---

* This article has no official character and the views expressed are the personal views of the author.

[1] See Article 53 CTMR and the decision of the First Board of Appeal of 30 September 2002 in R 16/2000-1 (NIKE/NIKE).

2. IMPACT OF COEXISTENCE OF TWO CONFLICTING MARKS ON THE OUTCOME OF DISPUTE

The coexistence of conflicting marks may be tolerated by the holder of the earlier rights, or it may be accepted by both parties by means of a coexistence agreement. The legal consequences of these two schemes differ.

One must consider the legal ground of the dispute, that is, likelihood of confusion (Article 8(1)(b) CTMR) or damage caused to the reputation (Article 8(5) CTMR).

2.1.1 The impact of coexistence on likelihood of confusion

Within the Community trade mark (CTM) system, the first decision to recognize the possible bearing of coexistence of conflicting marks on the outcome of a dispute was GOLDSHIELD/SHIELD.[2] There the Board of Appeal observed that the marks had coexisted in the marketplace for several years, with the opponent making no attempt to challenge the validity of the national registration of the applicant's mark. According to the Board, coexistence was 'highly persuasive' of the absence of likelihood of confusion:

> 22. ... where an opposition is based on a national trade mark, where the Community trade mark applied for is already registered in the Member State concerned for the goods or services covered by the Community trade mark application, where that mark and the opponent's mark have coexisted for several years and where the opponent has made no attempt to challenge the validity of the national registration of the applicant's mark, such a set of circumstances strongly suggests that a likelihood of confusion between the two marks will in all probability not exist in the relevant territory. That is particularly true when, as in the case of the United Kingdom, the national trade mark office in the relevant Member State raises relative issues of its own motion in the course of the registration procedure. While the Opposition Division may have been correct in stating that coexistence between the two marks in the relevant territory is not decisive, it is none the less highly persuasive.

As persuasive as it may be, proof of coexistence is nevertheless not decisive *per se*. Indeed the impact of coexistence has subsequently been greeted with scepticism. Thus in REGENT ASSOCIATES/MASTERCARD,[3] the Board of Appeal said:

> 126. The Board has some doubts whether the argument of coexistence on national markets could validly influence the prognosis on the existence of a likelihood of confusion in accordance with Article 8(1)(b) CTMR. This could possibly only be the case if one considered a decision of the competitors that there is no risk of

---

[2] First Board of Appeal, 12 September 2000, R 415/1999-1.
[3] Fourth Board of Appeal, 25 February 2004, R 264/2002-4.

confusion as the closest and most relevant assessment of the conditions on the respective market. Since the competitors know the conditions on that market best, their assessment might be considered a particularly strong indication and thus might (even decisively) influence the prognosis to be made by the Office. However, the reasons for a competitor not to take remedies against a conflicting sign on national markets may be manifold and quite different to those relevant on the Community market on the whole. More specifically, they might not have anything to do with the question of whether there exists a likelihood of confusion at all. Competitors might for instance not be interested to defend their CTM in those national markets but might very well see their economic interests at risk when the conflicting sign through a CTM registration (potentially) seeks to expand in the whole Community.

In other words, the Board of Appeal held that the decision to oppose or to tolerate the use of a junior mark in the Community or in a specific Member State is entirely within the opponent's discretion and cannot be taken as evidence of the degree of similarity, or lack thereof, between signs. The Board did therefore not consider that it was entitled to sanction the opponent's strategic business choices.[4]

The Board's statement explains that owners of quasi-identical trade marks covering identical or very similar goods are very much likely to compete with each other. Thus the coexistence of their respective marks may be explained by the owners' consent or by any other *subjective* reason, rather than by an *objective* absence of likelihood of confusion on the part of the public concerned.

The Court of First Instance (CFI) confirmed that the coexistence of the conflicting marks may be relevant in assessing the risk of confusion, even though the court's position appears to be restrictive. The CFI said:

> ... it is not impossible that such coexistence may possibly reduce the likelihood of confusion found by OHIM between two conflicting marks. Nevertheless, such a situation can be taken into consideration only if, at the very least, during the procedure concerning the relative grounds of refusal before OHIM the applicant for the Community trade mark has duly shown that that coexistence was based on an absence of likelihood of confusion in the mind of the relevant public . . .[5]

While the impact of coexistence on the finding of likelihood of confusion is accepted in theory, the conditions for this coexistence to be persuasive of the absence of a risk of confusion are in practice very difficult to establish.

---

[4] See also First Board of Appeal, 22 November 2006, R 718/2006-1 (SOL DE AYALA/AYALA), para. 35.

[5] See *Sadas SA v OHIM* (ARTHUR ET FELICIE) T-346/04 [2006] ETMR 27, para. 63 and *PepsiCo, Inc. v OHIM* (RUFFLES/RIFFELS) T-269/02 [2006] ETMR 94, para. 86.

First, as a matter of principle, it is no defence that the CTM applicant is the holder of a mark which is earlier than the earlier mark invoked in support of an opposition or action for invalidity. This is because opposition or invalidity proceedings at Community level do not attempt to analyse conflicts at national level. In such a case, the CTM applicant must prove that it had been successful in having the opponent's mark cancelled by the competent national authorities.[6]

In *HELLO!/HALLO*[7] the Second Board of Appeal took a different and, so far, unique position by holding that an opponent cannot have more rights when it files an opposition at Community level than at national level. Therefore, according to the Second Board, an opposition based on a national mark which is predated by an earlier right held by the CTM applicant must be dismissed. This position is now clearly contradicted by CFI case-law.

Secondly, coexistence may only have an impact on the assessment of likelihood of confusion if the marks are shown to coexist *in the market*. Coexistence should be understood as 'co-use' (concurrent use of the conflicting marks), rather than 'co-registration' (concurrent presence on the trade mark register). It is irrelevant that the marks coexist on the register, since that does not of itself reflect the actual market situation.[8]

This position introduces a nuance in the reasoning in *GOLDSHIELD*. After that decision, the coexistence of the marks on the register was a persuasive element provided the national Trade Mark Office examines relative grounds for refusal *ex officio*. Since the risk of confusion is assessed exclusively in the territory where the earlier mark is protected, coexistence outside this territory is irrelevant.[9]

---

[6] See RUFFLES/RIFFELS, cited above, paras. 24–26, Judgments of 25 May 2005, *TeleTech Holdings, Inc. v OHIM* (TELETECH GLOBAL VENTURES/ TELETECH INTERNATIONAL) T-288/03, unpublished, para. 29, and of 1 March 2005, *Vincenzo Fusco v OHIM*, (ENZO FUSCO/ANTONIO FUSCO) T-185/03, unpublished, paras. 61–63.

[7] See the decision of the 2nd Board of Appeal, 5 August 2004, in R 132/2002-2 (HELLO!/HALLO), paras. 16–21.

[8] See RUFFLES/RIFFELS, cited above, paras. 23–5. See also the decisions of the Boards of Appeal of 11 January 2007, in R 92/2006-1 (OHM/OHM), of 18 May 2004 in R 503/2003-2 (POLO/FARTONS POLO), of 30 September 2003 in R 60/2003-1 (GRENFELL/GREENFIELD), of 8 July 2003 in R 691/2002-2 (MX HONDA/HONDA), para. 16, of 5 March 2003 in R 860/2000-3 (BROOK & CROSSFIELD/BROOKFIELD), para. 23, of 8 January 2002 in R 360/2000-4 (NO LIMITS/ LIMMIT), para. 13, of 23 January 2002 in R 566/2001-3 (TORTI/TOSTI), para. 33, of 27 February 2002 in R 851/2000-3 (MAGIC/MAGIC BOX), para. 30.

[9] See, *José Alejandro, SL v OHIM*, (BUDMEN/BUD) T-129/01 [2003] ECR II-2251, para. 62. See also the decision of the 4th Board of Appeal of 15 January 2007, in R 27/2006-4 (LORAC/LIERAC), para. 32.

Thirdly, the CFI held in *GRUPO SADA/SADIA* that a condition for coexistence to be a persuasive factor in favour of the nonexistence of a risk of confusion is that 'the earlier marks in question and the conflicting marks must be identical'.[10] In *ARTHUR ET FELICIE/ARTHUR*, the CFI applied this principle literally, saying 'it is sufficient to state that the applicant's French trade mark and the intervener's [i.e. the opponent's] earlier mark are not identical'.[11]

One may object that the Court's requirement that 'the earlier marks in question and the conflicting marks must be identical' is likely to have been distorted in *ARTHUR ET FELICIE*. What the Court may have meant in *GRUPO SADA/SADIA* was that the marks which coexist at national level must be the same as those in conflict at Community level. The applicant's national trade mark which is shown to have coexisted with the earlier mark must therefore correspond to the CTM applied for.[12] Conversely, proof of coexistence must relate to the earlier mark invoked in support of the opposition rather than to any other mark held by the opponent.[13] This does not necessarily imply that the marks in dispute must be identical. Such a restrictive position may even lead to a *non sequitur* if the legal consequences of coexistence are discarded in the cases where it should be more reasonable to accept them, that is, where differences between the signs reduce the risk that the signs be perceived as originating from a unique commercial source.

Fourthly, in *GRUPO SADA/SADIA*, the CFI observed that:

> ... the applicant never claimed let alone proved that the marks SADA SOCIEDAD ANÓNIMA PARA LA DISTRIBUCIÓN ALIMENTARIA and LA DESPENSA DE SADA had an enhanced degree of distinctiveness which could diminish the risk of confusion between the intervener's [the opponent's] earlier mark and that applied for.[14]

The applicant must show that the public was exposed to the concurrent use of both trade marks, to be able to distinguish them and relate them to two different origins.[15] It is therefore not enough to prove that the national mark corresponding to that applied for at Community level was used on a small scale in the market; it must also be shown that it was used in such a manner that it now

---

[10] See judgment of 11 May 2005, *Grupo Sada, pa, SA v OHIM* (GRUPO SADA/SADIA) T-31/03, not yet published, paras. 86 and 88.

[11] See ARTHUR ET FELICIE, cited above, para. 64.

[12] See, for instance, the decisions of the Boards of Appeal of 8 June 2005 in R 764/2004-1 (BLUE ARC/ARC), para. 26, of 29 April 2003 in R 477/2002-1 (RUFFLES MAX/RIFFELS), para. 24.

[13] See, for instance, the decision of the 4th Board of Appeal of 16 June 2004 in R 952/2002-4 (LEE/LEE COOPER), para. 19.

[14] See GRUPO SADA/SADIA, cited above, para. 89.

[15] See the decision of the 3rd Board of Appeal of 24 April 2002 in R 907/2001-3 (GARO/GIRA), para. 43.

has market recognition (that is, 'an enhanced degree of distinctiveness' acquired through use which does not have to qualify a 'reputation' within the meaning of Article 8(5) CTMR). The underlying logic of this reasoning might be that the enhanced distinctiveness of *both* conflicting marks as a result of their use in the market may neutralize the risk of confusion because each one is known to identify and to belong to one single operator.

So far, it has been generally accepted that the analysis of the risk of confusion was confined to examining whether the later mark was included within the scope of protection of the earlier mark, irrespective of the later mark's scope of protection. CFI case-law may be interpreted as an indication that the degree of distinctiveness acquired through use of the mark applied for can also be relevant. In this respect, in three cases – *ARTHUR ET FELICIE, GRUPO SADA* and *TELETECH GLOBAL VENTURES* – the CFI dismissed the applicant's claim that the sign applied for had an enhanced degree of distinctiveness, but only insofar as this claim had not been properly substantiated. This claim was therefore not discarded on its merits.[16]

A consequence that derives from the principle that use of the mark applied for must not be confined to small-scale exploitation is that the CTM applicant must submit evidence that the opponent had reason to be aware of the existence of the applicant's mark.[17]

Furthermore, the existence of national disputes is sufficient reason for CFI to disregard arguments relating to the lack of confusion based upon the coexistence of the marks.[18]

Moreover, even though the CFI remained silent on this point, the duration of coexistence should be a relevant criterion in order to have a lasting effect on the views and attitudes of the relevant consumers.[19] Proof of coexistence must in any case be adduced for the period before the date of filing or priority date of the CTM.

Finally, the possible impact of coexistence is limited to the goods and services for which proof has been adduced, and it should be stated that the above principles apply both in opposition proceedings and in invalidity actions based on Article 52(1)(a) CTMR.

---

[16] See ARTHUR ET FELICIE, cited above, paras. 65–66, GRUPO SADA/SADIA, cited above, paras. 21–23, T-288/03, and TELETECH GLOBAL VENTURES/TELETECH INTERNATIONAL, cited above, paras. 98–100.

[17] See ARTHUR ET FELICIE, cited above, para. 64.

[18] See ARTHUR ET FELICIE, cited above, para. 64, and judgment of 8 December 2005, *Castellblanch, SA/OHIM* (CRISTAL CASTELLBLANCH) T-29/04, not yet published, para. 74. See also the decision of the Board of Appeal of 6 March 2006, in R 530/2004-2 (MARIE-CLAIRE/MARIE-CLAIRE), para. 26.

[19] See the decision of the 3rd Board of Appeal of 24 April 2002 in R 907/2001-3 (GARO/GIRA), para. 43.

2.1.2 The impact of coexistence on actions based on damage caused to, or on unfair advantage taken of, the repute or distinctive character of the earlier mark

The Boards of Appeal have scarcely addressed the defensive argument taken from the coexistence of trade marks in the context of Article 8(5) CTMR. However, in *MANGO*[20] the First Board of Appeal had to decide whether the use of the applied for CTM, MANGO for protective helmets, was likely to damage or take an unfair advantage of the reputation of the earlier Spanish registration MANGO for clothing. The applicant claimed in particular that, having used its trade mark in Spain since 1992 (that is, before the earlier mark could claim reputation), past detriment to the earlier mark was excluded and future detriment was unlikely. The applicant substantiated the coexistence claim by submitting documents for the first time before the Board of Appeal.

The Board of Appeal discounted those documents because they had not been submitted in due time before the Opposition Division,[21] but nevertheless held that, had the documents been admissible, they would not have been conclusive of the absence of detriment caused to or of unfair advantage taken from the earlier mark's repute:

> 24. . . . coexistence in Spain where the mark applied for has been used in the past for sports cycle helmets does not exclude the probability of unfair advantage or detriment occurring in the future. Indeed, the fact that the mark applied for may have enjoyed some success in the past in the Spanish market, might indicate to the contrary a 'free ride' on the success and reputation of the earlier mark.

In Article 8(1)(b) CTMR cases, coexistence may undermine the basic condition for likelihood of confusion to be found if proof is adduced that, because of the public's familiarity with the two marks, the products bearing one mark will *not* be related to the same origin as the products bearing the second mark. This is not the case for Article 8(5) CTMR, because the perception that both marks identify distinct commercial sources is irrelevant.

In *MANGO* the Board of Appeal apparently assumed that the success of the applicant's mark in the Spanish protective helmets market was due, at least in part, to an association with the earlier mark, given the (remote) connection between clothing articles and helmets. This reasoning is unsatisfactory: it amounts to holding that coexistence automatically plays in favour of dilution

---

[20] R 308/2003-1, 12 March 2004.
[21] See para. 25 of the decision. On the issue of the admissibility of additional evidence filed for the first time before the Boards of Appeal, see also A. Folliard-Monguiral and G. Bertoli '*Inter Partes* Proceedings and the Reform of the Community Trade Mark Implementing Regulation', (2006) 1 *Journal of Intellectual Property Law & Practice* 177–87.

when, in fact, it is possible to imagine that coexistence could play against such a finding.

Proof that the name *MANGO* was shared *before* the earlier right's reputation was acquired might have given credibility to the applicant's claim that there was no unfair advantage taken of the earlier mark's repute or at least no intention to so take advantage.

By the same token, the fact that the name *MANGO* exists in the Spanish language (as in English) could have reinforced the argument that the choice of that term in an economic field distinct from clothing was independent from any parasitism and was coincidental.

In an at first sight conflicting decision, *CAMELO*, the Second Board of Appeal gave effect to the coexistence in Spain between the earlier mark *CAMEL*, known for tobacco, and the mark applied for *CAMELO* for coffee. The Board of Appeal dismissed the opposition based on Article 8(5) CTMR on account of the absence of any 'link' between the marks, in spite of striking visual similarities.[22]

The Board based its finding on the coexistence of the marks on the Spanish market and on the substantial promotional investments made by the trade mark applicant. These factors tended to indicate a lack of parasitism on the part of the applicant:

> 63. This conclusion is corroborated by the fact that the parties admit the coexistence of the marks in at least part of Spain (Extremadura) over several years, as is confirmed by the judgment of the provincial Court of Madrid. In Extremadura the mark applied for has a leading position on the market of coffee since its market share amounts to 52% according to the Alimarket report. Such a market share must be the result of a long and public use of the mark applied for. Moreover, the opponent did not submit any argument or proof that would support its claim that use of the mark applied for would take profit from the repute of the earlier mark, notwithstanding the express request made by the Board in this respect.[23]

One may observe that the case-law of the Boards of Appeal lacks consistency in this area. Coexistence might undermine the conclusion that there is unfair advantage taken of the earlier mark's repute. This is because establishing parasitism requires one to have regard to the genuine intention of the later mark's holder, at least to some extent. It is however highly debatable whether coexistence has any impact on the blurring and tarnishment of the earlier mark's image since these harms need to be assessed on a more objective basis.

---

[22] Board of Appeal, decision of 22 February 2006, R 669/2003-2, (CAMELO/CAMEL).

[23] The Court of First Instance dismissed the action against this decision by its Judgment of 30 January 2008, *Japan Tobacco, Inc. v OHIM*, (CAMELO/CAMEL), T-128/06 (unpublished). The Court found that the opponent failed to substantiate parasitism; hence it did not find it necessary to adjudicate on the impact of the coexistence.

2.2 The Impact of Coexistence Agreements on Likelihood of Confusion

OHIM practice regarding the importance afforded to coexistence agreements remains unsettled. The Opposition Division generally refuses to give weight to private agreements when assessing likelihood of confusion.[24] Such agreements are enforceable in the competent national Courts, but the Opposition Division considers that it lacks jurisdiction to interpret and enforce them.

One reason for this is that OHIM's tribunals have jurisdiction to examine and weigh 'facts', but Article 74(1) CTMR does not recognize a competence to interpret 'deeds'. This distinction might be artificial since the CFI recognized OHIM's entitlement to interpret a 'declaration' in a case involving Article 8(3) CTMR (trade mark filed by an agent).[25]

Another reason is that there is no provision in the CTMR and its Implementing Regulation that would allow for an earlier right holder to be deprived of its capacity to file an opposition (or a request for invalidity), even if this holder had undertaken never to do so in an agreement with a CTM applicant or holder.[26]

Very few Board of Appeal decisions draw consequences from the provisions of civil agreements. However, in *COMPAIR/COMPAIR*[27] the Second Board of Appeal said:

> 19. In determining whether there exists a likelihood of confusion in Germany the Office must have due regard to the Agreement, which was clearly intended by the parties to be legally binding. The opponent cannot argue, without violating the Agreement, that there is a likelihood of confusion in Germany between its trade mark and the applicant's trade mark in so far as the latter is claimed in relation to the goods covered by German Registration No W 940945. Moreover, to argue that there is a likelihood of confusion would be to call in question the validity of the opponent's German registration (No 1.190.584), which is later in time than the applicant's registration. If the opponent's registration were challenged on that basis, the opponent could of course invoke the Agreement in its defence. It would be grossly inequitable to allow the opponent to invoke the Agreement in order to protect the opponent's

---

[24] See OHIM's *Opposition Guidelines*, Part 2, Chapter 2 D, point 6 ('Coexistence of the conflicting marks in the market in the same territory'), p. 285: 'Civil agreements between the parties of any kind are irrelevant in opposition proceedings.' However, OHIM's Cancellation Division will pay attention to the existence of contracts in actions in revocation based on bad faith and in actions involving claims of acquiescence, within the meaning of Articles 51(1)(b) and 53(2) CTMR, respectively.

[25] CFI, judgment of 6 September 2006, *DEF-TEC Defense Technology GmbH/ OHIM*, (FIRST DEFENSE AEROSOL PEPPER PROJECTOR/DEFENSE & FIRST DEFENSE) T-6/05, not yet published, paras. 45–9.

[26] See the decision of the Board of Appeal of 14 March 2006, in R 1257/2005-4 (YAGER/YAGA), para. 12.

[27] R 590/1999-2, 30 July 2002.

German registration and yet at the same time to refuse to allow the applicant to invoke the Agreement as a means of defeating an opposition to its CTM application based on the opponent's German registration. The issue is always whether there is a likelihood of confusion in Germany. The opponent cannot say, on the one hand, that there is no likelihood of confusion between the two German trade marks, because the parties have agreed otherwise, but there would be a likelihood of confusion in Germany between its own German trade mark and the applicant's trade mark if the latter became a CTM.

In *VICHY/VICHY CATALAN*[28] the First Board supported its dismissal of the opposition by referring to the measures taken by the parties to hamper likelihood of confusion:

> ... from the text of the agreement it transpires quite clearly that the consumers' interest not to be confused between the signs was also duly considered [since] the parties determined the conditions under which both parties could use their respective trade marks in Spain without any risk of confusion.[29]

Even though the Boards of Appeal may take unequivocal coexistence agreements into account, they are however reluctant to interpret provisions which leave room for ambiguity. For instance, in *OMEGA/OMEGA*[30] the Second Board of Appeal considered that the terms of the coexistence agreement between the parties were ambiguous. Observing that 'prima facie it would appear that the applicant has acted in breach of the agreement', the Board further stated that it is 'doubtful whether [the applicant] can invoke the agreement against the opponent' (paragraph 24).[31]

The Board took no position on the interpretation to be given to the agreement, but rather expressed that it could not be bound by the provisions contained in a private agreement, whatever its correct interpretation.

In the event that a party files an opposition or an action in invalidity in breach of a coexistence agreement, the CTM applicant or CTM holder may therefore find it useful to obtain a national court judgment giving a proper interpretation of the agreement and ordering the other party to withdraw its action before OHIM.[32]

---

[28] R 24/2003-1, 12 July 2004.
[29] See the decision of the First Board of Appeal of 12 July 2004 in R 24/2003-1 (VICHY/VICHY CATALAN), paras. 48–50.
[30] R 330/2002-2, 10 December 2004 (appeal to the CFI pending).
[31] See also decision of the 2nd Board of Appeal of 30 August 2004 in R 518/2002-2 (UTS/UPS), para. 18.
[32] The CTM applicant or CTM holder will also have to request the suspension of the proceedings before OHIM until a final judgment is handed down at national level.

3. IMPACT OF COEXISTENCE ON THE EARLIER MARK'S SCOPE OF PROTECTION

The limits of the principle under which third parties' marks may impact on the earlier mark's distinctiveness require clarification. We must also consider a complex issue addressed in a preliminary ruling of the European Court of Justice, Case C-145/2005, *Levi Strauss & Co v Casucci Spa*.

3.1 The Principle

The administrative bodies of OHIM were formerly reluctant to have regard to the possible impact of third parties' marks on the outcome of a dispute in which they were not involved. It is significant that the decision of the Third Board of Appeal in one of the *DEER HEAD* decisions states: 'Coexistence of similar marks in the market is *per se* irrelevant'.[33]

The case-law has changed in this respect and it is now accepted that the coexistence in the market of many marks similar to the one invoked in support of the opposition may affect its distinctiveness, and thus its scope of protection. The use of similar signs by a number of operators may indeed erode the uniqueness of a sign whose function is to guarantee the identification of a unique source.

In *FLEXI AIR/FLEX*[34] the Fourth Board of Appeal said:

> ... the earlier trade mark has been validly registered in the relevant territory and therefore enjoys the protection endowed on it by the CTMR. At the same time, it consists of a word which is not uncommonly used in relation to hair care products in general, and on the United Kingdom market in particular. The appellant validly demonstrates this in its grounds of appeal in response to the view expressed in the contested decision that 'FLEX' was uncommon in relation to hair care products because 'people do not talk about "flexible" hair'. The brands identified by the appellant suffice to demonstrate that that finding lacks substance. In view of the common occurrence of the word 'FLEX' in relation to hair care products, the distinctive character of the earlier trade mark consisting of the same word might in principle be deemed weak.

The CFI endorsed this finding, but confirmed the existence of likelihood of confusion. The weak distinctive character of the earlier mark FLEX, which

---

[33] See the decision of the 3rd Board of Appeal in R 213/2001-3, 4 June 2003, para. 33.
[34] See the decision of the 4th Board of Appeal of 15 January 2003, in case R 396/2001-4 (FLEXI AIR/FLEX), para. 27.

could lead to a lower degree of similarity between the signs, was outweighed by the high degree of similarity between the goods.[35]

In *FLEXI AIR/FLEX*, both the Board of Appeal and the CFI corroborated the finding that FLEX had a limited degree of distinctiveness *per se* by the fact that this sign was frequently used by operators on the market of hair care products. The limited degree of distinctiveness is therefore not the exclusive result of the common use of identical signs by competitors but rather, this common use supports the view that it is strongly allusive. The CFI has taken a similar position in a previous judgment NU-TRIDE[36] and lately in ECHINAID/ECHINACIN.[37] In the later judgment, the CFI found that the common element 'ECHINA' could not be the dominant element of the compared signs:

> The word 'Echinacea' is the scientific name in Latin of a plant used for pharmaceutical products and herbal medicine. It is common to use the Latin names of plants in those areas. That is confirmed by the large number of registrations of the prefix 'echin-' or 'echina-' in the territories concerned. OHIM was therefore justified in finding that the prefix 'echina-' refers, as far as the average consumer is concerned, to the composition of the product rather than to its commercial origin.

The same reasoning was developed by the Second Board of Appeal in RED STAR/BLUE STAR where it found that the degree of distinctiveness *per se* of the word STAR was rather low given that it may be perceived as referring to the high quality of the goods. The Board of Appeal corroborated the finding that STAR is laudatory by observing that there are:

> ... a large number of trade marks all over Europe, including in Germany, using the word 'star' as a sole component or in combination with others, as it appears from the excerpts of various trade mark registers (International Trade Mark Register, Seagis and Marquesa databases) filed by the applicant in the course of the opposition proceedings ... Therefore, if not totally descriptive of the 'star quality' of the goods, the word 'star' is at least strongly allusive to the superior quality of the goods at issue in Class 33 and thus of a weak distinctive character, as rightly held by the applicant.

In *FABER/NABER* the CFI went further as it drew inferences from the coexistence of numerous trade marks held by competitors and having the common sequence of letters 'A-B-E-R' in order to show that the presence of

---

[35] See judgment of 16 March 2005, *L'Oréal SA v OHIM*, (FLEXI AIR/FLEX) T-112/03, not yet published, para. 85 (appeal pending before the Court of Justice).

[36] See judgment of 9 April 2003, *Durferrit GmbH v OHIM*, (nu-tride/tufftride) T-224/01 [2003] ECR II-1589, para. 50.

[37] See judgment of 5 April 2006, *Madaus AG v OHIM*, (ECHINAID/ECHINACIN) T-202/04 [2006] ECR II-1115, para. 45.

this common sequence in the two conflicting marks is not conclusive *per se* of a high degree of similarity between them.[38] Similarly, in *QUICKY/QUICKIES*, the CFI confirmed that the frequent use of a given type of sign (in this case representations of animals) for the presentation of foodstuff may render the concept banal which may in turn diminish 'considerably' the distinctive character of the specific representation, in this case of a rabbit.[39] However, this judgment was annulled by the ECJ.[40]

However, in *VENADO*, the CFI nuanced this reasoning when applying it to the representation of a deer head. The CFI introduces a distinction between the general concept (that of associating a deer with beverages) and the specific concept (a deer head facing forward in a medal). The CFI considered that the existence of only eight trade marks containing the representation of a deer head (only three of which were in a frame) was not conclusive evidence of the earlier mark's low degree of distinctiveness. The distinctive character (or uniqueness) of the specific concept embodied by the earlier mark was not diminished by the coexistence with third parties' marks showing different embodiments of the general concept. The CFI therefore concluded that 'it is impossible to deny that the concept of a deer's head facing forward in a circle has at least average distinctive character for designating beverages'.[41]

Proof of use of the similar marks by competitors must be adduced in order to have a bearing on the claim that the earlier mark's distinctiveness is affected. Thus the CFI held in *CRISTAL CASTELLBLANCH/CRISTAL*:

> As for the applicant's argument that other marks exist which contain the word 'cristal' and are registered for goods in Class 33, thus showing the weak distinctive character of the earlier mark and that both of the marks in question coexist peacefully, it is sufficient to find that it is not established that those marks have their effects or correspond to a usage in relation to the goods in dispute and in particular to sparkling wines.[42]

An important issue which the CFI did not address is whether regard should be given to all competitors' marks or only to those which are earlier than that

---

[38] See judgment of 20 April 2005, *Faber Chimica Srl v OHIM* (FABER/NABER) T-211/03, not yet published, para. 40.

[39] See judgment of 22 February 2006, *Société des produits Nestlé SA v OHIM*, (QUICKY/QUICK, QUICKIES) T-74/04, not yet published, para. 51.

[40] See judgment of 20 September 2007, *Société des produits Nestlé SA v OHIM* (QUICKY/QUICK, QUICKIES) C-193/06 P, not yet published.

[41] See judgment of 14 December 2006, *Mast-Jägermeister AG v OHIM* (VENADO) Joined Cases T-81/03, T-82/03 and T-103/03, not yet published, para. 110.

[42] See CRISTAL CASTELLBLANCH, para. 71 (appeal pending before the Court of Justice) and judgment of 24 November 2005, *GfK AG v OHIM*, (Online Bus – a figure made up of three interlaced triangles) T-135/04, not yet published, para. 68.

invoked in support of the opposition. In other words, may the scope of protection of a mark suffer from the coexistence of signs which bear a later date of filing, irrespective of whether the owner of that mark consented to that coexistence? This is one of the issues raised in a preliminary question asked by the Court of Cassation of Belgium in Case C-145/2005, *Levi Strauss & Co v Casucci Spa*.

3.2 The Levi Strauss Preliminary Ruling Case C-145/05

On the basis of its earlier Benelux trade mark for the 'arcuate' device (that is, the 'seagull wings' device stitched on garments' back pockets), Levi Strauss & Co ('Levi Strauss') initiated a Court action against the use by Casucci of a pattern consisting of a double row of overstitching curving upwards towards the centre of garments' pockets (see Figure 4.1). The allegedly infringing use started in 1997.

Levi's claimed that there was likelihood of confusion in the Benelux pursuant to Article 13(A)(1)(b) of the Uniform Benelux trade marks law.

The action was dismissed at first instance and on appeal: given the low degree of similarity of the signs, a finding of likelihood of confusion would have required proof that the earlier mark was shown to enjoy an enhanced distinctiveness *when the decision was taken*. Although the earlier mark was recognized as having a reputation when the Court action started, its degree of distinctiveness was held to have diminished in the course of the Court proceedings.

In particular, the Benelux trial and appellate courts accepted Casucci's arguments that the widespread use of devices similar to the earlier 'arcuate' sign resulted in the weakening of its distinctive character because, in the

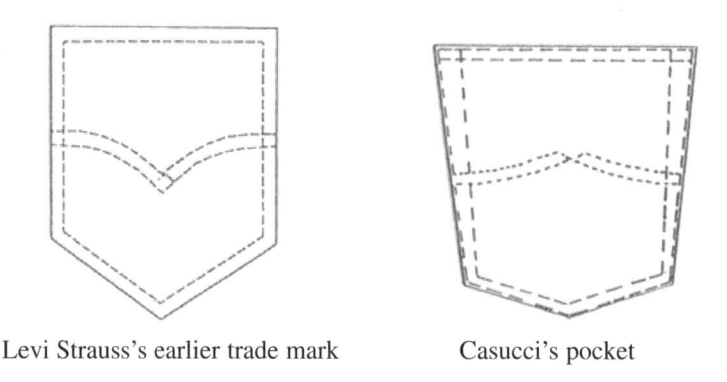

Levi Strauss's earlier trade mark   Casucci's pocket

Figure 4.1 Levi Strauss and Casucci's pocket stitching

public's perception, the elements composing the earlier sign became inseparable from the design of the garment to which it is affixed. The appeal court held that the device consisting of two parallel lines converging in the centre of the pocket was then so widely used that it merely signalled the fact that the garment belongs to the category of jeans. As a result, the common characteristics of the conflicting signs should be disregarded. The appeal court also held that a likelihood of association between the signs was insufficient to give rise to likelihood of confusion.

Levi further appealed against the appeal court's decision to the Belgium Supreme Court, which asked four questions to the Court of Justice concerning the interpretation of Article 5(1) of the Directive 89/104.

The first two questions deal with the point in time when the scope of protection of the earlier mark should be assessed. By its third question, the referring court asked in substance whether a finding of likelihood of confusion may or must result in an order prohibiting use of the infringing sign. By its fourth question, the referring court asked whether it is appropriate to order cessation of the use if the earlier mark has lost its distinctive character, wholly or in part, as a result of an act or omission of its proprietor.

The issue which underlies these questions is whether the mark's scope of protection may decrease after its filing date. In his opinion of 17 January 2006,[43] Advocate General Ruiz-Jarabo Colomer agreed that the perception of trade marks may evolve over time, 'depending in particular on the *behaviour of the other providers* of goods or services on the relevant market, which affect their distinguishing power'[44] (emphasis added). This observation makes good sense: it would be contradictory to the spirit of the Directive 89/104/EEC for the scope of protection of a trade mark to be defined once and for all in the light of the situation existing at an invariable point in time.

This can be contrasted with the scope of patent protection, which is 'frozen' at the time of filing because the scope is assessed only in the light of the prior art. Instead, the scope of protection of trade marks depends on the public's perception, which may vary over time.

The ECJ handed down its judgment on 27 April 2006.[45] The ECJ concurred with this principle, but seemed to require that the holder play a role in the loss of distinctive character in order for it to impact the outcome of infringement proceedings. As to the relevant point in time for assessing this

---

[43] See *Levi Strauss & Co v Casucci SpA* C-145/05 [2006] ECR I-3703 (AG) and A. Wood, 'Advocate General's opinion regarding challenges to distinctiveness' (2006) 1 *Journal of Intellectual Property Law & Practice* 303–4.
[44] See para. 23 of the Opinion.
[45] See *Levi Strauss & Co v Casucci SpA* C-145/05 [2006] ETMR 71 (ECJ).

scope of protection (first two preliminary questions), the ECJ endorsed the Advocate General Ruiz-Jarabo Colomer's Opinion,[46] saying that

> ... the proprietor's right to protection of his mark from infringement is neither genuine nor effective if account may not be taken of the perception of the public concerned at the time when the sign, the use of which infringes the mark in question, began to be used.[47]

It makes sense that a trade mark's scope of protection be assessed on the *starting point* of the use complained of.[48] This is because that point in time is also the starting point of the period taken into consideration for the assessment of the damages.

That said, the national court should also ascertain that the factual circumstances which led to a finding of likelihood of confusion before the action was initiated extend until the last reported act of infringement[49] and are still met at the time when the ruling is given. This is because the national court must not extend the trade mark protection 'beyond the date on which the holder ceases to benefit from its rights'.[50]

This is accepted by the ECJ. In its answer to the third preliminary question (that is, whether a finding of likelihood of confusion may or must result in an order prohibiting use of the infringing sign), the ECJ recognized that any remedy must be appropriate at the time when the decision is handed down.[51] If, in principle, an order prohibiting the use of the later mark is 'indeed a measure which genuinely and effectively safeguards those rights',[52] the fact remains that 'the competent national authorities retain a degree of discretion in that regard'[53] and that the prohibition of use *may*, but need not always, be ordered.[54]

Consequently, the national court must strive to avoid that a measure for the

---

[46] See para. 25 of the Opinion.
[47] See *Levi Strauss*, para. 17.
[48] See paras. 25–7 of the Opinion.
[49] This is because the national court must redress the infringement by granting corrective measures, among which are damages. The amount of damages to which the right holder is entitled will depend on, among other criteria, the duration of the infringement. See Art. 13 of the Corrigendum to Directive 2004/48/EC of the European Parliament and of the Council of 29 April 2004 on the enforcement of intellectual property rights which refers to 'the actual prejudice suffered by him/her as a result of the infringement'.
[50] See para. 25 of the Opinion.
[51] See also para. 33 of the Opinion,
[52] See para. 24 of the Judgment.
[53] See para. 23 of the Judgment.
[54] See para. 25 of the Judgment.

present (such as the recall from the channels of commerce, the definitive removal from the channels of commerce, or the destruction[55]) or a measure for the future (such as the prohibition of use) proves to be inadequate on the day the judgment is taken because the earlier mark has lapsed or has become liable to revocation in the course of the court proceedings.

This principle was reiterated in *NOKIA*. In this judgment, the ECJ interpreted the 'special reasons' allowing a national court to derogate from the obligation laid down in Article 98(1) CTMR, that is, to order cessation of an infringing mark. According to the ECJ, the impossibility of any further act of infringement would be a 'special reason', in particular where the earlier mark is revoked in the course of the proceedings, thus implying that the infringement is no longer existing at the time of the judgment.[56]

In other words, the ECJ held in its *Levi Strauss* and *NOKIA* judgments that the prejudice caused to the essential functions of an earlier trade mark (which is an essential requirement for an infringement action to be upheld)[57] ends at the point in time when this trade mark ceases to enjoy protection.

Likewise, where one of the conditions for an infringement action to be sustained is the enhanced distinctiveness of the earlier mark, the national court may be asked to verify that this condition is still satisfied at the time the order prohibiting future use is granted, that is, when the ruling is given.

Assuming the earlier mark has lost part or all of its attractive power in the eye of the consumers in the course of the proceedings, the question is now whether this loss of distinctiveness must be imputable to its holder in order for it to have a bearing on the outcome of an infringement case. This issue is addressed by the ECJ in its answer to the fourth preliminary question.

The ECJ distinguished two situations: the first in which the loss of the distinguishing power of the mark is imputable to the acts or inactivity of its holder. This is the revocation of the mark which has become generic within the meaning of Article 12(2)(a) of Directive 89/104. In such a case,

> after revocation in the particular case has been established, the competent national court cannot order cessation of the use of the sign in question, even if, at the time when that sign began to be used, there was a likelihood of confusion between the sign and the mark concerned.[58]

---

[55] See Art. 12 of Directive 2004/48/EC on the enforcement of intellectual property rights.

[56] See *Nokia Corp v Joachim Wärdell*, (NOKIA) C-316/05 [2007] ETMR 20, para. 35.

[57] See *Adam Opel AG v Autec AG*, (OPEL BLITZ) [2007] ETMR 33 (ECJ), para. 21 and the case-law cited therein.

[58] See para. 36 of the judgment. See also *Nokia Corp., Joachim Wärdell* (NOKIA), cited above, para. 35.

One may observe that the ECJ extends the scope of application of Article 12(2)(a) of Directive 89/104 to cases where the mark has become 'non-distinctive', which may encompass situations other than those where the mark 'has become the common name in the trade for a product or service in respect of which it is registered'.[59]

The second situation considered by the ECJ is that in which the attractiveness and uniqueness of the mark decrease in the public's mind as a result of the use by many operators on the jeans market of later signs incorporating the same concept (that is, the concept of having stitched rear pockets). In such a case, the ECJ considers that

> the loss of the distinctive character is linked to the activity of a third party using a sign which infringes the mark, [and thus] the proprietor must continue to enjoy protection.[60]

Under Article 12(2)(a) of the Directive 89/104/EEC, the rights cannot be revoked as a result of third parties' acts if the trade mark holder made attempts to defend its right. Nevertheless, even though the rights are maintained, one should have regard to the degree of protection the mark is now worthy of. This is because a distinction should be made between the validity of the right and its scope of protection. That the protection stands does not prevent a decline of its magnitude.

Even though the right is retained, its scope of protection may have suffered from the fact that the public no longer sees (or to the same extent as before) the sign as a business identifier but rather as a common name or, in the *Levi Strauss* case, as a standard feature of jeans. As the CFI put it in the BSS case,[61] 'initiatives by the proprietor are to be taken into consideration in so far as they produce objective results in terms of the perception of the sign amongst the relevant public'.

---

[59] Not least because a figurative sign cannot become the name for a product. The fact is, neither the Directive nor the CTMR foresee the possibility of cancelling marks which have become *non-distinctive* (or descriptive) when the absolute ground under Article 3(1)(b) of the Directive 89/104/EEC or under Article 7(1)(b) CTMR becomes applicable *after registration*. In such a case, an action for invalidity based on Article 3(1)(b) of the Directive or 7(1)(b) CTMR would fail since the lack of distinctiveness would have to be appreciated at the time of the filing of the mark rather than at any later stage. See Order of the Court of Justice of 5 October 2004, *Alcon Inc v OHIM*, (BSS) C-192/03P [2004] ECR I-8993, para. 39.

[60] See para. 19 of the Judgment.

[61] See judgment of 5 March 2003, *Alcon Inc. v OHIM*, (BSS) T-237/01 [2003] ECR II-411, para. 55. This quotation addresses the issue of whether the generic sign BSS has acquired distinctiveness after registration, pursuant to Article 51(2) CTMR. The reasoning is nevertheless transposable by analogy to the *conservation* of the distinctiveness after registration

Therefore, even though, according to the ECJ, the purpose of infringement actions 'is precisely to preserve the distinctive character of the mark in question',[62] the conservation of an enhanced distinctive character should not be automatically inferred from the holder's initiatives.

It might be that the ECJ considered that third parties' acts are, as a matter of principle, without effect on the scope of protection of an earlier mark. Such an interpretation of the preliminary ruling would be based on the assumption that those third parties' acts 'infringe the mark' (see paragraph 19 of the ruling). The Advocate General was also reluctant to admit that the decline of the mark's distinctiveness may be the result of the massive use of similar later marks by third parties, considering that 'an advantage obtained through unlawful acts would be granted to those third parties'.[63]

However, the presumption that the third parties' acts are unlawful lacks a legal basis. It is quite obvious that a defendant cannot refer to infringing acts, committed by itself or by third parties, in order to show the earlier mark's full or partial reduction in distinctiveness. That said, these third parties' acts should not be discarded unless they were sanctioned beforehand by a national court.

If the holder fails to start as many actions as necessary and if it is accepted that a national court lacks jurisdiction for adjudicating on the use of third parties' signs (which are not formally involved in the infringement proceedings), logic would therefore command that those third parties' acts be treated as lawful.

This can be the case in particular where a trade mark embodies a *concept* (that is, covering jeans' back pockets with stitching). Although that idea was originally very distinctive (why stitching? why on the back pockets?), the massive use by competitors of different embodiments of the same concept may imply that the stitching is now perceived as a standard characteristic for jeans. This can affect the degree of distinctiveness of the earlier mark which has *de facto* lost its uniqueness.

This is so even if competitors use very different patterns for the stitching, producing a notably different overall impression. Although an *air de famille* between signs used by different companies may be perceptible, this will be imputable to the concept which, as such, cannot be monopolized. This *air de famille* might therefore be insufficient so as to be captured by the notion of likelihood of confusion.

---

[62] See para. 34 of the Judgment.
[63] See para. 40 of the Opinion.

4. CONCLUSION

The analysis of the case-law shows that the coexistence between two conflicting marks has at best a marginal influence on the assessment of likelihood of confusion, despite the theoretical effect that the CFI recognized for it. The indirect impact of the coexistence with third parties' marks appears to be more important.

One may regret that the ECJ leaves the door open to doubts as to whether the scope of protection of an earlier mark may be diminished by later acts of third parties. Opponents of this concept will argue that the expropriation of trade mark rights requires the holder's consent or its blameful inactivity. In turn, advocates will claim that reputation is not a right that is acquired forever. Reputation cannot be fictitiously maintained by initiating court actions if the perception of the consumers on the market concerned has evolved.

It is noteworthy that the same issue arises in very similar terms in design law. Whereas the validity of a design is assessed against the prior art existing at the date of filing or date of priority, the scope of protection is measured at a later stage against the impression left on the informed user by the two conflicting designs. In order to assess the scope of protection of an earlier design, neither Article 9 of Directive 98/71/CE[64] nor Article 10 of the Community Design Regulation[65] specifies whether the perception of the user is likely to be affected by the profusion of shapes that are disclosed after the filing date or priority date of a design whose rights are enforced.

---

[64] Directive 98/71/EC of the European Parliament and of the Council of 13 October 1998 on the legal protection of designs.
[65] Council Regulation (EC) 6/2002 of 12 December 2001 on Community Designs.

5. The approach of the UK-IPO to co-ownership of registered trade marks: nanny leaves the Registry, but not completely

Edward Smith*

1. INTRODUCTION

It is perhaps an exaggeration to say that 'nanny' left the United Kingdom Intellectual Property Office (UK-IPO) in 1994 but there is nevertheless some truth in the statement. Of course, 'nanny' is not so much a person as an approach or underpinning assumption to the law governing the registration of trade marks. The 'nannying' approach, more precisely, the approach which regards consumer protection as paramount or at least a crucial Registry consideration, is in some respects still in evidence at the Registry and in its practices. In the main, however, traders who are already involved in, or anticipate co-proprietorship, coexistence or some other form of 'sharing' marks will find that the UK-IPO is accommodating in its practices and generally untroubled by private agreements of this nature.

'Nannying' reveals itself in different guises, and as suggested above, our concern here is the tension between (i) what has been called a 'permissive'[1] regime in terms of its approach to trade marks as items of property and co-proprietorship, and (ii) the underlying function of a trade mark namely to guarantee the origin (and quality) of goods or services of a single undertaking.

2. USE WITH THE CONSENT OF THE PROPRIETOR

This 'tension' finds an expression in *Continental Shelf 128 Ltd v Hebrew*

---

* The views expressed are personal and not necessarily those of the UK-IPO.

[1] *Kerly's Law of Trade Marks and Trade Names* (14th edn, Sweet & Maxwell, London, 2005), Chapter 13, para. 13-003.

University of Jerusalem, sub nom Continental Shelf 128 Ltd's Trade Mark Application, Einstein Trade Mark.[2] In this revocation case before the appointed person,[3] the issue was whether the registrar's hearing officer had been right to require the proprietor to establish that the use made of the mark had not just been 'genuine', but that the use made was *both* with the consent of the proprietor *and* under its control. For the purposes of this article, the appointed person found, first, that the 'consent of the Proprietor' as it has been interpreted (a) in relation to a claim for protection defined by reference to use, (b) to defeat an application for revocation on the basis of non-use, and finally (c) in relation to the requirements for exhaustion, ought to have a consistent meaning in all three contexts.

Second, he found that ECJ case law and the development of Articles 7(3) and 10(3) of the Directive[4] and Articles 13(1) and 15(3) of the Regulation[5] provide support for the position that there is no need for the Proprietor to have approved or exercised quality control over the relevant goods sold under the mark, so long as he has allowed or authorized the person with whom he is 'economically linked' to use the mark.

Third, Articles 21 and 19(2) of the TRIPS Agreement[6] cannot be said to require the Community or Member States to regard authorization unaccompanied by quality control as insufficient. Fourth, there is no express or implied prohibition in the Directive or CTMR against regarding a trade mark as an asset which the proprietor may authorize others to exploit on such terms and conditions as he legitimately sees fit to impose. Fifth, again based on case law including *Scandecor Development AB v Scandecor Marketing AB*[7] the current UK Act countenances bare licensing, that is, licensing without quality control.

The last finding has been quoted directly. This is because the words 'current' and 'countenances' suggest a nuance of wistfulness, not to say regret, that we now have a regime which, allows bare licences. It would seem that the system has effectively abandoned consumer protection as an underlying legal principle, in the face of practical reality that a registered trade mark nowadays simply comprises another item of property.

---

[2] [2007] RPC 23.

[3] The appointed person is a senior trade mark lawyer who hears appeals from the hearing officers of the Trade Mark Registry – see the 1994 Act, ss. 76 and 77.

[4] First Council Directive 89/104 of 21 December 1988 to approximate the laws of Member States relating to Trade Marks.

[5] Council Regulation 40/94 of 20 December 1993 on the Community Trade Mark.

[6] Agreement on Trade-Related Aspects of Intellectual Property Rights concluded as part of the Uruguay Round of GATT.

[7] [2002] FSR 7.

The appointed person nevertheless recognizes, quoting from the Paper entitled 'Reform of Trade Marks Law',[8] that it ill becomes a proprietor to tolerate 'uncontrolled' use of his trade mark, which use may damage the reputation of the mark with the ultimate arbiter, the consumer. It is not the responsibility of the registrar, the Paper notes, but that of the proprietor to prevent the devaluation of his own property. Indeed, the liberalizing nature of the Act, as compared to the strictures and bureaucracy of the Trade Marks Act 1938 in respect of licensing in particular, bears testament to this underlying 'transfer' of responsibility, some would say, simply a recognition that the law needed to catch up with everyday practical reality.

The *Einstein* decision relates to a situation where the 'proprietor' and 'user' are 'economically linked', but the Trade Marks Act 1994 (and Registry practice) has also actively encouraged those who engage in the registration process to accommodate each other in relation to conflicting marks. The Act provides for consent to registration[9] (which overcomes all objection), or reliance on 'honest concurrent use' as a means of clearing the *ex officio* examination phase where marks conflict.[10] Quite how that consent is obtained is not something that concerns the registrar, so there is no need to present any underlying agreement, for example a licence or co-ownership or coexistence agreement, to indicate how that consent came about.

There are other, less well known, equitable practices which the Registry has adopted in order to ensure that the fruits of registration are not unjustly denied – even at the expense of possible customer confusion or inconvenience. These will be dealt with later, but first we need to look at honest concurrent use.

3. HONEST CONCURRENT USE

Pirie's Application,[11] which provides the basis for an understanding of the application of honest concurrent use, recognized as long ago as the 1930s that a measure of possible consumer confusion may be outweighed by the inequity of a refusal of registration benefits. Honest concurrent use survived into the

---

[8] (Cmnd 1203). The paper was also quoted by the Court of Appeal in *Reed Executive Plc v Reed Business Information Ltd* [2004] RPC 40.
[9] Exercising the option given in Art. 4(5) of the Directive. The position contrasts with that under the 1938 Act, whereby consent was not conclusive but merely a factor in the question whether there may be confusion between the marks (*British Lead Mills Ltd's Application* (1958) 17 RPC 425).
[10] 1994 Act, s. 37.
[11] (1933) 50 RPC 147.

1994 Act, some may say,[12] controversially, as there is no clear basis for it in the Directive. That it did survive and that its existence has been tied to the existence of *ex officio* refusal on relative grounds testifies to the need to provide balance in a regime where applicants could be denied beneficial rights on the basis of ever-increasing earlier registered rights which themselves were not subject to relative grounds examination, that is, Community trade marks. Additionally, at the time the 1994 Act came into force many of those earlier registered rights would have been assumed to be 'dead wood' on the register.[13]

That 'balance' provided by honest concurrent use only took the applicant as far as publication for opposition, and it could not be relied upon as decisive in an opposition. Now it has gone completely as a result of the new notification regime which has been introduced in the UK. Earlier registered rights no longer form a barrier to acceptance of a mark for registration, unless and until they form the basis of a successful opposition. With the introduction of the new notification regime, honest concurrent use as a means of overcoming 'citations' is now consigned to history.[14]

4. COEXISTENCE

That said, it is and always has been open to an applicant in an opposition to plead 'peaceful coexistence' as a factor mitigating against the likelihood of confusion. This factor was recently pleaded and found sympathy in *Fiorelli Trade Mark*,[15] a case on appeal from the Registry to the Court. There is a tendency for the Registry to be somewhat unsympathetic to this argument as the reasons for apparent lack of factual confusion or deception may be varied, for example as was noted in *The European Ltd v The Economist Newspaper Ltd*.[16] If the tribunal is persuaded that actual side-by-side use can be proven to

---

[12] *Kerly*, n. 1, para. 9-150.

[13] Art. 8(1) CTMR provides that CTM applications can only be refused on relative grounds upon opposition by the proprietor. The imbalance between this regime and the UK's previous regime of *ex officio* refusal on relative grounds was a main (and anticipated) factor in the change to the current system of notification in the UK, see for example paras. 14–19 of the Consultation Paper 'Relative Grounds for Refusal: The Way Forward' published on the UK-IPO website (www.ipo.gov.uk) dated February 2006. Likewise, the fact that many CTMs would not necessarily have been used and yet still they would have blocked the registration of UK applications, see paras. 20ff. of the Consultation Paper.

[14] On the development and ultimate demise of honest concurrent use, see Chapter 3 of this volume.

[15] [2007] RPC 18.

[16] [1998] FSR 283.

have taken place without confusion occurring then the case for finding no likelihood of confusion becomes much stronger.[17]

'Consent' of course retains a place in the Act, and if an applicant shows that the owner of an earlier mark has consented to the registration then this will result in notionally conflicting marks existing on the Register. As far as the Registry is concerned, all that is required is an appropriate[18] letter or document showing that consent to the registration has been given. The Registry is not troubled by the terms under which that consent has been given. If, however those terms result in the applicant limiting the specification it is important to recognize that the Registry will bear in mind the *Postkantoor*[19] dicta as regards the legal certainty of limitations and exclusions. The fact that the parties appear to understand the terms used to delineate goods or services would not preclude the Registry from objecting to a particular limitation or exclusion which it feels would be legally uncertain.

Mention of limitation also draws attention to section 13 of the Act as another mechanism for facilitating the coexistence of marks. It is important to make a distinction between limitations which go to the *nature* of the goods and services which, assuming they are *Postkantoor* compliant, should be entered in the specification, and those limitations which are more properly entered under section 13, that is to say that they limit the *rights* conferred by registration listed in section 9. So, for example the specification in class 28 of 'Games, none being darts' would be a limitation in relation to the nature of the goods, whereas a limitation 'None of the specified games for sale in Northern Ireland' would be a limitation under section 13.[20]

5. THE REGISTRY'S 'EQUITABLE DISCRETION'

As well as these express provisions, the Registry has in the past, and continues in some cases, to exercise an 'equitable discretion' in allowing potentially conflicting marks onto the register. For example, the Registry will allow the registration of both (or all) marks when conflicting marks are filed on the same day. Furthermore, though the practice has ceased with the introduction of the notification[21] regime, the Registry used to allow an applicant to rely upon an

---

[17] The role of peaceful coexistence before OHIM is considered in Chapter 4 of this volume.
[18] See the UK-IPO's *Manual of Trade Marks Practice*, Chapter 3, para. 56.2.1, available from http://www.ipo.gov.uk/tm/t-decisionmaking/t-law/t-law-manual.htm.
[19] Case C-363/99, paras. 114 and 115.
[20] See also *Nestlé SA's Trade Mark Application* [2005] RPC 5 para. 32.
[21] As explained in n 9, the UK has moved from a regime based on *ex officio*

earlier mark in his ownership to 'overcome' potential earlier conflicting marks where the applicant's earlier mark predates the potential citations. At least it could be said to have some 'equitable' basis.[22]

6. AVOIDING MERE NOTIONAL CONFLICTS

Finally on this issue, and also now abandoned with the coming of the new notification regime, the Registry was not above 'fine tuning' its cross-search list in places to permit marks having notionally conflicting specifications onto the register at the same time. This would have happened in circumstances where either the application or potential cite did not mention certain specific goods (though they may have been covered in a broader term) and no clash was assumed. For example, if an application had the specification 'Clothing, footwear and headgear' in Class 25, then the goods of an earlier mark in class 18 would only be considered 'similar' if 'purses, handbags for women and girls' were specifically mentioned. 'Leather goods at large' would not have been considered similar goods. In the main, with the exception of same day filing treatment, these could be considered equitable practices borne out of an *ex officio* relative grounds refusal regime which is now no longer in existence.

7. PRIVATE AGREEMENTS

When exercising its tribunal function however, the Registry is inevitably engaged in adjudicating between two or more parties and must decide in favour of the rights of one or the other. Should the parties settle by whatever means, including coexistence agreements, then there will in general be no issue remaining before the Registry, save occasionally that of costs. In particular, the Registry will not interfere in a private agreement or contract which may well undermine the essential function of a trade mark to guarantee the origin of goods and services of a single undertaking. Is this a good or bad thing? Perhaps this is for others to say but it certainly is a reflection of a shift in onus away from the Registry to rights holders in terms of policing the use of marks.

---

refusal on relative grounds to a notification system, whereby those earlier rights holders who have opted into the system are notified of later marks against which the earlier registered marks may be successful in an opposition. Earlier rights can only then be invoked in an opposition, thus mirroring the CTM Regulation and most other European States.

[22] The UK-IPO's *Manual of Trade Marks Practice*, Chapter 3, para. 51 (now superseded).

Having said that, the terms of a private agreement may well subsequently in *inter partes* actions form the basis of an action for invalidation or opposition based upon 'bad faith' before the Registry or Court. Disputed terms may also be argued to give rise to an estoppel based upon abuse of process, see, for example, *Fenchurch Environmental Group Ltd v Ad Tech Holdings Ltd, sub nom Bactiguard Trade Mark*.[23] This interlocutory decision involved construing a delimitation agreement, and in particular the question whether the agreement, involving a no challenge clause, prevented revocation proceedings based on non-use, and if so, whether such an effect would have constituted an unreasonable restraint of trade by virtue of such a clause. The appointed person concluded on appeal that the agreement did prevent revocation proceedings, but that it was wrong to assume that such a conclusion necessarily constituted an unreasonable restraint of trade. The correct position was to presume that the agreement represented a reasonable division of the parties' interests unless the tribunal could be persuaded that the agreement could be avoided. Further, that in the specific case there were grounds to suppose that there was no reasonable basis for including such a clause, or that the clause was contrary to the public interest, as it went beyond the legitimate purpose of seeking to avoid confusion or conflict between the parties. However, a finding on this point demanded further investigation of the factual circumstances and thus the case was remitted to the registrar.

This case can be contrasted with *Omega SA (Omega AG) (Omega Ltd) Application*[24] in which the hearing officer concluded that the giving of consent some years earlier and without designating the actual application numbers in suit nevertheless gave rise to an estoppel based on equity which prevented the opponent from opposing the relevant applications.

8. THE ROLE OF THE ESSENTIAL FUNCTION BEFORE THE REGISTRY

It is however rare to find Registry decisions which even refer to the essential function of a trade mark as defined by the ECJ. One such rarity is the recent decision in *Thomas Plant (Birmingham) Ltd v Rousselon Freres et Cie* concerning use of the mark *Sabatier*.[25] In this case the hearing officer found that genuine use, sufficient to defeat an application for revocation based on non-use, had not been made as the multiple use made by many undertakings

---

[23] BL O/236/05, dated 25 August 2005 (Appointed Person).
[24] BL O/554/01, 10 December 2001.
[25] BL O/288/07, 28 September 2007.

undermined the essential function as defined by the ECJ. It did not matter that the average consumer would have assumed on seeing the word 'Sabatier' that it indicates origin, what mattered was whether the use was genuine, that is, in accordance with the essential function. At the time of writing the final outcome of this case is not known.

9. THE DANGER OF DECEPTION

Finally, as other commentators have pointed out,[26] it is important to appreciate that a consequence of having a liberal regime in terms of the treatment of registered trade marks as items of property is that the proprietor is well advised to ensure that the mark in use does not become deceptive. This is especially the case where the mark comprises the name of an individual (such as in the *Elizabeth Emanuel* case[27]) and the continued use of such a mark when the person concerned no longer has any links with the user would result in deception. This is really a matter for the new owners, but if referred to the Registry or Courts by another party, such deception could well result in invalidation – although as has also been pointed out, it is almost inevitable that some measure of consumer confusion would be tolerated in such circumstances.[28]

10. CONCLUSION

As we have seen, for the most part the Registry is 'liberal' in outlook and tolerant of multiple ownership and absence of quality control, simply because that is the way the law appears to be framed and interpreted. The Registry does not in general see itself as guardian of the essential function of a trade mark and as a result, of consumers, but instead, regards consent as determinative and thus coexistence as natural, even desirable. It is preferred that the parties come to their terms of settlement but in rare cases, should those terms become the subject of dispute in the context of any action which the Registry is entitled to hear, then such terms will have to be construed and their effect assessed.

---

[26] *Kerly*, n, 1, para. 13-043ff.
[27] C-259/04.
[28] *Kerly*, n. 1, para. 10-129.

6. The business end of collective and certification marks

Dev Gangjee

In the semiotic ecosystem of European trade mark law, certification and collective marks are shy beasts, rarely sighted in law reports or administrative decisions. According to Jeremy Phillips, 'taking a panoramic sweep across the peaks and troughs of . . . trade mark law, they are few in number and cast almost no shadow',[1] while the editors of *Kerly* more sedately observe that there 'has been little litigation concerning certification trade marks'.[2] Such marks, jointly referred to as association marks for the purposes of this chapter,[3] facilitate voluntary name sharing and have existed for over a century. Yet a recurring lament is that they remain underutilized and underappreciated.[4] This is unsurprising, considering their unusual functional niche and tentative integration into a system of protection historically premised on a sign's ability to indicate a single trade origin. There have been few decisions concerning the registration of such signs or on the scope of protection afforded to them, but this state of affairs may finally be changing. This chapter explores the assimilation of association marks into the mainstream of European registered trade mark law by drawing on a series of recent registry-level decisions in the UK[5] and at the Office for Harmonization in the Internal Market (OHIM) Registry,[6]

---

[1] J. Phillips, *Trade Mark Law: A Practical Anatomy* (Oxford University Press, Oxford 2003), p. 621.

[2] D. Kitchin et al., *Kerly's Law of Trade Marks and Trade Names* (14th edn, Sweet & Maxwell, London, 2005) at para. 12-023.

[3] In doing so I adopt Stephen Ladas's usage. See generally Ch. 35 of S.P. Ladas, *Patents, Trademarks and Related Rights: National and International Protection* (Harvard University Press, Cambridge, MA, 1975).

[4] See for example J. Belson, *Certification Marks* (Sweet & Maxwell, London, 2002), p. 1.

[5] The UK decisions considered here are available from the UK Intellectual Property Office website at: http://www.ipo.gov.uk/tm/t-decisionmaking/t-challenge/t-challenge-decision-results.htm (all internet references are accurate as of 30 April 2007).

[6] The Office of Harmonization for the Internal Market (OHIM) registers the

along with comparative insights from decisions of the US Trademark Trial and Appeal Board (TTAB)[7] where relevant.

Part 1 introduces certification and collective marks while emphasizing their unique requirements for registration. Part 2 reviews recent disputes before the UK and OHIM registries. Its purpose is to discern whether there are any teachings applicable to the infringement tests for such marks. Broadly speaking, association marks are treated akin to regular trade marks for most purposes, but they throw up the occasional surprise as well. The analysis includes a comparative glance at US decisions, which have covered territory as yet unfamiliar in the European context. Several recent developments including the rise of voluntary industry-wide benchmarking standards,[8] the growing interest in the protection of geographical indications[9] via such association marks and the use of certification in the global information technology industry[10] have led to a renewed interest in such marks. The time is ripe for a reassessment of their potential.

1. THE CHARACTERISTIC FEATURES OF CERTIFICATION AND COLLECTIVE MARKS

Under the Trade Marks Act 1994, regular trade marks, collective marks and certification marks each have a discrete signalling function in the marketplace. Before commencing with the analysis two limitations are acknowledged. While this chapter focuses on registered protection, unregistered association marks may be protected under the common law of passing off,[11] which is

---

pan-European Community Trade Mark. Decisions of the Office can be accessed at: http://oami.europa.eu/en/mark/aspects/default.htm.

[7] Recent decisions of the TTAB are available at: http://www.uspto.gov/web/offices/dcom/ttab/index.html.

[8] One such example of voluntary certification is the 'ENEC' mark (European Norms Electrical Certification) which covers product categories such as luminaries, transformers and switches for appliances, based on testing to harmonized European safety standards.

[9] See below at section 2.3, pp. 96–8.

[10] A theme developed by Belson n. 4 in Ch. 7, 'Authentication for Digital Products'.

[11] Many such cases concern collectively used geographical indications of origin such as 'Champagne'. See C. Wadlow, *The Law of Passing-Off: Unfair Competition by Misrepresentation* (3rd edn, Sweet & Maxwell, London, 2004) pp. 125–33 (trade associations and collective goodwill), pp. 510–19 (actionable misrepresentations as to origin or nature or products). In the US, the consensus appears to be that unregistered signs which function as certification marks are entitled to protection under the common law. See *Florida v Real Juices Inc* 330 F. Supp. 428, 171 USPQ 66 (MD Fla. 1971)

subject to an important caveat. It presently appears doubtful whether the representative body has the *locus standi* to sue in its own capacity.[12] Furthermore, this chapter can only selectively outline the registration requirements for such marks. A more detailed account is available in the specialized body of literature on this topic.[13] The modest aim here is restricted to identifying the emerging trends for harmonized European trade mark law via recent decisions.

1.1 Certification Marks

A certification mark informs purchasers that the goods or services certified by it possess certain characteristics or meet certain standards.[14] As opposed to regular trade marks which reliably indicate consistent quality, this sign provides a qualified guarantee that certain specific standards have been met.[15] It is defined in s. 50(1) of the Trade Marks Act 1994 as: '[A] mark indicating that the goods and services in connection with which it is used are certified by the proprietor of the mark in respect of origin, material, mode of manufacture of goods or performance of services, quality, accuracy or other characteristics.'

Familiar examples include the Underwriter's Laboratory 'UL' certification mark[16] for the non-profit organization which conducts product safety evaluations, the 'Woolmark'[17] denoting specific wool content and fibre quality

---

(unregistered mark 'Sunshine Tree' used to certify Florida citrus products); *Institut National Des Appellations d'Origine v Brown-Forman* 47 USPQ 2d 1875 (TTAB 1998) ('Cognac' recognized as a term certifying specific French geographical origin).

[12] It may lack the appropriate goodwill. At present, the authority on this point is *Chocosuisse Union des Fabricants Suisse de Chocolat v Cadbury* [1999] ETMR 1020. Attempts are under way to rectify this. See UK Patent Office *Consultation Paper: Representative Actions for the Enforcement of Intellectual Property Rights* (Sept. 2006), p. 4.

[13] See generally Belson n. 4; Ch. 12 of *Kerly* n. 2; N. Dawson *Certification Trade Marks Law and Practice* (Intellectual Property Publishing, London, 1988); A. Firth 'Collectivity, Control and Joint Adventure: Observations on Marks in Multiple Use' in N. Dawson and A. Firth *Perspectives on Intellectual Property: Trade Marks Retrospective*, Vol. 7 (Sweet & Maxwell, London, 2000), p. 171; see also Appendix II: 'Joint Interest in Marks, Names and Symbols' in W.R. Cornish and D. Llewelyn *Intellectual Property* (5th edn, Sweet & Maxwell, London, 2003) 859.

[14] Special rules for such marks are elaborated in Schedule 2 to the Trade Marks Act 1994.

[15] The question of whether this guarantee takes the form of a contractual obligation owed to the buyer of a certified product is explored further in J. Belson 'Certification Marks, Guarantees and Trusts' [2002] EIPR 340.

[16] UK TM No. 1177428. This mark has been the subject of litigation in the US. See *Midwest Plastic Fabricators Inc. v Underwriters Laboratories Inc.*, 906 F.2d 1568, 15 USPQ2d 1359 (Fed. Cir. 1990).

[17] UK TM Nos. 885752 to 885755.

assurance and the Stilton certification mark[18] for blue-veined cheese with a specific geographical origin and production method. Signs which certify that products meet defined criteria have been registrable under UK trade mark law for over a century, with the earliest iteration being the 'standardization trade mark' in the Act of 1905.[19] Writing around the time of its enactment, a leading commentator welcomed this development as a 'new and useful provision'[20] but subsequent registration statistics did not match up to this optimism.[21] This is partly due to the unusual evolutionary niche occupied by such marks in the trajectory of trade mark law's history. Scholars tend to characterize these marks as occupying the interstitial space between guild marks of the Middle Ages[22] and modern trade marks.[23] Shortly after the Lanham Act was enacted, Rudolph Callmann, when commenting on the equivalent US provision,[24] suggested that:

> Such [a] mark more closely resembles the guild mark of the Middle Ages than the modern trade-mark. It is similar to the guild mark in that the user is first required to subscribe to or satisfy certain standards of the organisation before he is entitled to use the mark and must then submit to the supervision of the organisation in his use

---

[18] UK TM Nos. 831407, 1267276. For details on the traditional production method, see *Stilton* [1967] RPC 173.

[19] As per s. 62 of the Trade Mark Act 1905, 5 Edw VII c 15:

> Where any association or person undertakes the examination of any goods in respect of origin, material, mode of manufacture, quality, accuracy, or other characteristic, and certifies the result of such examination by mark used upon or in connexion with such goods, the Board of Trade may, if they shall judge it to be to the public advantage, permit such association or person to register such mark as a trade mark in respect of such goods, whether or not such association or person be a trading association or trader or possessed of a goodwill in connexion with such examination and certifying.

[20] L.B. Sebastian, *The Law of Trade Mark Registration under the Trade Marks Act, 1905* (Stevens and Sons, London, 1906), p. 11.

[21] In 1906 there were 63 applications under s. 62 but 50 of them were from the same organization. The following year saw 11, while 1911 saw 16 such applications. See F.G. Underhay, *Kerly's Law of Trade Marks and Trade Names* (4th edn, Sweet & Maxwell, London, 1913), p. 92.

[22] Generally accepted as the predecessors to modern trade marks in light of Frank Schechter's extensive historical research. See F.I. Schechter *The Historical Foundations of the Law Relating to Trade Marks* (Columbia University Press, New York, 1925).

[23] See Ladas n. 3, p.1289; Firth n. 13, p. 176.

[24] Certification and collective marks are defined in s. 45 of the Lanham Act, 15 U.S.C.A. §1127.

thereof. Its purpose, like that of the guild mark, is to preserve certain standards of quality or craftsmanship as well as the reputation of the organisation in the market.[25]

From the examples above, it is evident that while the Underwriter's Laboratory mark certifies product safety compliance and its unauthorized use is policed by the proprietor, the Stilton mark also functions as a commercially valuable 'brand' in the marketplace for cheese, much like a regular trade mark. As far as consumers are concerned, the former lies closer to the regulatory end of the spectrum while the latter has a more familiar commercial goodwill cachet. Those who have sought to benefit from occupying this interstitial space have historically been few in number.[26] However what is common to all association marks is that they do not indicate origin in a single commercial or proprietary source, instead being utilized by a group of users. As the UK Registry notes: 'Certification and collective marks therefore differ from "ordinary" trade marks because an ordinary trade mark is one that distinguishes the goods and services of one particular trader (a single trade source) from those of other traders.'[27]

One of the aims of this volume is to explore how the essential function of a trade mark, with its commitment to a single trade source,[28] may be reconciled

---

[25] R. Callmann 'The New Trade-Mark Act of July 5, 1946' (1946) 46 *Columbia L Rev* 929, 935.

[26] Reasons given in support of adopting such marks include 'greater assurance against infringement, more effective protection . . . benefits of common advertising, and the like'. See Ladas n. 3, p. 1289.

[27] See Ch. 4: 'Certification and Collective Marks' in the UK Registry's *Manual of Trade Marks Practice* at para. 1.2 (hereinafter *Registry Manual*) http://www.ipo.gov.uk/tm/t-decisionmaking/t-law/t-law-manual.htm. For the US response to such applications, see Ch. 1300 of the *Trademark Manual of Examination Procedures* (TMEP) 4th edn http://tess2.uspto.gov/tmdb/tmep/1300.htm.

[28] As the ECJ held in *Arsenal Football Club v Matthew Reed* C-206/01 [2002] ECR I-10273 at para. 48:

[T]he essential function of a trade mark is to guarantee the identity of origin of the marked goods or services to the consumer or end user by enabling him, without any possibility of confusion, to distinguish the goods or services from others which have another origin. For the trade mark to be able to fulfil its essential role in the system of undistorted competition which the Treaty seeks to establish and maintain, it must offer a guarantee that all the goods or services bearing it have been manufactured or supplied under the control of a single undertaking which is responsible for their quality.

The interdependence of origin and quality is considered in W. Cornish and D. Llewellyn *Intellectual Property: Patents, Copyright, Trade Marks and Allied Rights* (6th edn, Sweet & Maxwell, London, 2007) at p. 621.

with a collective interest in the use of a sign. A preliminary issue therefore concerns the integration of such collectively used signs into the logic of the essential function.

When the 'essential function' is considered teleologically, the short answer is that signs may not have to always point to a single trade origin in order to fulfil the rationale underpinning distinctiveness. Identifying a single trade source is a stepping stone in order to achieve the more significant goal of ensuring that a consistent message of product quality can be communicated.[29] A certification mark by definition ensures that a consistent and specific message about certain characteristics of the product can be communicated, regardless of the fact that the use of the mark is usually open to anyone who can demonstrate that their goods or services have that characteristic.[30] The entire group of certified users can then be distinguished from those with similar non-certified products. This is reflected in para. 2 of Schedule 2 to the Trade Mark Act 1994:

> In relation to a certification mark the reference in section 1(1) [signs of which a trade mark may consist] to distinguishing goods or services of one undertaking from those of other undertakings shall be construed as a reference to distinguishing goods or services which are certified from those which are not.

Thus the single commercial origin requirement is replaced by one where association marks distinguish on the basis of qualities or membership.

As a result of this functional difference, there are at least three significant ways in which such marks diverge from standard trade marks.

(1) Unlike an ordinary trade mark, a certification mark must be applied for by an association or person not engaged in trade in the goods or services in connection with which the mark is used. This 'arm's length' requirement is intended to ensure objectivity in the certification process.[31] A consequence of the proprietor's inability to use it is

---

[29] In a marketplace characterized by imperfect information available to consumers, the economic justification for trade mark protection is based on granting exclusive rights in order to preserve the communicative integrity of the sign. By allowing consumers to rely on the sign's ability to indicate a single trade origin this lowers consumer search costs with regard to product quality, while also reducing the risk that competitors will free-ride on investments in product quality that the mark proprietor has made. See W.M. Landes and R.A. Posner 'The Economics of Trademark Law' (1987) 30 *Journal of Law and Economics* 265.

[30] See Ch. 4 of the *Registry Manual* at para. 3.4.2: 'Most certification marks are available for use by any person whose goods or services demonstrate the relevant characteristic being certified'. (Emphasis in the original).

[31] The UK Registry is clear that 'the proprietor of the certification mark cannot

that for the purpose of avoiding revocation by non-use, its adoption by authorized users counts.[32] These authorized users also have rights akin to licensees.[33]

(2) In addition to this communal aspect, such applications have to clear two distinct sets of hurdles. The sign applied for must satisfy the general criteria for registrability under the Act, including the definition and absolute grounds.[34] An illustration centred on distinctiveness is where the UK Registrar initially held that the Legal Aid Board had not managed to educate the relevant public that 'the term "legal aid" has acquired a distinctive character as a mark which certifies the quality of legal and conciliation services provided to the public because they appear to have no effective control of a significant number of users of the mark.'[35] This was subsequently overturned by the finding that acquired distinctiveness had been achieved.[36] Besides these standard requirements, the regulations which govern the use of the certification mark are also separately examined.[37] These regulations must set out certain basic requirements such as who is entitled to use the mark, the characteristics to be certified (for example, origin, mode of manufacture, quality, accuracy and so on), testing and supervision systems, fee structures and dispute resolution mechanisms.[38]

(3) Finally, since there is a regulatory interest in such marks, they are subject to heightened scrutiny. Assignment and transmission of certification

---

be engaged in the supply of the goods being certified . . . potential applicants should be wary that if this requirement is not met then the mark may be challenged by a third party through invalidity or revocation procedures. A *prima facie* objection will however be raised if the applicant for a certification mark is also the owner of an ordinary trade mark for the same goods and services as those being certified'. See Ch. 4 of the *Registry Manual* at para. 3.4.1.

[32] This was specifically raised, albeit in the context of collective marks, in *NF/MF* OHIM Opposition Division, No. 1702/2005, of 23 May 2005. (When evaluating the necessary proof of use under Art. 64(3) of the Community Trade Mark Regulations, a list of persons authorized to use the mark would satisfy the use requirement.)

[33] Authorized users are given the same rights as a licensee under ss. 10(5), 19(2) and 89. Any loss suffered by them as a result of infringement is a factor to be considered under s. 30 as well. See paras. 13 & 14 of Sch. 2 to the TMA 1994.

[34] Specifically, the requirements in ss. 1 and 3 of the TMA 1994.

[35] *Legal Aid* BL O/056/00, decision of the UK Trade Marks Registry of 27 January 2000 at p. 8.

[36] *Re Legal Aid Trade Mark Application* (High Court 2000, No. 00817), unreported but noted in Ch. 4 of the *Registry Manual* at para. 2.1.5.

[37] These need to be filed within nine months of the application. See para. 6(1) of Sch. 2, TMA 1994.

[38] *Ibid.* at para. 6(2).

marks require the Registrar's consent,[39] where the competence of the assignee to certify is ascertained. If the certification process is inadequately managed, this is grounds for possible revocation.[40] Certification marks should also be open to all those who satisfy the specified criteria.[41] In this context, an interesting issue which has arisen in the US is whether licensee estoppel applies to certified users. In a dispute involving the geographical certification mark for 'Idaho Potatoes', the proprietor sought to exclude a former authorized user, who in turn challenged the specifications.[42] Usually trade mark licensees cannot challenge the validity of the registered mark in question.[43] However the Second Circuit struck down an explicit 'no contest' clause in the license agreement and opened up the possibility of challenging the registration. The court held that in these circumstances, the public interest outweighed the policy of enforcing contractual provisions. The challenge implicated 'the public interest in maintaining a free market for the certified product unaffected by the possible competing interests of the certification mark owner.'[44]

Having identified the key features of certification marks, we now turn to collective marks, which, although overlapping in some respects, enjoy a greater degree of flexibility.

1.2 Collective Marks

A collective mark should indicate to the relevant public that goods or services originate from a member of a particular association. It is therefore 'a sign of membership'.[45] Such a mark is defined in s. 49(1) as: 'a mark distinguishing

---

[39] *Ibid.* at para. 12.
[40] *Ibid.* at para. 15. An isolated instance of an unsuccessful attempt under the Act of 1938 was *Sea Island Cotton* [1989] RPC 87.
[41] See *Registry Manual* at para. 3.4.2: ('Most certification marks are available for use by any person whose goods or services demonstrate the relevant characteristic being certified').
[42] See *Idaho Potato Commission v M & M Produce Farm & Sales* 335 F.3d 130 (2d Cir. 2003), cert. denied, 541 U.S. 1027 (2004). [Hereinafter *Idaho Potato Commission.*]
[43] A form of estoppel since a licensee is prevented from challenging the validity of the licensed trade mark, because the licensee enjoys the benefits of the mark and is presumed to have admitted its validity by entering into the license agreement.
[44] *Idaho Potato Commission* at p. 139.
[45] See Ch. 4 of the *Registry Manual* at para. 1.2. In the US, the difference between certification and collective marks has been drawn out in *American Speech-*

the goods or services of members of the association which is the proprietor of the mark from those of other undertakings.'

Apart from this modified distinctiveness standard, collective mark applications have to satisfy all the other absolute and relative grounds.[46] The provisions applying to such marks are set out in Schedule 1 to the Act and applicants for collective marks are often professional bodies or trade associations, where levels of proficiency or quality requirements are specified for membership. Examples include the registration by the Institute of Trade Mark Attorneys (ITMA) for 'Fellow of ITMA'[47] and the Scottish Federation of Meat Traders Association's 'Scottish Craft Butchers' mark.[48]

While in many respects, the registration process is similar, collective marks differ from certification marks in important ways. They are better established and accommodated within the Paris Convention of 1883.[49] Article 7*bis*, introduced at the Washington Revision Conference in 1911,[50] states that the 'countries of the Union undertake to accept for filing and to protect collective marks belonging to associations'. Perhaps because of the lighter regulatory touch for such marks when compared to certification marks, they find a place in the Community Trade Mark Regulation.[51] As to who may apply for a collective mark, it can be any 'association',[52] which is defined in Article 64(1) of the CTMR as an entity legally recognized as having the capacity for rights and

---

Language-Hearing Association v National Hearing Aid Society, 224 USPQ 798, 806–808 (TTAB 1984).

[46] For a CTM example, see OHIM Third Board of Appeal, 12 March 2001, R 865/1999-3 (MEMBER OF THE SOCIETY OF FINANCIAL ADVISERS). The issue was whether the application for 'Member of the Society of Financial Advisers' fell foul of the prohibition in Art. 7(1)(c) as it described the characteristics of the services claimed in the application.

[47] UK Reg. No. 2001536.

[48] UK Reg. No. 2404758.

[49] The Paris Convention for the Protection of Industrial Property, 20 March 1883 as revised at Stockholm on 14 July 1967, 828 UNTS 305 (1972). (Hereinafter, the Paris Convention.) The Convention presently has 171 Contracting Parties and was incorporated into the TRIPS Agreement.

[50] For its introduction, see Ladas, n. 3, pp. 1289–90.

[51] Council Regulation (EC) No 40/94 of 20 December 1993 on the Community Trade Mark [1994] OJ L 11, 1. (Hereinafter CTMR.)

[52] This requirement has been considered somewhat superficially in OHIM Third Board of Appeal, 3 March 2000, R 359/1999-3 (IKZ). The examiner's refusal was based on the grounds that the Dutch applicant did not have 'members' whereas the counterargument was that the applicant was a foundation formed by a group of manufacturers, producers and service providers, which fit the profile of a collective mark. Since the examiner had not given reasons, the refusal was set aside and resubmitted for further prosecution.

obligations in its own name.[53] These collective marks can then be granted for the whole of the Community,[54] such as the figurative Ducal Crown for Prosciutto di Parma.[55] This raises the possibility that a collective mark can be a vehicle to escape the more onerous requirements of a certification mark. While the conditions of membership for the club of authorized users must still be registered,[56] the applicant has far more flexibility in drawing up these criteria. As in the case of Parma ham, they could take on a certification aspect, requiring production in a specific region and according to particular methods as part of the membership requirements. Additionally, unlike certification marks, the assignment of collective marks does not require the Registrar's consent and the proprietor does *not* have to admit anyone who satisfies the membership criteria as an authorized user. The elements of discretion and exclusivity are largely retained.[57] There is no 'arm's length' requirement and the proprietor may also use the mark. Since collective marks may effectively perform a certification function, these silences and ambiguities could be problematic.

Having identified the key features of the regime governing the registration of association marks, we now turn to the scope of protection. Although there has been little reported litigation regarding the infringement of such marks, there have been registry-level disputes invoking the relative grounds for refusal of registration under EU trade mark law. Since the criteria under the relative grounds mirror the infringement provisions, the administrative deci-

---

[53] For the UK, the TMA 1994 doesn't define association, but Ch. 4 of the *Registry Manual* at para. 3.3.1 states that:

[T]he key factor to consider will be whether the claimed association has a form of membership and can point toward the normal indications present in any form of association with members, examples include payment of membership fees, issuing of membership card/numbers, membership meetings, conditions of membership. The fact that an association may be a Limited Company has no bearing on this matter; it is the manner of organisation and operation of the applicant that is important.

[54] The relevant provisions are contained in Arts. 64 to 72 of the CTMR.
[55] CTM No. 1116201.
[56] See Para. 5 of Sch. 2, TMA 1994.
[57] One possible check is where a collective mark gives the impression that it is open to all who qualify, when in fact it is more exclusive, it may be misleading. This is a ground for refusal or revocation under EU law. See *OHIM Examination Guidelines* at para. 11.4. A specific situation where membership must be open to all who satisfy the criteria is where a collective mark is applied for a geographical indication of origin. See *OHIM Examination Guidelines* at para. 11.5.2(g). The Guidelines are available at: http://oami.europa.eu/en/mark/marque/directives/exam.htm.

sions which address such disputes are instructive. There appears to be a tacit assumption that the rules for relative grounds/infringement will seamlessly apply to association marks. This is made explicit in the US Lanham Act,[58] whereas in the UK, in contrast to the old regime for standardization marks regulated by the Board of Trade, 'the whole emphasis of the certification mark as a special mark has changed and most provisions of the Act apply'.[59] Thus Section 2 sets out to test this assumption of 'business as usual'.

2. ASSOCIATION MARKS AND THE TESTS FOR INFRINGEMENT

A preliminary note of caution must be sounded since the ensuing analysis draws on Registry level decisions. These are indicative of present practice, but are not charged with precedential value. Nevertheless they do showcase instances where the unique characteristics of association marks assert themselves within the architecture of a regime primarily dedicated to individual trade marks. The analysis is divided into situations (1) where confusion is alleged and (2) those where detriment to distinctive character or repute, or unfair advantage is raised. It concludes in (3) with the observation that producer collectives for geographical indications of origin appear to be resorting to this system, in addition to protection under national or EU-wide regimes.

2.1 Association Marks and the Test for Confusion

European trade mark law exhibits an expedient symmetry whereby the tests for the relative grounds for refusal mirror those for infringement. In both situations the registered proprietor seeks to prevent others from registering or using the same or a similar sign. This is successful where:

---

[58] See §4 of the Lanham Act, 15 U.S.C.A. §1054, which provides that:

Subject to the provisions relating to the registration of trademarks, so far as they are applicable, collective and certification marks, including indications of regional origin, shall be registrable under this Act, *in the same manner and with the same effect as are trademarks*... and when registered they shall be *entitled to the protection provided herein in the case of trademarks*. (Emphasis added.)

[59] *Kerly* n. 2 at para. 12-018.

(1) The signs and the goods or services are identical for both parties.[60] Confusion is presumed in these 'double identity' situations.[61]
(2) Where the signs may be similar or identical *and* where the goods or services may be similar or identical *and* there exists a likelihood of confusion on the part of the relevant public, which includes the likelihood of association.[62]

UK Registry practice suggests that for association marks, when 'assessing potential conflict the same principles apply as they do to the examination of ordinary trade marks, namely, after considering the similarity between the respective marks and their goods and services, is there a likelihood of confusion between them'.[63] With one intriguing exception considered below, recent decisions concerning a certification or collective mark have applied these provisions in an uncontroversial manner.

In *Customer First*,[64] the proprietor of a series of two figurative certification marks for 'Putting the Customer First' was a benchmarking organization which certifies levels of customer service. It opposed Devon County Council's application for a certification mark for a stylized 'Customer First' logo. The Hearing Officer was of the opinion that the two marks were not similar, so there was no likelihood of confusion. Interestingly, the certification specifications for the applicant's mark were used to develop the context of notional use on goods and services (here limited to 'business to consumer' transactions),[65] but otherwise the global likelihood of confusion test was followed.[66] A fairly standard application of this analysis is found in other Registry decisions as well.[67] At the OHIM Registry, one finds the standard approach to 'likelihood

---

[60] This exists as a relative ground for opposing a subsequent application in Art. 4(1)(a) of the TM Directive and Art. 8(1)(a) of the CTMR. It is mirrored in the infringement provisions in Art. 5(1)(a) of the TM Directive.

[61] See *LTJ Diffusion SA v Sadas Vertbaudet SA* C-291/00 [2003] ETMR 83 (ECJ).

[62] See Art. 4(1)(b) of the TM Directive and Art. 8(1)(b) of the CTMR. It also exists as the basis for infringement in Art. 5(1)(b) of the TM Directive.

[63] Ch. 4 of the *Registry Manual* at para. 2.3.

[64] *Customer First* BL O/048/06, decision of the UK Trade Marks Registry of 14 February 2006 (unreported).

[65] *Ibid.* at pp. 9–10.

[66] The familiar triumvirate of authorities relied upon for the global likelihood of confusion are *Sabel BV v Puma AG* C-251/95 [1998] RPC 199, *Canon Kabushiki Kaisha v Metro-Goldwyn-Mayer Inc* C-39/97 [1999] RPC 117, *Lloyd Schuhfabrik Meyer & Co. GmbH v Klijsen Handel BV* C-342/97 [2000] FSR 77.

[67] See for example *Star Pads* BL O/156/03 decision of the UK Trade Marks Registry of 11 June 2003; *WiFi/WISI* BL O/290/06 decision of the UK Trade Marks Registry of 16 October 2006. (Here the applicant unsuccessfully argued that because

of confusion' followed in Opposition Division decisions,[68] while the First Board of Appeal has considered conflicts concerning collective marks in a dispute between the Wi-Fi Alliance and the proprietor of the prior mark 'WISI'.[69] In a similar vein, the US position is that the equivalent test for confusion (the *Dupont* analysis) applies to certification marks.[70]

Amidst all this harmonious conformity, the one verdict which stands out is the GRÜNE PUNKT decision of the OHIM Fourth Board of Appeal.[71] Duales System Deutschland AG was the proprietor of the community collective mark for the Green Dot (Figure 6.1) and opposed the application for a figurative mark (Figure 6.2) by Mayocéan Mermonde, where the Green Dot is reproduced on the bottom right.

Figure 6.1 Green Dot mark   *Figure 6.2 Mayocéan Mermonde mark*

---

its mark was used as a Certification Mark, there was less of a likelihood of confusion. See para. 23.)

[68] *Culatello di Zibello* OHIM Opposition Division, No. 981/2001 of 19 April 2001; *DIN/Din-Lock* OHIM Opposition Division, No. 464/2002 of 28 February 2002; *CBF/CBI* OHIM Opposition Division No. 2510/2002 of 26 August 2002; *NF/MF*, n. 32.

[69] OHIM First Board of Appeal, 26 October 2006, R 1365/2005-1 (*Wi-Fi/WISI*) (Application for 'Wi-Fi Zone' as a collective mark and no similarity between the signs); OHIM First Board of Appeal, 26 October 2006, R 864/2005-1 (*Wi-Fi/WISI*) (Application for 'Wi-Fi' as a collective mark and no likelihood of confusion); OHIM First Board of Appeal, 28 February 2007, R 243/2006-1 (*Wi-Fi/WISI*) (Application for 'Wi-Fi Protected Access' as a collective mark and no similarity between the signs).

[70] Most recently summarized in *Tea Board of India v The Republic of Tea, Inc.* 80 USPQ2d 1881 (TTAB 2006).

[71] OHIM Fourth Board of Appeal, 10 January 2006, R 345/2003-4 (*Mermonde/DER GRÜNE PUNKT* (The Green Dot)). (Hereinafter *Green Dot*).

Mermonde's figurative mark application was for classes 29 (cocktails based on seafood and derivatives thereof) and 30 (mayonnaise; dressings) while the Green Dot was a registered community collective mark representing compliance with nationally recognized systems set up in EU Members to implement the Packaging Waste Directive.[72] Valid licensees of the collective mark were those who had paid a contribution to a qualified national packaging recovery organization.[73] Duales unsuccessfully argued that there was a likelihood of confusion within the meaning of Article 8(1)(b) of the CTMR, since the earlier CTM was totally incorporated within the contested sign. Both before the Opposition Division[74] and on appeal the signs were considered dissimilar.[75] The Board was otherwise emphatic that 'the same rules and standards must be applied when making the assessment of a likelihood of confusion between conflicting signs within the meaning of Article 8(1)(b) CTMR, irrespective of whether the signs at issue are individual or collective trade marks'.[76] But what is remarkable about this decision is the way in which it applies a conventional approach to distinctiveness[77] for collective marks when determining the likelihood of confusion.

The Opposition Division had found that since the Green Dot indicated recyclable packaging

> on a large variety of packaging types and products and in association with a large number of other proprietor's trade marks, (it) had a *low level of distinctiveness*. The consumer was *less likely to regard it as a trade mark in its own right* and more likely to regard it as a label indicating the nature and quality of the packaging.[78]

---

[72] European Parliament and Council Directive 94/62/EC of 20 December 1994 on Packaging and Packaging Waste [1994] OJ L365 at p. 10.

[73] See *Green Dot* at para. 13. For further information on this scheme see: www.pro-e.org.

[74] *Mayocéan Mermonde/DER GRÜNE PUNKT OHIM* Opposition Division No.740/2003 of 31 March 2003.

[75] The result may be a function of the operation of the relative grounds for refusal, where the contested sign (as applied for) must be compared with the prior mark (as registered). In an infringement action Duales would not have been compelled to compare their sign with Mayocean's entire mark.

[76] *Green Dot* at para. 19 prior mark. Duales therefore had no option but to compare Mermonde's complex figurative mark wit.

[77] According to the conventional analysis, there is a greater likelihood of confusion where the earlier trade mark has a highly distinctive character (that is, ability to indicate a single trade origin), either *per se* or because of the use that has been made of it. See *Sabel BV v. Puma AG* C-251/95 [1998] RPC 199, 224.

[78] *Green Dot* at para. 6 (emphasis added).

Based on this reasoning, since no collective mark, by definition, can ever indicate a single trade source all such marks are condemned to a twilight realm of insipid signification of origin. The additional insult to injury was the finding that the incorporation of the Green Dot would 'be viewed by consumers in the same way as the copyright symbol ©'.[79]

Duales appealed on the basis that 'the contested decision has not correctly evaluated the fact that the appellant's mark was a collective mark with a special function'.[80] Given its special characteristic identifying function,[81] it would still lead to a likelihood of confusion, not as to trade source but with regard to the characteristics of Mermonde's products. Furthermore, the © analogy was erroneous. While a © symbol would not meaningfully distinguish between goods on the market,[82] the Green Dot satisfied the specific distinguishing function of a collective mark by differentiating the products of members from those who were not members of the association.[83] Consumer understanding is different for collective marks in the sense that such marks speak directly to product qualities rather than origin.[84] Based on the widespread use of such marks, they were factually distinctive in the sense that consumers understood the packaging recycling message communicated by the sign. Duales then moved beyond distinctiveness and took the argument one step further, proposing a modified likelihood of confusion test, both in terms of the comparison between signs and the nature of the confusion:

> Hence, for a likelihood of confusion, the question to be answered is not whether the younger trade mark as a whole is likely to be confused with an older trade mark but whether that mark contains the collective mark, 'the green dot' as an element. A different approach would result in a complete worthlessness of collective marks in general ... If only the overall impression of a combination mark was relevant, a likelihood of confusion in all these cases would have to be denied with the consequence that the owners of such collective marks could not successfully claim any rights, either in official or in court proceedings, if third parties used the collective marks in the usual way.[85]

---

[79] *Ibid.* at para. 7.
[80] *Green Dot* at para. 11.
[81] That is, that the products thus marked are produced by members who have signed up to a specific recycling system.
[82] Although Ilanah Simon Fhima has observed that the © symbol would continue to distinguish between goods which were and those which were not protected by copyright.
[83] *Green Dot* at para. 12.
[84] Otherwise such marks follow the conventional logic of trade marks, allowing consumers to rely on product attributes while enabling producers to distinguish their products from others which do not bear the collective mark. *Green Dot* at para. 14.
[85] *Ibid.*

The Board remained unimpressed by the integrated argument that the likelihood of confusion operated differently in these cases. It held that the 'mere fact that the earlier mark is a collective mark does not alter the outcome of the assessment'.[86] Although there were certain special rules in Title VIII of the CTMR, the regular confusion analysis continued to apply to collective marks. A different sort of confusion (the product possesses the characteristics indicated by the mark) was not the test here. The inquiry was whether

> the goods or services in question come from the same undertaking or, as the case may be, from economically-linked undertakings. It is not sufficient that the relevant public perceive, if at all, 'the green dot' in the mark of the application, since the only conclusion a well-informed consumer might draw from this is that the undertaking providing the marked good and the packaging thereof, respectively, participates in a recycling system.[87]

The primary message of the Green Dot would be recycling and the details of the specific parallel garbage collection system would be unknown to most consumers.

Since collective marks appeared alongside regular trade marks on packaging, 'consumers are deemed to be able to distinguish between an indicator of origin and an indicator of common characteristics . . . and are not likely to be misled as to the origin of the product if its label contains a sign which they are also confronted with on a variety of other goods and packaging.'[88] The Board thus remained committed to an idea of *confusion as to specific commercial origin* even for collective marks.

If collective marks are to have any teeth, the approach to distinctiveness and therefore conventional confusion as to origin is unsustainable. The Board could have arrived at a more harmonious interpretation by reminding itself of the reason why commercial origin is valued by trade mark law. When it is viewed as a proxy for consistent quality, incorporating association marks is straightforward. Such marks assure quality without having to rely on the anchor of origin, by virtue of the membership specifications. By adopting the collective mark (presumably without a licence), Mermonde was interfering with Duales' ability to control the quality message. The resulting confusion could have amounted to an infringement.[89] The concern here is that the Board

---

[86] *Green Dot* at para. 17.
[87] *Ibid.* at para. 21.
[88] *Green Dot* at para. 22.
[89] A more unorthodox alternative would have been for the Board to consider that collective marks fulfil the requirements of differential distinctiveness (differentiating between signs) but not source distinctiveness (differentiating on the basis of a particular origin). I adopt this terminology from B. Beebe 'Search and Persuasion in

was doing a disservice to collective marks precisely by treating them like any other trade marks in these circumstances. Whether this approach will be followed remains to be seen.[90]

2.2 Association Marks and the Tests for 'Dilution'

'Dilution' is found in both the relative grounds and infringement provisions of EU trade mark law.[91] It is somewhat inelegantly applied to the three separate actions for blurring, tarnishment and taking unfair advantage, while traditionally mapping on to the first of these.[92] The application of these provisions to collective marks has been considered in *Tudapetrol*.[93] The applicant had applied for stylized protective hands cupping a black drop while the opponent was the owner of prior Benelux and community collective marks for stylized protective hands cupping an atomic model on dissimilar goods and services, which represented membership in the Responsible Care programme for the chemical industry.

At issue, under Art. 8(5) of the CTMR, was whether the opponent's Benelux collective mark had a reputation. The Board followed the *Chevy* criteria,[94] to ascertain whether 'the earlier mark is known by a significant part of

---

Trademark Law' 103 *Michigan Law Review* 2020, 2028–31 (2005). An alternative approach may have been found within the likelihood of commercial association amounting to confusion.

[90] As one of the few cases concerning the nature of a collective mark, the decision was reported in the *Alicante News*, Newsletter No. 03 (2006) at http://oami.europa.eu/en/office/newsletter/06003.htm.

[91] Taking s. 5(3) of the TMA 1994 as a representative provision:

A trade mark which . . . is identical with or similar to an earlier trade mark, shall not be registered if, or to the extent that, the earlier trade mark has a reputation in the United Kingdom (or, in the case of a Community trade mark, in the European Community) and the use of the later mark without due cause would take unfair advantage of, or be detrimental to, the distinctive character or the repute of the earlier trade mark.

[92] Summarized by Advocate General Jacobs in *Adidas-Salomon v Fitness World* Case C-408/01 [2004] FSR 21 at paras. 36–9. For further details, see I. Simon 'Dilution in the United States and European Union (and Beyond) Compared, Part I: International Obligations and Basic Definitions' (2006) 1 *Journal of Intellectual Property Law and Practice* 406 and 'Part II: Testing for Blurring' (2006) 1 *Journal of Intellectual Property Law and Practice* 649.

[93] OHIM Second Board of Appeal, 13 March 2006, R 214/2004-2 (*TUDAPETROL/Hands Logo*).

[94] Set out in *General Motors Corporation v Yplon SA* C-375/97 [1999] ECR I-5421 at paras. 22–8. (In particular the market share held by the trade mark, the intensity, geographical extent and duration of use, and the size of the investment made by the undertaking in promoting it.)

the public ... either by the public at large or by a more specialised public depending on the product or service marketed and covered by that mark'.[95] The decision confirms the disturbing trend made possible by *Chevy*, that is, that a product with 'niche' reputation in one sector (here the chemical industry) can nevertheless claim strong protection in non-confusing situations across all market sectors.[96] Another preliminary matter considered by the Board was that although the goods were dissimilar, there was a sufficient nexus between them for Art. 8(5) to operate.[97]

However the decision turns on a core argument which will no doubt surface in future collective mark actions as well. While the Responsible Care programme had been widely adopted by significant portions of the Benelux chemical industry, from 'the mere fact that the *programme's objectives* are well known and largely adhered to, it cannot be automatically inferred that the *earlier mark* upon which the present opposition is based, has been largely used and is well known by a significant part of the relevant public'.[98] The focus of the enquiry was whether the sign, as registered, was widely used in practice[99] and the Board engaged in a wide-ranging review of the documentary evidence submitted. While it proved the successful adoption of the programme 'it has not been proved that the pure device trade mark *per se* has been largely promoted and used by ... licensees (national chemical federations) and sub-licensees (national chemical industries), in the Benelux countries, within the relevant period.'[100] The result was that no reputation for the registered collective mark was established[101] and the opposition failed. Therefore distinguishing between the reputation of a collective association and the project which its membership is built around is a relevant yet distinct enquiry from whether the sign in question has managed to encapsulate this reputation.

2.3 Association Marks and Geographical Indications

This chapter concludes by touching upon the use of the registered trade mark

---

[95] *TUDAPETROL* at para. 27.
[96] In 2006, the US has unambiguously retreated from niche fame. As a threshold requirement for a blurring or tarnishment action, the mark must be famous. According to 2006 amendment 'a mark is famous if it is widely recognized by the general consuming public of the United States'. See §43(c)(2)(A) of the Trademark Act of 1946 (15 U.S.C. §1125(c)(2)(A)).
[97] *TUDAPETROL* at para. 31.
[98] *Ibid.* at para. 42 (emphasis added).
[99] *Ibid.*, n. 97 at para. 44.
[100] *Ibid.*, n. 97 at para. 51.
[101] *Ibid.*, n. 97 at para. 53–4.

system to protect Geographical Indications (GIs).[102] Europe has distinct regimes governing the labelling of wine with reference to place names[103] and the registration of geographical names for agricultural products and foodstuffs.[104] However the TRIPs Agreement has left open the possibility that the obligations for the protection of GIs can be fulfilled by a variety of means and GIs are registered under both *sui generis* registration systems as well as via certification or collective marks.[105]

This reliance on both categories of rights in opposition proceedings is beginning to surface in registry decisions. The UK Registry was the site for an unsuccessful challenge to an application for 'Madara Rock' on Bulgarian table wines by the *Instituto Do Vinho Da Madeira* based on a prior certification mark for 'Madeira' wine.[106] The OHIM Second Board of Appeal recently considered an appeal concerning 'Geronimo Stilton'.[107] The opposition was *inter alia* based on White Stilton and Blue Stilton, which are registered Protected Designations of Origin under Regulation 2081/92.[108] Similarly, 'Grana Biraghi' was opposed by the *Consorzio per la Tutela del Formaggio*

---

[102] Geographical Indications are defined in Art. 22.1 of TRIPs as 'indications which identify a good as originating in the territory of a Member, or a region or locality in that territory, where a given quality, reputation or other characteristic of the good is essentially attributable to its geographical origin'. Examples drawn from the names of wines, spirits, agricultural products and foodstuffs include Bordeaux wine, Darjeeling tea and Havana tobacco. They function as valuable, collective brands in a manner similar to a trade mark. For an overview, see WIPO Secretariat *Document SCT/6/3 Rev. on Geographical Indications: Historical Background, Nature of Rights, Existing Systems for Protection and Obtaining Protection in Other Countries* (SCT/8/4) 2 April 2002.

[103] The legislative framework is principally set out by Council Regulation (EC) No. 1493/1999 of 17 May 1999 on the Common Organisation of the Market in Wine [1999] OJ L179/1.

[104] Initially established by Council Regulation (EC) No. 2081/92 of 14 July 1992 on the Protection of Geographical Indications and Designations of Origin for Agricultural Products and Foodstuffs [1992] OJ L208/1. (Hereinafter Regulation 2081/92.) In light of a recent WTO Panel Ruling, several amendments have been carried out and it has arisen, phoenix like, as the similarly titled Council Regulation (EC) No. 510/2006 of 20 March 2006 [2006] OJ L93/12. (Hereinafter Regulation 510/2006.)

[105] For an analysis of the consequences of this overlap and possible pre-emption issues, see L. Bently and B. Sherman 'The Impact of European Geographical Indications on National Rights in Member States' 96 Trademark Rep 850 (2006).

[106] *MADARA ROCK* BL O/215/05, decision of the UK Trade Marks Registry of 29 July 2005. (Madeira's reputation seems to have worked against it in this decision, making it less likely that there would be any confusion.)

[107] OHIM Second Board of Appeal, 26 July 2006, R 982/2002-2 (*Geronimo Stilton/STILTON*) (French only). (The matter was settled, so the opposition was withdrawn.)

[108] See http://ec.europa.eu/agriculture/qual/en/194_en.htm.

Grana Padano on the basis of both community collective marks and protected designations of origin for 'Grana Padano' cheese.[109] The Board was clear that Art. 14 of Regulation 2081/92, specifying that an application for a trade mark which would infringe a registered Geographical Indication should be refused, also applies to the CTM regime.[110] Finally, prior registrations of appellations of origin have been referred to in a series of relative grounds challenges between Anheuser-Busch and Budějovický Budvar over the registration of variants of 'Budweiser' and 'Bud'.[111]

3. CONCLUDING OBSERVATIONS

As industry sectors and producer cooperatives continue to rally under collective banners, the utility of certification and collective marks appears to be growing. Given the proliferation of self-governing industrial codes and regulatory compliance requirements, such marks may be experiencing a renaissance, as evinced by the recent increase in registry level skirmishes. However this turns the spotlight on to the message communicated by such association marks and the need to more fully integrate them within the mainstream of trade mark law. Perhaps more significantly, such signs also pose a more serious question to the fundamentals of conventional trade mark doctrine. How meaningful is it to speak of commercial origin if it is merely a proxy for quality? The question is all the more relevant in an era when most consumers are blissfully unaware of the commercial origin of goods and licensing agreements proliferate. If the purpose of trade mark law is to enable the relevant public to distinguish between the goods and services of producers, is a sign's ability to indicate a single trade origin the only way to go about this? If relevant quality standards are assured, should a specific trade origin continue to be the baseline? Association marks may be living in and possibly even the cause for interesting times ahead.

---

[109] OHIM First Board of Appeal, 16 June 2003, R 153/2002-1 (*Grana Biraghi/GRANA PADANO*) (Italian only). The dispute turned on whether 'Grana' was included in the scope of registered protection or was a generic term for a type of cheese.
[110] *Ibid.* at paras. 33–5. The equivalent provision is Art. 14 of Regulation 510/2006.
[111] See the series of proceedings between these parties in: OHIM Second Board of Appeal, 11 July 2005, R 509/2004-2 (BUDWEISER/BUDWEISER BUDVAR et al.); Second Board of Appeal, 11 July 2005, R 514/2004-2 (BUDWEISER/ BUDWEISER BUDVAR et al.); Second Board of Appeal 14 June 2006, R 234/2005-2 (BUD/BUD); Second Board of Appeal, 28 June 2006, R 241/2005-2 (BUD/BUD) and Second Board of Appeal, 20 March 2007, R 299/2006-2 (BUDWEISER/ BUDWEISER BUDVAR et al.).

PART III

Shared name litigation

7. Same name, different goods – death of the principle of specialty

Ilanah Simon Fhima

1. INTRODUCTION

In a nutshell, the principle of specialty dictates that a mark's scope of protection will be limited to combating later use on identical or similar goods and services. As a corollary of this principle, mark owners cannot prevent later users from using their marks on dissimilar goods and services. Thus, the principle of specialty forces mark owners to 'share' the names of their goods and services on certain goods.

This chapter will begin by briefly considering the background to the specialty principle, and the effect that this forced sharing of names has. It will go on to argue that specialty has been eroded in two, ultimately distinct, ways:

1. by an expansion of the situations in which the courts hearing both passing off cases and registered trade mark cases are prepared to recognize the existence of actionable confusion and
2. through the adoption of dilution and unfair advantage as independently actionable forms of registered trade mark infringement.

However, it will conclude that the principle of specialty never really went away. Although it no longer has the 'veto power' it once did over registered and unregistered trade mark infringement actions, specialty remains alive and well, if somewhat reduced, not only in confusion-based infringement, particularly in the field of passing off, but also where one might least expect it – in dilution cases.

2. WHAT'S SO SPECIAL ABOUT SPECIALTY?

2.1 Specialty – A Very Brief History

The specialty rule has been influential in many jurisdictions.[1] It requires that the owner of a trade mark or protected sign only be protected against later uses on goods or services which are identical or similar to those for which the owner holds a registration, or which he uses his mark on. Perhaps the most basic reason for this is that the key interest of trade mark law has historically been to protect consumers and the earlier user from confusion. It appears to have been assumed that this confusion could only happen if the two parties were active in the same or a very similar product market. Associated with this reasoning is the idea that a trade mark should not give rise to an absolute right. To grant protection against all second uses of the same mark would grant its owner greater protection than he needed to protect his ability to continue using the mark as he previously had, and would be tantamount to creating a 'property right' in the mark.[2]

The influence of the rule is highlighted in Art. 6*bis* of the Paris Convention. That article outlines the protection that Paris Union members should give to 'well-known' marks. Even though it may be easier to demonstrate that consumers believe that goods come from the same source across a wider range of goods when the goods are well known,[3] that article limits the special protection afforded to well-known marks to situations where the mark is 'used for identical or similar goods'.

More recently, the international *zeitgeist* has changed, and there is a greater willingness to look beyond the formalities of assessing the degree of similarity between the parties' products. Instead the focus is more on whether the actual harm has occurred, that is, whether consumers are confused. Moreover, the law has gone beyond protection against confusion, and is now willing to recognize other types of harms, most notably dilution of the earlier mark's distinctiveness. These new types of harm do not necessarily require a connec-

---

[1] For example, So Young Yook in 'Trademark Dilution in the European Union' 11 Int'l Legal Persp 223, 256 (2001) details its influence in France and C. McManis, states of the US in *Intellectual Property and Unfair Competition in a Nutshell* (West, St Paul MN, 2004), 'The original common-law view was that there could be no infringement except by use of a confusingly similar mark or name on a competing product, service of business' (p. 175).

[2] B. Patishall documents these fears in 'Trade-Marks and the Monopoly Phobia' 42 TMR 588 (1952).

[3] On the reasons for giving extra protection beyond similarity good goods to well-known marks, see A. Kur, 'Well-Known Marks, Highly Renowned Marks and Marks Having a (High) Reputation. What's It All About' 32 IIC 218, 220 (1992).

tion between the parties' goods or services to occur. These changes are exemplified in Art. 16(3) of the TRIPs Agreement. This applies Art. 6*bis* of the Paris Convention to situations where the goods are not similar. It has also been argued that Art. 16(3) requires WTO Members to provide dilution protection,[4] although a clearer expression of the international will to provide measures against dilution can be seen in the Joint Recommendations Concerning Provisions on the Protection of Well-Known Marks.[5] As we shall see, the UK has also taken a more flexible approach, but does not appear to have gone as far in all respects.

2.2 Specialty and Sharing Names

The continued existence of a specialty rule forces trade mark owners, and those who hold indicia protected by unfair competition or passing off, to share their marks with other traders who use the marks on dissimilar or even allied, but not quite similar, goods. This can harm the earlier user in situations where, even though the goods are not similar, consumers are confused into thinking that the original user has produced, or is responsible for those goods. Additionally, a specialty rule could thwart the prevention of types of harm which do not require confusion, such as harming the distinctiveness of the earlier user's mark on the market (i.e. dilution) or allowing the later user to take advantage of the earlier user's mark and the efforts he has put into publicizing the 'brand' that the mark is part of. The earlier user may also be prevented from expanding into a new field of activity if other traders are allowed to use the mark in those areas before the earlier trader is ready to enter the new area.

3. SPECIALTY AND PASSING OFF

The high point of the specialty principle in the context of passing off came in

---

[4] See N. Pires de Carvahlo, *The TRIPs Regime of Trademarks and Designs* (Kluwer Law International, The Hague, 2006), pp. 286–7, and D. Gervais, *The TRIPs Agreement: Drafting History and Analysis* (Sweet & Maxwell, London, 2003), p. 174. However, I have argued in that, by making Art. 6*bis* of the Paris Convention apply *mutatis mutandis*, the drafters have imported a confusion requirement, removing Art. 16(3) from the scope of traditional dilution actions – see I. Simon, 'Dilution in the US, Europe, and beyond: international obligations and basic definitions' (2006) 1 JIPLP 406, 407.

[5] See in particular Art. 4(1)(b)(ii). These are non-compulsory recommendations for the level of protection to be given to well-known marks, formulated by the WIPO Standing Committee on Trade Marks.

McCulloch v May.[6] It appears that previously, there had not been a particular focus on the relationship between the parties' goods or services.[7]

In this 1947 case, the children's radio personality Derek McCulloch (known affectionately to his fans as 'Uncle Mac') brought a passing off action against the producer of 'Uncle Mac's Puffed Wheat'. McCulloch alleged that in naming the cereal, which was aimed at children, 'Uncle Mac's Puffed Wheat', the defendant would benefit from his reputation as a children's radio presenter. McCulloch's case was rejected on grounds which are capable of being interpreted as giving a prominent role to the specialty principle.

Wynne-Parry J identified two requirements for a successful passing off action:

1. a protectable proprietary right of the claimant in the form of reputation in a name in relation to a profession or business;
2. an invasion of that proprietary right which has caused, or is likely to cause, damage to that profession or business in the form of confusion.

It was in relation to the second element, damage, that specialty was brought in. After noting that, in order to show damage to the claimant's business, there must be a connection between the claimant's and defendant's business, the judge stated:

> [O]n analysis I am satisfied that there is discoverable in all those [cases] in which the court has intervened the factor that there was a *common field of activity in which, however remotely, both the plaintiff and the defendant were engaged* and that it was the presence of that factor which grounded the jurisdiction of the court. [Emphasis added]

This is not the bright line rule that it is sometimes represented as being.[8] Read literally, Wynne-Parry J does not require that the two parties' goods or services be identical. Instead, he merely called for some commonality or connection between the fields of goods of the two parties that will make it possible for there to be damage in the form of confusion to the earlier user's indicia.

---

[6] *McCulloch v Lewis A May (Produce Distributors) Ltd* (1948) 65 RPC 58.

[7] See J. Phillips and A. Coleman, who in 'Passing Off and the "Common Field of Activity"' (1985) 101 LQR 242 detail the previous passing off case law before concluding, 'From the foregoing cases it can be stated categorically that "common field of activity" was not an accepted doctrine of passing-off law . . . This relatively settled view of the law of passing off was undermined quite spectacularly, however, in the case of *McCulloch v May*' (p. 252).

[8] See for example J. Andrew, 'The Necessity for "A Common Field of Activity" in the British Law of Passing Off' 53 TMR 1, 3 (1963).

3.1 The Backlash Against Specialty

3.1.1 An Australian intervention

It is therefore ironic that the strictest view of the common field of activity came in the case in which it was most vehemently rejected. In the Australian *Henderson v Radio Corporation* case,[9] Manning J condemned *McCulloch v May* as wrongly decided, based on the argument that 'The ratio of the decision in that case [*McCulloch v May*] was that the plaintiff failed because the parties were not business rivals, having no common trading activities.'[10]

It can be argued though that Manning J has constructed a straw man. As has already been stated, Wynne-Parry J stopped short of requiring direct business rivalry, only needing a field of activity that both parties are 'remotely' involved in. Likewise, Evatt CJ and Myers J in the same case criticize the supposed need in *McCulloch* for conflicting activities.

However the better reading of *McCulloch*, and the one that has gained currency in the predominant majority of subsequent cases is that a strict view of common field of activity, in the sense of a direct conflict between the parties' goods and services is *not* needed, although it may be helpful in showing the deception that is needed to establish passing off. Put another way, the general trend that is being argued for in this chapter has been followed: the principle of specialty is no longer a 'dead hand' on passing off actions, but it has made a swift reappearance because the closer goods are, the easier it will be to establish an actionable case.

To some extent, this is acknowledged in *Henderson*. Evatt CJ and Myers J identified the defendant's activity of providing records for dancing and the teaching of dance to be 'broadly competitive' with the Hendersons' occupation of performing dance, and consequently to fall within *McCulloch*.[11] This suggests that even the *McCulloch* common field of activity requirement was not incredibly exacting.

3.1.2 The slow demise of the common field of activity

In form, if not in substance, the sidelining of the common field of activity requirement happened incrementally. Earlier[12] English cases did not directly reject the term 'common field of activity', but interpreted it relatively widely. In the *Wombles* case, Walton J stated categorically 'there must be a common

---

[9] *Henderson and another v Radio Corporation Pty Ltd* [1969] RPC 218.
[10] P. 242.
[11] P. 235.
[12] Surprisingly, there do not seem to have been many cases on this issue between *McCulloch v May* and the *Wombles* case. Phillips and Coleman (n. 7, at p. 257) detail only one, reported in 1968.

field of activity'.[13] However, he did not require the two parties to be in direct competition with each other for there to be this common field. Instead, he held that it was sufficient if there was a common field 'which is not actual, but which is reasonably to be assumed by the reasonable man from the use of the same or similar name'.[14] Here Walton J is, while paying lip-service to the common field of activity requirement, being led by the presence of confusion on the part of consumers. Likewise, in *Tavener Rutledge v Trexapalm*,[15] Walton J again noted the need for a common field of activity, but the comparison of fields was not limited to the goods or services which the parties are actually offering. Instead, he states that one must 'look and see what ordinary, reasonable people, the man in the street, would consider to be within the relevant field of activities'.[16] Once again, instead of being driven by a rigid rule akin to specialty, the judge is prepared to look at consumer perception, and to define which goods 'clash' impermissibly based on those consumer beliefs.

Having said this, in neither of these two cases did the claimant manage to overcome the problems posed by the common field activity. Both cases involved fictional characters – the Wombles in the *Wombles* case and the television detective Kojak in *Tavener Rutledge*. In both cases, the later users' goods had a conceptual connection with the characters in question. In the *Wombles* case, the later goods were skips and the Wombles are famed for their altruistic tidying of their Wimbledon Common home. In *Tavener Rutledge*, Kojak was known for sucking on lollipops, and the later user started producing lollipops which he called KOJAKPOPS and KOJAK LOLLIES. Yet, in neither case was the conceptual link considered sufficient. In both cases, the earlier user's activity was identified as being the licensing of the fictional character and this was not close enough to the production of actual goods.

The reasoning behind this is particularly clear in *Tavener Rutledge*, where Walton J said that consumers would not believe that all products bearing the name or likeness of a fictional character would be licensed by the copyright owner who would exert quality control over the goods. This displays a particularly English breed of scepticism towards character merchandizing (indeed, in *McCulloch v May*, Wynne-Parry J did not believe that a radio presenter could have an professional interest in the production of goods such as puffed wheat) which clearly was not present in Australia in the *Henderson* case. Nevertheless, the fact remains that a distinctly flexible approach was taken, at least in principle, to what constitutes the common field of activity.

---

[13] *Wombles Limited v Wombles Skips Limited* [1977] RPC 99, 101.
[14] *Ibid.*
[15] *Tavener Rutledge Limited and anor v Trexapalm Limited* [1977] RPC 275.
[16] *Ibid.*, p. 279.

In fact, the Court of Appeal in the slightly earlier case of *Annabel v Schock*[17] adopted an even more ambivalent approach to the common field of activity requirement. The court did not expressly denounce common field of activity as a prerequisite for passing off, but nor did they state that it was needed either. Instead, Russell LJ, delivering the leading judgment, emphasized the connection between confusion and any association between the parties' goods, stating

> In this question of confusion of course, as a matter of commonsense one of the important considerations is whether there is any kind of association, or could be in the minds of the public any kind of association, between the fields of activities of the plaintiff and the field of activities of the defendant – as it is sometimes put: Is there an overlap in the fields of activity?[18]

Russell LJ appears to be implicitly rejecting the common field of activity as a rigid rule. Rather than describing it as a prerequisite, he views it as a 'consideration', suggesting that it is one of a number of factors which may be helpful in establishing the confusion that will lead to a finding of passing off. This is clearer in his next comment: 'But of course, when one gets down to brass tacks this is simply a question which is involved in the ultimate decision whether there is likely to be confusion.'[19]

In other words, the common field of activity is, according to the Court of Appeal, a pragmatic indicator of confusion, rather than a strict requirement. Moreover, it appears that the court was willing to take a relatively wide view[20] as to what constituted a common field. In this case, the claimant ran a high-class nightclub, while the defendant ran an escort agency. These were considered to be within an associated field since both concerned 'night life'. More specifically, the escort agency provided ladies for *inter alia* dining and dancing, while the nightclub offered dining and dancing facilities for gentlemen and their female partners. While the services are quite different in terms of what the proprietor delivers to his customers, the conceptual link between them, and their complementary natures led to a finding of likely confusion.

3.1.3 An express rejection

A clear English rejection of the common field of activity as a prerequisite

---

[17] *Annabel's (Berkeley Square) Limited v G Schock (Trading as Annabel's Escort Agency)* [1972] FSR 261.
[18] P. 269.
[19] *Ibid.*
[20] Although this was not without its limits. Russell LJ rejected the prospect of a hairdresser called Annabel's being confused with the nightclub because of the lack of any overlap between the services (p. 269).

came in *Lyngstad v Anabas*.[21] There Oliver J criticized the *Henderson v Radio Corporation* court for their 'misconception' that *McCulloch v May* established such a rule. Instead, he claimed that the expression 'common field of activity' was a 'convenient shorthand term for indicating . . . the need for a real possibility of confusion', rather than a 'term of art'.[22] With respect to Oliver J, Wynne-Parry J's articulation of the common field of activity standard appears a good deal stronger than that, but this is to some extent by-the-by. Both approaches mean that a lack of specialty will not be fatal to a passing off case, but the presence of a link between the goods will be helpful in establishing the confusion that leads to passing off.

This new approach was followed by Falconer J in *Lego v Lemelstrich*,[23] where the judge added that the most up-to-date and authoritative formulation of the law of passing off was to be found in the House of Lords' decision in the *Advocaat* case.[24] There no mention was made of any need for a common field of activity, and so it could not be said as a matter of law that a common field was required. Nevertheless, such a common field could be helpful as a matter of fact in establishing misrepresentation. To prove the point, Falconer J found that there was a likelihood of misrepresentation leading to confusion with Lego's plastic bricks if Mr Lemelstrich was allowed to market his irrigation equipment in the UK. This case highlights that, while a relationship between the goods is important, its absence can be overcome in some cases, particularly where the earlier indicia has a strong reputation. The judge held that the fact that 'everyone'[25] associated LEGO with a particular company, meant that misrepresentation was easier to prove. We will see that reputation has also played a role in diminishing the role of specialty in the registered trade mark confusion cases.

This area of passing off is characterized by steps forward being followed by slight steps backwards, and indeed that is what happened following *Lego v Lemelstrich* in *Stringfellow v McCain*.[26] Here the Court of Appeal did not expressly reject the common field of activity requirement, particularly in its broadest sense of requiring an association between the parties' activities,

---

[21] *Lyngstad and others v Anabas Products Ltd* [1977] FSR 62.
[22] P. 67.
[23] *Lego System Aktieselskab and another v Lego M Lemelstrich Ltd* [1983] FSR 155.
[24] *Erven Warnick BV v J Townsend & Sons (Hull) Ltd* [1980] RPC 31. The common field of activity requirement also does not appear in the other major House of Lords statement of passing off principles, *Reckitt & Colman Products Ltd v Borden Inc* (the 'JIF Lemon case') [1989] 1 WLR 491.
[25] *Lego v Lemelstrich* p. 187.
[26] *Stringfellow and another v McCain Foods (GB) Limited and another* [1984] RPC 501.

rather than direct competition. Having said that, Slade LJ did point out that there is no need for direct diversion of trade, ruling out a strict specialty requirement. He went on to label an association between the parties' activities as 'an important and highly relevant consideration'[27] and continued by saying that confusion is increasingly less likely the further the parties' activities are from each other. In terms of result therefore, the position is the same as in *Lego v Lemelstrich*. However, this case does demonstrate the argument being proposed in this chapter – although specialty was no longer a requirement, its complete absence meant that there was no confusion. Here the court found that the claimant's nightclub and the defendant's oven chips were just too far apart for consumers to draw the inference that a nightclub owner would be responsible for the chips. It also demonstrates the point made immediately above that other factors, particularly the reputation of the earlier mark, can alter the importance of specialty in any given case[28] since Slade LJ noted that, unlike LEGO, STRINGFELLOW was not a 'household' word, and in fact was a relatively common surname.

Despite this setback, the common field of activity requirement was decisively cast out by the majority of the Court of Appeal in *Harrods v Harrodian*.[29] Leaving no room for doubt, the Court labelled Wynne-Parry J's approach 'contrary to numerous previous authorities . . . and now discredited'.[30] Nevertheless, the court affirmed the role of an association between the goods (and hence, to some extent at least, specialty) in showing that confusion is likely, describing the lack of a common field as 'not fatal'.[31] The court went on to label any kind of association between the parties' activities as 'important and highly relevant'[32] and in the absence of such association, 'the burden of proving the likelihood of confusion and resulting damage is a heavy one'.[33]

This is very visible in this case, perhaps even more so than in *Stringfellow v McCain*. According to Millett LJ, the lack of a common field of activity meant that, as a matter of fact, there was no likelihood of confusion. The claimant was the proprietor of Harrods, the luxury department store, while the defendant had opened a preparatory school named the Harrodian School on the grounds of the former sports ground for Harrods employees. Harrods the shop had no reputation for running a school. Its reputation for running a

---

[27] P. 534.
[28] See the discussion of this point by Phillips and Coleman, n. 7, pp. 260–2.
[29] *Harrods Limited v Harrodian School Limited* [1996] RPC 697.
[30] P. 714, above.
[31] *Ibid.*
[32] *Ibid.*, n. 29 above.
[33] *Ibid.* On the continued relevance of common field, see Christopher Wadlow, *The Law of Passing Off: Unfair Competition by Misrepresentation* (Sweet & Maxwell, London, 2004), pp. 341–2.

department store would have no bearing on the running of a school and consequently consumers would be 'incredulous' if told that Harrods had opened a school. Thus, Harrods' immense reputation could not compensate for the lack of a common field of activity. This highlights that the relationship between the reputation of the earlier indicia and the distance between the parties' goods and services is a subtle one. In fact, the two are interrelated, with the need to look not only at whether the mark is well known, but also at *what goods or services* the reputation is for. We will see that this is also true of the registered trade mark decisions which are discussed below.

Most recently, Laddie J in *Irvine v Talksport*[34] also rejected the approach taken in *McCulloch v May*. This case demonstrates just how far passing off has come. There was no whisper of a commonality of overlapping fields. The claimant, Eddie Irvine, was a Formula 1 motor racing driver, while the defendant was the broadcaster of a radio station. The defendant featured doctored pictures of Irvine listening to a radio in its promotional materials. Despite the lack of any overlap, passing off was found on the basis that consumers would wrongly believe that Mr Irvine had endorsed the radio station. This makes it clear that, even though previous courts have strongly stated that an overlap will be helpful in demonstrating the presence of the misrepresentation that is vital to a successful passing off action, its absence is not fatal in exceptional cases.

3.2   Protection against Dilution through Passing Off

Irvine v Talksport is interesting because it stands at the crossroads of the two themes explored in this chapter: a wider conception of confusion and the willingness to accept dilution as actionable. Laddie J appears to expand the rationale behind passing off by defining it as follows: 'If someone acquires a valuable reputation or goodwill, the law of passing off will protect it from unlicensed use by other parties.'[35]

This is certainly wider than protection against confusion (although that will of course be covered) and instead appears to provide a monopoly right in an acquired reputation. However, he goes on to require a little something extra to trigger the passing off action, in a paragraph that is somewhat confused.

Laddie J recognizes the blurring or reduction of a mark's exclusivity as a type of harm that will be caught by passing off. This type of harm does not require a common field. However, he goes on to require misrepresentation

---

[34]   *Irvine and anor v Talksport Ltd* [2002] 1 WLR 2355. The case is put in its passing off context in Brian Cordery and Kirsty Sloper, 'Personality Endorsement – New Brands Hatch' (2002) 13 Ent LR 106.

[35]   P. 2368, above.

because 'it is misrepresentation which enables the defendant to make use of or take advantage of the claimant's reputation'.[36] Here Laddie J has effortlessly slipped from one justification of the action (blurring, which focuses on harm to the indicia in which the goodwill resides) to another (unfair advantage, which focuses on the benefit to the defendant).

This has serious consequences on the ability of passing off to escape the specialty rule. As we will also see in the registered trade mark cases, it is far easier to demonstrate that the later user has obtained an unfair advantage if there is some link between the two parties' goods or services. Moreover, a continuing need for misrepresentation,[37] despite the supposed protection of goodwill from blurring, will send the courts back to the cases which propose that it is far easier to find the confusion that results in a misrepresentation where the parties' offerings are in some way linked. Granted, in this case it was possible to find misrepresentation without this link, but it could be objected that this is an exceptional case, since consumers have an expectation that those who are famous will expand into the endorsement of products that they could not make or control the quality themselves. It is not necessarily the case that consumers will routinely believe that companies involved in more conventional types of production and marketing will expand into areas in which they have no experience, or with which there is no natural linkage to their current businesses.

3.3 The Role of Speciality in Passing Off: the Prognosis

We have seen that although specialty (in the form of the common field of activity) is no longer a strict requirement in passing off cases, it is still extremely helpful in demonstrating the misrepresentation that is a requirement of a successful passing off case. Moreover, it took a long time for the courts to

---

[36] *Ibid.*
[37] This continuing need has been confirmed forcefully by the Court of Appeal in *L'Oreal SA and ors v Bellure SA and ors* [2008] ETMR 1. It was also evident in one of the first cases to recognize the avoidance of dilution as a protected interest under passing off law – *Tattinger SA and others v Allbev Ltd and another* [1993] FSR 641, particularly *per* Sir Thomas Bingham MR. There the damage identified was that the later use of the term CHAMPAGNE on a sparkling elderflower drink would 'erode the singularity and exclusiveness of the description Champagne and so cause the first plaintiffs damage of an insidious but serious kind' – in other words, a form of blurring. However, the Court of Appeal still required misrepresentation, which in that case was found since consumers would think that the product was in some way associated with Champagne, even though they would probably know that it was not Champagne. It was particularly possible to find this association because the two products were beverages, and were both at the high end of their respective markets.

dispense with the common field of activity, particularly when one bears in mind that it seems pretty much to have appeared out of nowhere in the 1940s. Likewise, passing off is making efforts to provide protection against dilution, which, as a matter of principle, does not have confusion as its basis and so should not require the parties' goods to be related. However, the continued need to show misrepresentation on top of dilution in all passing off cases, together with a very narrow conception of unfair advantage, mean that specialty is not absent completely, even in cases where the real harm is dilution. In terms of sharing names, following the discrediting of *McCulloch v May*, it is no longer the case that there is a formal rule which would force mark-holders to share their marks if the later use is on non-identical, or even dissimilar goods. Equally well, as a practical matter, mark-holders may be forced to share their marks, even when their marks are being harmed, if they cannot demonstrate confusion.

4. SPECIALTY AND REGISTERED TRADE MARKS UNDER THE DIRECTIVE

Similarity between the goods, and hence the principle of specialty, also has a reduced role in registered trade mark law following the harmonization of European trade mark law. This can be attributed to two causes: a widened definition of infringement and within that widened definition, a more flexible approach to detecting the presence of likely confusion. The new European approach means that confusion can be found and stopped in more cases, cutting the number of situations in which trade mark owners will be forced to share their marks with users on goods which are in some way associated with their own.

4.1 Specialty Prior to Harmonization

While s. 4 of the pre-harmonization Trade Marks Act 1938[38] purported to

---

[38] The relevant subsection (s. 4(1)) reads in full:

Subject to the provisions of this section, and of sections seven and eight of this Act, the registration (whether before or after the commencement of this Act) of a person in Part A of the register as a proprietor of a trade mark (other than a certification trade mark) in respect of any goods shall, if valid, give or be deemed to have given to that person the exclusive right to the use of the trade mark in relation to those goods and, without prejudice to the generality of the foregoing words, that right shall be deemed to be infringed by any person who, not being the proprietor of the

grant proprietors the 'exclusive right' to use their marks, the right was rather limited, since it was expressly only an exclusive right to use the mark 'in relation to *those goods*', i.e. the goods for which it was registered. Thus, the rule of specialty governed trade mark infringement.

The law on the registration of conflicting marks was not so strict when it came to specialty. Under s.12, trade marks which were identical to or resembled earlier trade marks could not be registered for either the same goods, goods of the same description as those for which the earlier mark was registered, or goods which were associated with the earlier goods, where deception or confusion was likely. As we will see though, the test for determining whether goods were of the same description was more rigid than that used for detecting whether goods are similar under the post-harmonization Trade Marks Act 1994. However, under s. 11, there was a general bar on the registration of marks which were 'likely to deceive or cause confusion', without reservation as to the goods of the later user. This might appear to be a complete abandonment of the specialty principle, and as a matter of theory, it does appear to come close to this. However, in practice, as the authors of *Kerly* point out, just like in passing off, factors indicating a closeness between the goods were helpful in establishing association.[39] Moreover, the authors of the 1986 edition of *Kerly* identify only four cases between 1898 and 1986 which they describe as involving goods which 'were clearly not "of the same description" '.[40]

Finally, there was the possibility of filing a defensive registration under the 1938 Act. This enabled the owners of marks with a reputation to register their marks for goods which were dissimilar to those for which they used their marks. Again though, there was a need to show that use in respect of the goods for which registration was sought was likely to confuse consumers. Since this

---

trade mark or a registered under thereof using by way of the permitted use, uses a mark identical with or so nearly resembling it as to be likely to deceive or cause confusion, in the course of trade a mark, in relation to any goods in respect of which it is registered, and in such manner as to render the use of the mark likely to be taken either –
 (a) as being used as a trade mark; or
 (b) in a case in which the use is use upon the goods or in physical relation thereto or in an advertising circular or other advertisement issued to the public as importing a reference to some person having the right either as proprietor or as registered user to use the trade mark or goods with which such a person as aforesaid is connected in the course of trade.

See further T.A. Blanco White and Robin Jacob, *Kerly's Law of Trade Marks and Trade Names* (12th edn, Sweet & Maxwell, London, 1986), §§14–15.

[39] *Ibid.*, §§10–13.
[40] N. 72, accompanying §§10–13.

was necessarily speculative (taking place before the later use had begun), a tricky guessing game was involved, and only about a hundred registrations were filed between 1938 and 1974.[41] Even these were mostly for goods similar to those for which the earlier mark was registered, prompting Amanda Michaels to conclude in an earlier edition of her book written during the currency of the 1938 Act that 'All in all, the advantages of this statutory provision over the common law are not overwhelming particularly as the common law seems to be widening on this point.'[42]

4.2 The Expanded Definition of Confusion

The advent of European harmonization of trade mark law brought with it a more fluid approach to establishing confusion. While similarity of goods remains necessary in order to demonstrate confusion-based infringement, the degree to which it needs to be shown has been reduced by its treatment as just one factor in a global assessment of confusion. At the same time, the European Court of Justice has drawn up a wide-ranging list of facts that can contribute to a finding that goods are similar, making it easier to prove that similarity in less obvious cases. We will see though that, behind these changes, the principle of specialty lives on, although in a greatly weakened form.

4.2.1 Global appreciation and interdependence

From the point of view of weakening the specialty principle, global appreciation works by de-emphasizing the importance of similarity of goods. The global appreciation approach, and more specifically, the idea of interdependence, means that a lower degree of similarity between the goods can be compensated for by a more convincing showing on the other factors relevant to confusion. This makes it possible to demonstrate likely confusion, as is required by the head of infringement in Art. 5(1)(b) of Directive 89/104, even when the goods are not particularly similar if the marks are very similar.

This was first made explicit by the ECJ in *Canon*, where the court said

> A global assessment of the likelihood of confusion implies some interdependence between the relevant factors, and in particular a similarity between the trade marks and between these goods or services. Accordingly, a lesser degree of similarity between these goods or services may be offset by a greater degree of similarity between the marks, and vice versa.[43]

---

[41] Mathys Committee Report on British Trade Mark Law & Practice 1974, Cmnd. 5601, cited by Amanda Michaels in *A Practical Guide to Trade Marks* (ESC Publishing Limited, Oxford, 1982), p. 51.
[42] *Ibid*.
[43] *Canon Kabushiki Kaisha v Metro-Goldwyn-Mayer Inc* C-39/97 [1999] ETMR 1, para. 17.

From the point of view of sharing names, this partial withdrawal from the principle of specialty means that there will be more situations in which the owner of an earlier mark will be able to block either the use or registration of a conflicting mark, and so there will be fewer situations in which an earlier mark-holder will be forced to share his name with a second-comer.

The ECJ's approach can be contrasted with that which prevailed (briefly) between the passing of the Act[44] implementing Directive 89/104 and the ECJ ruling on the issue. In *British Sugar v Robertson*,[45] the court was required to rule on whether the use of ROBERTSON'S TOFFEE TREAT on a sweet spread would cause confusion with TREAT, registered for 'dessert sauces and syrups'. Jacob J (as he then was) found that there was no infringement, despite the near identity of the most distinctive element of the two trade marks. In fact, the confusion case never got beyond a comparison of the similarity of the parties' goods. Jacob J found that the goods were not similar. Armed with that finding, the judge ruled that there was no infringement, without going on to consider the effect on any other factors on whether consumers would be confused by the concurrent use of the two sets of marks on the two sets of goods. To do so, he said, would illegitimately 'elide the questions of confusion and similarity',[46] in a way that ignored the fact that the relevant provision of the UK Act (and indeed Directive 89/104) asks three separate questions: (i) are the marks similar or identical; (ii) are the goods similar or identical and (iii) is there a likelihood of confusion? Jacob J's approach left each of the questions as 'stand alone' questions, which had to be answered affirmatively before proceeding to the next relevant question.

It is submitted that the ECJ's approach is the better one. The harm that is being addressed in this sub-article of the Directive is consumer confusion. Such confusion can occur regardless of the relationship between the goods or services on which it is used. While it may be sensible to use similarity of goods as a limiting factor to ensure that trade mark holders do not get overly wider protection, unlike preventing confusion, the similarity of goods requirement is not an end in itself.

4.2.2 The role of reputation

Additionally, in *Sabèl v Puma*,[47] the ECJ introduced an extra factor to the

---

[44] The Trade Marks Act 1994.
[45] *British Sugar Plc v James Robertson & Sons Ltd* [1996] RPC 281, [1997] ETMR 118.
[46] Pp. 124–5.
[47] *Sabèl BV v Puma AG, Rudolf Dassler Sport* C-251/95 [1998] ETMR 1, para. 24.

analysis of confusion: the reputation of the earlier mark, stating 'the more distinctive the earlier mark, the greater will be the likelihood of confusion'.

In so doing, the Court has added another element to the confusion text. This further dilutes the importance of similarity of goods, particularly since all the factors which determine confusion are interdependent. It is worth noting that this reflects (presumably unconsciously) the approach taken in the passing off cases, where an earlier mark's reputation, particular if that earlier mark is a household name, makes misrepresentation more likely. Moreover, the importance of the distinctiveness of the earlier mark (and consequent potentially reduced role for similarity of goods) was given a boost in *Canon*,[48] where the court confirmed that both inherent and acquired distinctiveness can contribute to making confusion more likely.

4.2.3 A liberal test for similarity of goods

The ECJ has further loosened the grip of the specialty principle by instructing us to conduct a wide-ranging investigation into establishing whether the two parties' goods are similar. Rather than merely looking at whether the parties' goods are physically similar, the *Canon* court has instructed us to consider the following:

- the nature of the goods;
- the intended purpose of the goods;
- their method of use;
- whether they are in competition with each other; and
- whether the goods are complementary.[49]

The ECJ's test shifts the focus away from a mechanistic test of whether the goods are physically similar, and looks instead at the circumstances in which the goods are used and sold. This allows us to reach a more considered opinion on whether there are links between the goods or their surrounding circumstances that will lead consumers to be confused. For the most part, this approach does not treat specialty as an end in itself, but instead gives it a secondary role as one of the elements that can be used to establish the real harm that the legislation is trying to prevent – confusion. This liberal approach to similarity of goods should make it easier to demonstrate actionable confusion, and consequently will reduce the number of situations in which trade mark owners will have to tolerate others from sharing their marks.

---

[48] At para. 18.
[49] Para. 23.

4.3 ... But Specialty Never Completely Leaves the Picture

4.3.1 The test for similarity of goods

As ever though, specialty retains a role. In a line of cases, the Court of First Instance has explained that at least some of the *Canon* factors must be met, and to a meaningful standard.[50] The issue has arisen in particular in relation to the question of whether the parties' goods are complementary. In *MISS ROSSI/SISSI ROSSI*, the Court of First Instance[51] defined complementarity for these purposes as the situation in which 'one [set of goods] is indispensable or important for the use of the other so that consumers may think that the same undertaking is responsible for the production of both goods'. This necessity to use the two sets of goods together could be either functional in nature, or could be aesthetic. In this case, the parties' goods were handbags and shoes. There was no functional necessity for the two to be worn together – one's shoes will protect one's feet whether or not one's valuables are safely and portably stowed away and vice versa. The CFI, in what must have been a testosterone-charged courtroom, was also of the opinion that there was no aesthetic necessity, as it would be neither 'unusual' nor 'shocking' for a lady to be seen with shoes and a handbag which did not match perfectly.[52]

MISS ROSSI/SISSI ROSSI demonstrates that the standard adopted in relation to complementarity is a high one. The standard meaning of the word might suggest goods which are commonly used together, but the CFI appears to want more, that is, that consumers have no real choice but to use them together. This is also apparent in subsequent CFI cases. In *TOSCA BLU*,[53] the goods were perfumery products and leather goods. The opponent argued that they were complementary because the public was accustomed to fashion items being sold under the trade marks of perfume companies, since it was a common industry practice for the perfume trade marks to be licensed. The CFI again repeated the need for genuine aesthetic necessity for such goods to be used together. However, in this case it added a further requirement that consumers must consider it normal for the two sets of goods to be sold under the trade mark. For consumers to have such a perception, it would need to be

---

[50] In addition to the cases discussed in the text, the complementary goods factor has been discussed recently by the CFI in *Assembled Investments (Proprietary) Ltd v OHIM; Waterford Wedgwood plc intervening* (WATERFORD STELLENBOSCH), T-105/05, 12 June 2007 (unreported).

[51] *Sergio Rossi SpA v OHIM; Sissi Rossi intervening* (SISSI ROSSI), T-169/03 [2005] ECR II-685, para. 60. This case was subject to an appeal to the ECJ on procedural grounds. The ECJ upheld the CFI's decision.

[52] Para. 62.

[53] *Mülhens v OHIM; Minoronzoni intervening* (TOSCA BLU) T-150/04, 11 July 2007, (unreported), paras. 36 and 37.

the case that a large number of companies used or licensed their marks against the two product markets. This development means that there is a stringent two-stage test for showing that goods are complementary from an aesthetical point of view, making it particularly difficult to show similarity of goods in these circumstances. Significantly, the CFI justifies its stringent approach by expressly referring to the principle of specialty, stating that '[I]t is clear from Article 8(1)(b) of Regulation No 40/94 that a likelihood of confusion between two identical or similar marks can exist only within the limits of the principle of speciality.'[54]

This is surprising, as the ECJ and CFI seldom, if ever, make mention of the principle.[55] However, the CFI's statement demonstrates that even under the relatively liberal approach to testing for confusion, specialty has a restraining influence, limiting the scope of protection for trade mark owners.

Having said this, it is important to keep the issue in perspective. The CFI has adopted a hard-line view of the meaning of this factor in the *Canon* test, and this will lead to fewer findings of similarity between goods and consequent confusion than a lower standard would have done. This will mean that a greater number of undertakings will be unable to restrain the sharing of their names than under a lower standard. However, the inclusion of complementarity as a factor in the assessment of similarity of goods considerably expands the comparison between goods in a way that was far from necessary on the plain meaning of the similar goods requirement.

4.3.2 Similarity of goods as a threshold requirement

Specialty retains a more fundamental role in confusion-based infringement actions. Although the *Canon* court led the way towards loosening specialty's grip, it also stressed that in every case, there must be some degree of similarity between the parties' goods, stating,

> It is, however, important to stress that, for the purposes of applying Article 4(1)(b) [the relative ground for the refusal of registration which is identical to Art.5(1)(b)], even where a mark is identical to another with a highly distinctive character, it is still necessary to adduce evidence of similarity between the goods or services

---

[54] Para. 34.

[55] A search of the ECJ's case law database (www.curia.europa.eu) which includes all case law from 1997 onwards revealed the term only being used twice, in *Budějovický Budvar, národní podnik v OHIM; Anheuser-Busch, Inc. intervening* (BUDWEISER) Joined Cases T-53/04 to T-56/04, T-58/04 and T-59/04, 12 June 2007 (unreported), para.184 and *Budějovický Budvar, národní podnik v OHIM; Anheuser-Busch, Inc. intervening* (BUD) Joined Cases T-60/04 to T-64/04, 12 June 2007 (unreported), para. 177, and even then it was in a quote from a WIPO Standing Committee report, which was cited 'for the sake of completeness'.

covered ... Article 4(1)(b) provides that the likelihood of confusion presupposes that the goods or services covered are identical or similar.[56]

The *Canon* court's approach is consistent with that later taken to similarity of marks. In *Vedial*,[57] the ECJ held that a tribunal should not embark on the interdependence analysis where it is satisfied that there is absolutely no similarity between the marks. This appears to be a real barrier to embarking on the interdependence-based analysis since the fact that both marks shared the common element of the word HUBERT did not stop the ECJ from finding that the marks were not similar, and so it was unnecessary to consider the relationship between the two parties' goods. This has been interpreted in the UK[58] as introducing a threshold level of similarity between marks (albeit a low one) under Art. 5(1)(b). Thus, a complete lack, or a very low level of either of the types of similarity will form an absolute bar to infringing infringement.

The *Canon* court's comments mean that, subject to the availability of a cause of action under Art. 5(2), where a later user uses the same or a similar mark on dissimilar goods, the owner of the earlier mark will be powerless to stop that later use, even where it causes confusion. In other words, the proprietor of the earlier mark will be forced to share his mark in a way that will harm that ability of his mark to act as a sign which designates only his goods. In this respect, infringement under Art. 5(1)(b) is narrower in its scope of protection than passing off. As has been discussed above, under the law of passing off, although it is assumed to be harder to show misrepresentation where the parties' goods are dissimilar (i.e. where there is no common field of activity), if it is possible to show that misrepresentation then the later user's use will be stopped, whatever sector of trade he is operating in.

4.4 Dilution – the Death of Specialty?

European harmonization also appeared to bring with it a measure which would

---

[56] Para. 22.
[57] *Vedial* v *OHIM* Case C-106/03 P [2004] ECR I-9573, [2005] ETMR 23, paras. 51–54. The marks were the word SAINT-HUBERT and the word HUBERT in fancy script and a cartoon picture of a chef. However, the Court of Appeal has subsequently held that there is no minimum threshold of similarity – see [2008] EWCA Civ 842.
[58] *Esure Insurance Ltd v Direct Line Insurance Plc* [2007] EWHC 1557 (Ch), 29 June 2007 (unreported). Here the threshold was met where the marks were an angular and quite realistic telephone on wheels and a rather more impressionistic computer mouse on wheels. This case suggests that the threshold is rather low, since visually, the only thing the two marks really had in common was the existence of wheels and conceptually, they were united by the somewhat abstract concept of both being electronic communication devices on wheels.

sound the death-knell for specialty: a new form of actionable harm which did not require any link between the parties' goods. Under Art. 5(2) of Directive 89/104, the owner of a trade mark can prevent later uses which either (a) harm the distinctive character of his mark; (b) harm the reputation of his mark or (c) take unfair advantage of the reputation or distinctive character of his mark. The important element from the specialty point of view is that, on its express wording at least, the protection is limited to situations where the parties' goods are dissimilar. This is anathema to the principle of specialty: whereas specialty has always limited protection to goods of the same type, this form of infringement ostensibly withholds protection where the goods are of the same time.

Art. 5(2) was never going to completely oust specialty since its protection is limited to marks with a reputation. Thus, 'ordinary' trade marks would still have to be dealt with under Art. 5(1)(a) if both the goods and signs are identical or Art. 5(1)(b) in other situations. We have already established above that specialty remains relevant under this article, albeit with a lesser role. However, we might have expected that for Art. 5(2) cases, specialty would have no role. This though has not been the case. As we will see, not only has the ECJ read the article so as to make it possible to rely on Art. 5(2) where there is specialty between the goods, but also, certain courts have taken the view that a link between the goods will make it *easier* to show that harm of the sort envisaged by Art. 5(2) is present. This is most surprising, bearing in mind that the literal wording would appear to suggest that such a link would take the situation outside the scope of the article, and demonstrates that specialty continues to work its way back into the trade mark system, even when it appears to have been (partially) dispensed with.

4.4.1 Why was specialty eliminated from the original dilution law?

The definition of dilution which focuses its protection on dissimilar goods can probably be attributed to Frank Schechter's article, 'The Rational Basis of Trademark Protection',[59] in which he offered the first definition of trade mark dilution, stating

> The real injury in all such cases can only be gauged in the light of what has been said concerning the function of a trade mark. It is the gradual whittling away or dispersion of the identity and hold upon the public mind of the mark or name by its use upon non-competing goods.[60]

---

[59] F. Schechter, 'The Rational Basis of Trademark Protection' 40 Harv. L. Rev. 813 (1926–27).
[60] P. 825.

The type of harm that is identified is the diminution of distinctiveness, but what is important for our purposes is that he specifically refers to this harm being caused by use on *non-competing* goods, i.e. in situations where the principle of specialty is not operative.

As an aside, it is worth noting that Schechter may well not have intended for his theory to be limited to uses on non-competing goods. Absent in cases where the later use causes confusion (and the use is thus attributed back to the mark-owner), it is hard to see why use on identical or similar goods should not also harm the earlier mark's distinctiveness. Instead, his focus on non-competing goods can be attributed to the fact that he perceived a lacuna in the law, *viz*, that the law would only provide protection where the parties' goods were competing, and only against confusion, leaving no protection against use on non-related goods. Schechter's aim in this article was to advocate for protection against non-competing uses, and it is on these uses that he focuses. That does not mean that, had he been asked, he would have said that the harm could not happen where the goods are competing or are similar.[61]

Be that as it may, many US commentators viewed Schechter's new form of trade mark protection as being limited to use on dissimilar goods.[62] The various states, when passing individual anti-dilution legislation (federal action did not follow until 1995) were split, with some limiting their protection to dissimilar goods, and others taking the opposite approach. However, when federal legislation was finally passed, its protection was '. . . regardless of the presence or absence of . . . competition between the owner of the famous mark and other parties . . .'.[63]

Europe, on the other hand, initially adopted an approach which would seem faithful to a literal reading of Schechter's article, and which would therefore run directly counter to the principle of specialty. As has already been mentioned, Art. 5(2) of Directive 89/104 only expressly prohibits use of a sign 'in relation to goods or services which are not similar to those for which the mark is registered'.

---

[61] A hint that Schechter did not intend to grant differential protection against use on similar and dissimilar goods can be seen from his amendments to the Vestal Bill which he unsuccessfully proposed to Congress in 1932 (reproduced in F. Schechter, 'Fog and Fiction in Trade-mark Protection' 36 Colum. L. Rev. 60, 86 (1936)). These would have granted identical protection against harm to goodwill and reputation to goods of the same and different 'descriptive properties'.

[62] See for example J.T. McCarthy, *McCarthy on Trademarks and Unfair Competition* (4th edn, West, St Paul, MN, 2000 and updates), who states at 24:74 that 'Like an attorney who wears his shoes on his hands for a court appearance, antidilution law is out of its proper place in a case of competing parties'.

[63] Lanham Act 1946 (prior to the 2006 revision), §45. US federal protection against dilution was comprehensively revised by the Trademark Dilution Revision Act 2006.

This caused puzzlement,[64] as trade mark lawyers had difficulty believing that the legislator intended to provide wider[65] protection against use on dissimilar goods than in the arguably more deserving situation of use on similar or identical goods. In the UK, some judges took matters into their own hands, and introduced a confusion requirement into Art. 5(2).[66] Although this could not reintroduce specialty, it at least put dissimilar goods situations on a par with the protection afforded to similar and identical goods.

A reference to the ECJ followed, in *Davidoff v Gofkid*, in which Advocate General Jacobs[67] adopted an approach that suggested that, far from being an oversight, the decision to cut the expanded protection of Art. 5(2) free from the traditional limits of trade mark protection was deliberate. The wording of the Directive was clear, and the legislative history showed that a suggestion had been made to broaden the protection of Art. 5(2) to similar and identical goods, but this had been rejected. Moreover, the legislative history showed a clear reason why Art. 5(2) was kept narrow: to encourage those who valued such protection to apply for a Community trade mark, rather than a national trade mark. Consequently, extending protection beyond dissimilar goods could only be justified if there was a clear gap in protection, which there was not since the ECJ test for confusion is wide, particularly in the light of the global appreciation doctrine. Moreover, confusion was meant to be the keystone of infringement under the European regime, and harm to reputation and distinctiveness was only afforded protection exceptionally because of the risk limited to later uses on dissimilar goods which would not cause confusion but would cause harm to the earlier mark. Thus, under the Advocate General's conception, the abandonment of specialty was not a principled decision, but rather a pragmatic one, which was designed to fill a gap in the case of dissimilar goods which essentially only arose because of an abortive decision to favour Community trade marks over national marks.

However, the ECJ[68] differed from the Advocate General, laying the groundwork for the reintroduction of specialty. The court said that the Directive had to be read in the light of 'the overall scheme and objectives of the system of which it is a part'. This meant that it could not be the case that

---

[64] This is documented by H. Norman in '*Davidoff v Gofkid*: dealing with the logical lapse or creating European disharmony?' [2003] IPQ 342, 343.

[65] Wider in the sense that confusion is not required under Art. 5(2), according to *Sabèl BV v Puma AG, Rudolf Dassler Sport* C-251/95 [1998] ETMR 1.

[66] See for example *Baywatch Production Co. Inc. v The Home Video Channel* [1997] FSR 22.

[67] *Adidas-Salomon AG and Adidas Benelux BV v Fitnessworld* C-408/01, [2003] ETMR 91 (AG), paras. 33–54.

[68] [2004] ETMR 10 (ECJ).

it was intended to give wider protection against use on dissimilar goods than against use of similar or identical goods. Because there was the possibility of a situation where a mark could be used on identical or similar goods without confusion being caused, the protection afforded under Art. 5(2), which does not require confusion, had to be extended to cover identical or similar goods.

The ECJ reiterated its position in *Adidas v Fitnessworld*.[69] If the case law on this subject had stopped there, this would have left us in the optimal situation for minimizing name sharing. The ECJ would have read into the Directive a cause of action which could stop the later use of a mark on all types of goods, be they identical, similar or dissimilar to those for which the earlier mark is registered. Granted, the remedy would be limited under the terms of Art. 5(2) to marks with a reputation, but the ECJ has taken a relatively liberal approach to finding that a mark has a reputation.[70] However, as we will see, the ECJ's decision has allowed the British courts to reintroduce a form of specialty through the back door, and has resulted in a reference to the ECJ which could lead to a stronger role for specialty under Art. 5(2) across Europe.

4.5 The Reincarnation of Specialty

4.5.1 The UK

A clear example of the way in which the *Davidoff* decision has enabled the British courts to give a more prominent role to specialty can be seen in *Esure v Direct Line*.[71] Here both marks were in the field of insurance services. The earlier mark consisted of a telephone on wheels while the later applied-for sign was a computer mouse on wheels. There Lindsay J stated 'The risk of relevant unfair advantage being taken, perhaps also of relevant detriment being suffered, is, I would think, likely to be greater where the goods or services are identical.'[72] This clearly would give greater protection under Art. 5(2) in

---

[69] *Adidas-Salomon AG and Adidas Benelux BV v Fitnessworld* C-408/01 [2004] ETMR 10 (ECJ).
[70] *General Motors Corp v Yplon SA* C-375/97 [1999] ETMR 950, para. 31, states that for a mark to have a reputation for the purposes of Art. 5(2), there is no set percentage of the public amongst which it must be known. Instead, it need only be known amongst a significant section of the public, and that public need only consist of the consumers of the goods or services covered by the earlier mark.
[71] Para. 90. Dilution was not considered by the Court of Appeal.
[72] See also *Wheels 'R' Us Limited v Geoffrey Inc.*, BL O/296/06, decision of the UK Trade Marks Registry of 19 October 2006 (unreported), where at para. 73 the hearing officer, after noting that identical and similarity goods are now covered, states that, in establishing unfair advantage 'the proximity of the goods or services is a factor which has to be taken into account' and seeks a 'close association' between the parties' businesses.

specialty-type situations, but it would not have been possible for the judge to made this statement were it not for the ECJ's *Davidoff* decision.

An equally overt example of at least the partial reintroduction of specialty can be seen in the Court of Appeal's reference to the ECJ in *Intel v CPM*.[73] Here the goods were dissimilar (computer microprocessors and telephone marketing services). Jacob LJ, mindful of the fact that in the past the UK has taken a cautious approach to the interpretation of Art. 5(2), composed three questions which it is hoped will clarify, but equally well could limit the scope of Art. 5(2). For our purposes, the most important is the first question, where he asks

> For the purposes of Art. 4(4)(a) of the First Council Directive 89/104 of 21st December 1988, where:
> (a) the earlier mark has a huge reputation for certain specific types of goods or services,
> (b) *those goods or services are dissimilar or dissimilar to a substantial degree to the goods or services of the later mark,*
> (c) the earlier mark is unique in respect of <u>any</u> goods or services,
> (d) the earlier mark would be brought to mind by the average consumer when he or she encounters the later mark used for the services of the later mark,
> are those facts sufficient in themselves to establish (i) 'a link' within the meaning of paragraphs [29] & [30] of *Adidas-Salomon AG v. Fitnessworld Trading Ltd*, Case C-408/01, [2003] ECR I-12537 and/or (ii) unfair advantage and/or detriment within the meaning of that Article? [Emphasis added][74]

Jacob LJ appears to be inviting the ECJ to find that dissimilarity of goods will either make the types of harms which are outlawed under Art. 5(2) less likely, or that the dissimilarity will even step in to prevent consumers from linking the two parties' marks together in a way that could result in the types of harm. He explains his thinking when he states his proposed answers to his questions. In his opinion, most marks are 'robust enough' to withstand their being brought to mind through being used a second time, giving as an example the fact that JIF cleaning fluid and JIF lemon juice managed to coexist on the UK market for many years. Only where the earlier mark is particularly strong would use on dissimilar goods be likely to cause actionable harm, since such use could 'cause the consumer to think there is a trade connection between the owner of the former mark and the user of the later mark'.[75]

The situation we would find ourselves in under Jacob LJ's approach is most surprising. Whilst the express wording of the Directive would limit Art. 5(2) protection to later use on dissimilar goods, he would make this type of use the

---

[73] *Intel Corp Inc v CPM United Kingdom Ltd* [2007] ETMR 59.
[74] Para. 28.
[75] Para. 30.

exception rather than the rule. Moreover, he appears to only be convinced that there is actionable harm in cases where there is confusion between the two marks, even though the ECJ has said (discussed above) that confusion is not required under Art. 5(2). In terms of name sharing, this would be a step backwards because it would suggest that later users can use earlier marks, as long as they do not cause confusion.

To be fair, the reintroduction of similarity of goods cannot be wholly attributed to *Davidoff*. Even before that case, the British courts were making moves of this nature. For example, in *Premier Brands v Typhoon*,[76] although the earlier mark-holder was ultimately unsuccessful under Art. 5(2), the judge found that the fact that there was a connection between the parties' goods (tea and kitchenware respectively) contributed towards showing whether there was an association between the use of the signs that could ultimately lead to one of the kinds of harm covered by Art. 5(2).[77] Likewise, in *Pebble Beach*,[78] the relationship between the parties' products (a golf course and whisky) was not close enough for it to be likely that consumers would associate them in a way that would lead to the whisky taking unfair advantage of the golf course. In both cases, the court correctly did not require a likelihood of confusion. Instead the courts saw a relationship between the goods as a helpful (and in the case of *Pebble Beach*, perhaps necessary) factor in demonstrating that the later mark could bring the earlier mark to mind in a way which would either harm the earlier mark or benefit the user of the later sign. At the time of those cases though, the dissimilar goods requirement remained, and so the courts could, in theory at least, only require a somewhat vague link between the parties' goods. In the light of *Davidoff*, this limitation has been removed, allowing the courts to move closer towards the position in which they have historically felt most comfortable in both registered trade mark law and passing off – where the parties' goods are directly connected.

4.5.2 ... and OHIM

However, it would be a mistake to think that this phenomenon is limited to the UK. The same trend is apparent in the decisions of OHIM, particularly in the field of establishing unfair advantage. On repeated occasions, the Boards of Appeal have identified a proximity between the goods as contributing to the association between the two parties' signs which will lead

---

[76] *Premier Brands UK Ltd v Typhoon Europe Ltd & Another* [2000] ETMR 1071, p. 1102.
[77] The need for such an association has subsequently been confirmed by the ECJ in the *Adidas v Fitnessworld* decision mentioned above.
[78] *Pebble Beach Co v Lombard Brands Ltd* [2003] ETMR 21, para. 19.

to unfair advantage. For example, in *SER/SER (FIG. MARK)*,[79] the Fourth Board of Appeal stated

> The greater the proximity between the goods and services and the circumstances in which they are marketed, the greater is the risk that the relevant public will make a link between the conflicting signs, and that unfair advantage will be taken of the earlier marks.

Although this does not eliminate Art. 5(2) protection in dissimilar goods situations (indeed, the services were not particularly similar in that case), it leaves us in a situation where the closer the parties' goods, the greater the likelihood of a finding of infringement or a successful opposition. The paradigm example of proximate goods is where they are either identical or similar.

An even more audacious example can be seen in *MARIE CLAIRE/MARIE CLAIRE*. In this decision, the Board devotes a separate subsection to the issue of 'nexus between the goods', where the Board highlights the points of proximity between the parties' goods (fashion magazines and swimwear), i.e. that fashion magazines often contain articles about clothing, including swimwear, and that such magazines often licence their names for items of clothing. Consequently

> ... the public could believe that the goods bearing the contested trade mark were produced under the control of the opponent, since, although clothing products covered by the mark are not similar to the goods covered by the earlier reputed mark, the distance between them is not sufficiently great to prevent the public from establishing a certain link between them.[80]

Although the Board goes on to state that it is not requiring confusion, this does not seem to be correct, since under *Canon* (discussed above), confusion includes a mistaken belief that the parties are economically linked. A false belief that the earlier mark-holder is controlling the quality of the later goods would appear to fit within that definition. This subtle reintroduction of confusion echoes Jacob LJ's approach in *Intel v CPM*, and could also give a greater role to similarity of goods, because such confusion will be most likely where the goods are similar.

---

[79] Fourth Board of Appeal, 17 January 2006, R 0404/2004-4 (SER/SER (FIG. MARK), CADENA S.E.R), para. 34. See also for example Second Board of Appeal, 19 June 2007, R 1136/2006-2 – (LIFESPA/SPA et al.), para. 24.

[80] Second Board of Appeal, 6 March 2006, R 530/2004-2 (MARIE CLAIRE/ MARIE CLAIRE et al.), paras. 56–9. The term 'nexus' is also used, together with similar reasoning in decision of the First Board of Appeal, 17 November 2004, R 237/2004-1 and R 299/2004-1 (OPIUM/OPIUM), paras. 39–41.

4.5.3 ... but not in the US?

Finally, it is interesting to note that the US appears to have avoided this pitfall. Under the 1995 Act, similarity of goods was, following the intervention of the courts, a factor favouring a dilution finding.[81] However, in passing its new anti-dilution Act,[82] no mention has been made of the relationship between the goods in the definitions of dilution. Also, it is not mentioned as a factor helpful to showing dilution by blurring in the newly created six-part test for proving that blurring is likely to occur. In the light of the controversy created when similarity of goods was used under the 1995 Act, it seems likely that this omission was deliberate. Perhaps the US really is willing to kill off specialty.

5. CONCLUSION

There can be no doubt that the past couple of decades have seen a more flexible approach towards the specialty principle, both in registered and unregistered trade mark law. This should translate into fewer situations in which traders are forced to share their marks with later users in a way which might either cause confusion or damage the distinctiveness of the mark, and its ability to identify a single undertaking to consumers.

However, as we have seen, specialty does retain a role in both types of law. Although in passing off, specialty is no longer a 'dead hand' with its absence preventing a successful claim, as a practical matter, it will be difficult to demonstrate the confusion which is needed for a passing off claim if the parties' goods are far apart. This situation is unlikely to change, as the courts have steadfastly required misrepresentation in passing off cases. Even their acceptance of dilution as a process that passing off will recognize has not led to a loosening of the misrepresentation requirement.

Under registered trade mark law though, specialty does remain a 'dead hand', though it has become far more flexible than it was in the past. It remains the case that a confusion-based claim cannot succeed unless there is similarity between the goods which exceeds the threshold level, even though consumers may be duped and the earlier trade mark and its owner may be harmed. Moreover, while Directive 89/104 appears, on a literal reading, to have introduced a cause of

---

[81] *Nabisco, Inc and Nabisco Brands Company v PF Brands Inc and Pepperidge Farm, Inc* 191 F.3d 208, 219 (CA2, 1999): 'The closer the junior user comes to the senior's area of commerce, the more likely it is that dilution will result from the use of a similar mark.'
[82] Trademark Dilution Revision Act 2006.

action which is completely divorced from specialty, the approach of the judiciary appears to be reintroducing specialty via the back door. It seems therefore that, despite the progress that has been made, trade mark owners will be forced to share their names in a significant number of situations.

8. Is there an own-name defence in the common law tort of passing-off? The implications of *Asprey*, *Reed* and *Newman v Adlem*

Christopher Wadlow

1. INTRODUCTION

That there is a defence of the use of one's own name in the law of registered trade marks is plain on the face of the relevant legislation.[1] In passing-off, however, the existence of the defence is anything but clear. It undoubtedly enjoyed some support in the nineteenth century, occasionally being asserted in terms which suggested it was something akin to an inalienable natural right.[2] In due course we shall see something of this approach reasserting itself in the judgment of Arden LJ in the latest of the three recent Court of Appeal cases with which this chapter is principally concerned.[3] In the intervening century, however, the defence has led a precarious existence, even by reference to the restrictive terms in which it had been restated by Romer J in *Rodgers v Rodgers*.[4]

---

[1] Trade Marks Act 1994, s.11(2)(a) giving effect to the First Directive 89/104/EEC of the Council, of 21 December 1988, to Approximate the Laws of the Member States Relating to Trade Marks, Art. 6(1)(a); Council Regulation (EC) 40/94 of 20 December 1993 on the Community trade mark, Art. 12(a). See also Chapter 9 of this volume, which considers the subject in detail.

[2] *Burgess v Burgess* (1853) 43 ER 90, especially *per* Knight Bruce LJ; *Turton v Turton* (1889) 42 Ch D 128, CA, especially *per* Lord Esher MR.

[3] *Asprey & Garrard Ltd v WRA (Guns) Ltd and Asprey* [2002] FSR 31, [2002] ETMR 47; *Reed Executive plc v Reed Business Information Ltd* [2004] ETMR 56; and *I N Newman Ltd v Adlem* [2006] FSR 16.

[4] *Joseph Rodgers & Sons Ltd v W N Rodgers & Co* (1924) RPC 277. The quotation is not directly from Romer J's judgment in *Rodgers v Rodgers*, but is a paraphrase taken from the headnote, which has gained currency and widespread judicial acceptance, most significantly in *Parker-Knoll v Knoll International* [1962] RPC 265 (HL).

To the proposition of law that no man is entitled to carry on his business in such a way as to represent that it is the business of another, or is in any way connected with the business of another, there is an exception, that a man is entitled to carry on his business in his own name so long as he does not do anything more than that to cause confusion with the business of another, and so long as he does it honestly. To the proposition of law that no man is entitled so to describe his goods as to represent that the goods are the goods of another, there is no exception.

There are many judicial *dicta* about the defence, but no unambiguous example of it ever succeeding on the facts.

2. THE RECENT CASES: *ASPREY, REED* AND *NEWMAN v ADLEM*

Between the decision of the House of Lords in *Parker-Knoll v Knoll International*[5] in 1962 and the end of the twentieth century, there were occasional attempts to invoke the defence in passing-off, but none of those in England resulted in any systematic attempt to re-evaluate or restate it. The reasons why this should have changed in the twenty-first century are obscure. Certainly, none of the three cases discussed below actually required the Court of Appeal to opine on either the scope or the continued existence of the defence, whether because the defence was premature, or inapplicable for extraneous reasons, or because it would not have been determinative on the facts.[6] Perhaps the underlying reason for the increased discussion is the renewed prominence of the defence in trade mark law following European harmonization.[7]

2.1 *Asprey*

There were two defendants in *Asprey & Goddard v WRA (Guns) Ltd and William Asprey*.[8] The first defendant was a company which operated a retail shop for luxury goods in London's Mayfair district, under the name *William R Asprey Esq.*, and the second (individual) defendant was its founder, managing

---

[5] *Supra*.
[6] In *Asprey* the Court of Appeal refused to give any opinion on the defence, treating it as premature; in *Reed* the defence was superfluous, since the relevant claims for passing-off all failed; in *Newman v Adlem* the irrelevance of the defence to the final result is demonstrated by the fact that the third member of a divided court expressed no opinion on it.
[7] As to which see Chapter 9.
[8] [2002] ETMR 47, reversing [2002] FSR 30.

director, and majority shareholder. As such the first defendant competed directly with the claimant company, which had bought out the interests of the Asprey family in the long-standing business of *Asprey & Co*. William Asprey had worked for the family business, but had become disenchanted with the takeover and subsequent merger with Goddard, and had left to set up his own business.

At first instance, Jacob J gave summary judgment in favour of the claimants.[9] On the passing off claims, he held that despite the best efforts of the personal defendant to avoid or rectify confusion, nonetheless mistakes indicative of some likelihood of confusion had already occurred, and confusion on an actionable scale was inevitable from the choice of name and trading strategy. Rejecting the argument that the company could benefit from the own-name defence when its trading name was so different from its corporate name, he went on to consider whether the second defendant would have the benefit of the defence if he were to take over the running of the shop as a sole trader. He held that despite the personal defendant's good intentions it would be impossible to avoid confusion in these circumstances, and that an injunction should be granted against the second defendant as well as the first.

The main issue on appeal was whether Jacob J's finding of a likelihood of confusion was supported by the evidence, and on this issue of fact or inference he was upheld. So far as the own-name defence was concerned, the Court of Appeal roundly dismissed its relevance in respect of the first defendant:[10]

> The first question that arises on this is whether the first defendant can take advantage of this defence. ... In my judgment it is plain that the defence is not available to the first defendant. Its own name is WRA (Guns) Ltd. The fact that it has chosen to adopt the trading name of William R Asprey Esquire does not enable it to rely on the own name defence.
>
> As the judge said, the defence has never been held to apply to names of new companies as otherwise a route to piracy would be obvious. For the same reason a trade name, other than its own name, newly adopted by a company cannot avail it. Further, as the judge also pointed out, because a company can choose to adopt any trading name, there could be an own name defence in almost every case if Mr Bloch were right. In my judgment he is not.

Turning to the availability of the defence to the second defendant, Peter Gibson LJ disapproved the decision of the judge below to grant summary judgment against him on an assumed but hypothetical set of facts. It was one thing to assume that Mr Asprey might set up business on his own account and

---

[9] [2002] FSR 30.
[10] Para. 42, *per* Peter Gibson LJ.

under his own name, but on the *Rodgers*[11] formulation the court would have needed to know precisely what Mr Asprey would be doing in detail, if it was to deprive him of his prima facie benefit of the defence.[12]

In the final analysis, and so far as the own name defence in passing-off is concerned, the *Asprey* case is of limited direct relevance. The only defendant actually trading was WRA (Guns) Ltd, and no conventional formulation of the defence could have allowed the company to trade under a name which was not its own, but simply that of an individual with which it was closely associated, and who might have been able to assert the defence (such as it was) had he operated as a sole trader. So what if William Asprey had decided to divest himself of his corporate veil and trade in his own right, and under his own name? Such a scenario was hardly implausibly remote, and the fact that the Court of Appeal pointedly refused to answer it will be interpreted by some as avoiding the question as to whether this would have been a proper occasion to apply the defence or not. At the very least it would have required reconsideration of Jacob J's seemingly paradoxical conclusion, that although the individual defendant was entirely honest in both motives and conduct, nonetheless he lacked the necessary *bona fides* for the defence to apply, in so far as it would not have been honest for him to trade under his name if any significant degree of confusion resulted.

2.2 Reed

The second of these cases to consider the defence is *Reed Executive Plc v Reed Business Information Ltd*,[13] and once again it is obscured by other, more material, issues. The dispute arose when the defendants Reed Information decided to exploit their long-standing business as publishers of professional journals to set up an internet service advertising job vacancies in related professional fields, thereby coming into conflict with the claimants' employment agency. Although the defendants' site had the entirely distinct name *totaljobs.com*, occurrences of the word *Reed* in its content and metatags caused *totaljobs.com* to be returned against searches for *Reed*. There were claims in trade mark infringement and in passing-off, with the own name defence being raised in respect of both causes of action. So far as passing-off was concerned, Pumfrey J as trial judge initially held:[14]

---

[11] *Joseph Rodgers & Sons Ltd v W N Rodgers & Co* (1924) RPC 277. See above, n. 4.
[12] Para. 44, *per* Peter Gibson LJ. Chadwick LJ expressly agreed: *ibid.* para. 53.
[13] [2004] ETMR 56, reversing [2003] RPC 12.
[14] At para. 136.

This is not a case of deliberate passing off in the sense that the defendants were willing to accept confusion in the hope that it would bring them more business than would otherwise be the case. All the defendants were emphatic that they were aware of the possibility of confusion and did not wish to contribute to it. I accept this evidence. But the evidence of a risk of passing off is strong in those cases where I have identified infringement, with the exception of the metatags. This is not an action in respect of mere confusion. So far as the use of the logos and the copyright line on the website is concerned, it is an action in respect of confusion giving rise to a risk of deception. The classical trinity of ingredients in a passing off action, reputation, confusion leading to deception, and damage, are present.

That led to the question of whether the own-name defence was available to the defendants:[15]

A defendant may not use his own name if to do so results in deception. In *Rodgers (Joseph) & Sons Ltd v WN Rodgers & Co*, Romer J put it this way in a phrase frequently cited and approved by the House of Lords, at least by a majority, in *Parker-Knoll Ltd v Knoll International Ltd*: . . .

The defence afforded by this passage is narrow. The reference to honesty is key, and in my judgment the same considerations apply as apply in respect to the proviso to s 11(2). The test is objective, and in any event cannot be satisfied if the defendant knows of a risk of deception in fact. . . .

In other words, the only defence is 'no passing off', because there is no deception leading to damage to the relevant goodwill.

So in the result the so-called 'defence' failed, as it was bound to do on this formulation, once there was any liability to set it against.

On appeal,[16] all the remaining passing off claims were held to fail on the facts, and strictly speaking the defence did not arise. It was, nonetheless, addressed in *obiter* terms by the Court of Appeal, with their relatively brief treatment of the common law defence concluding that the defendants were responsible for nothing more than 'some minimal degree of confusion', so that the exception acknowledged by Romer J in *Rodgers* was applicable.

2.3 *Newman v Adlem*

The most recent, and most interesting of these three cases is *I N Newman Ltd*

---

[15] *Ibid.* at para. 137. Internal citations have been omitted. For the quotation from *Rodgers*, see above at n. 4.
[16] See para. 109 *et seq.* (own-name defence to passing off) and para. 114 *et seq.* (defence to infringement).

v Adlem.[17] Although the supposed defence was no more determinative in *Newman* than in the previous two cases, the former did at least provide an occasion for the expression of two quite radically different opinions within the Court of Appeal.

The defendant, Richard Adlem, had sold his funeral director's business in 1993 to a Mr Beckwith, who carried on the business under the name 'Richard T Adlem Funeral Director' until he in turn sold the goodwill of the business to the claimants, another local undertakers' firm, in 2000. In the meantime, a restrictive covenant given by Mr Adlem on the occasion of the original sale had expired, and in 2001 he re-established himself in business under the former name, and asserted that Newmans had no right to use it.

The trial judge[18] held that the 1993 Agreement had vested in Mr Beckwith the whole of the goodwill in the funeral business, including that relating to the name Richard T Adlem, but that the defendant had concurrent rights in it. Since the name did not exclusively denote either the claimant, or the defendant, the passing-off action failed. The major issue in the appeal was again the construction of the 1993 Agreement, and specifically whether it transferred the whole of the goodwill in Mr Adlem's former undertaking business to Mr Beckwith; or whether Mr Adlem had retained a non-exclusive right to carry on business as 'Richard T Adlem Funeral Director', subject only to the restrictive covenant.

The Court of Appeal was divided. For the majority, Jacob LJ, with whom Tuckey LJ briefly agreed, held that Mr Adlem had retained no relevant rights under the 1993 Agreement, and that Newmans, as successors to Mr Beckwith, had exclusive rights to the name and the goodwill. Arden LJ, in the minority, would have held that the 1993 Agreement had never conveyed the exclusive right to use the name in the undertaking business to Mr Beckwith, that Newmans had no better title, and that Mr Adlem had always retained a concurrent right to use the name without liability. Both Jacob and Arden LJJ addressed the own name defence, but neither would have made it decisive. According to Arden LJ there was no liability for passing-off, and the defence simply did not arise, although Mr Adlem could probably have claimed the benefit of it, had it been necessary. According to Jacob LJ, the defence did not arise and did not need to be considered in any detail, because on any analysis the defendant had forfeited it by asserting that the claimants were usurpers with no right to use the name.[19]

---

[17] [2002] ETMR 47, reversing [2004] EWHC 2006. See also R. Moscona 'The Sale of Business Goodwill and the Seller's Right to Use his Own Name' [2006] EIPR 106–110.

[18] David Young QC, Deputy Judge.

[19] Tuckey LJ, who agreed with Jacob LJ in the result and on the issues of construction and misrepresentation, did not express any opinion on the own-name defence as such.

3. A CHAMPION FOR THE DEFENCE AT LAST?

The actual decision of the Court of Appeal in *Newman v Adlem* turned principally on the interpretation of a contract by which the defendant had sold all (*per* the majority) or part (*per* Arden LJ, in the minority) of the goodwill of his undertaker's business to the claimants' predecessor. However, although the views expressed by Arden LJ on the own name defence are *obiter*, they are nonetheless of considerable interest as being probably the most sympathetic to have been heard in a superior court since *Parker-Knoll v Knoll International*.[20] Had the defence been relevant, Arden LJ would have held:[21]

> Argument has been directed to the scope of the own name defence. It is clear that if the defendant is able to say that the name he is using for trading purposes is his own name which he had before the trading in question began, it will in practice be less difficult for him to show that the adoption of that name as a business name was not passing off. He would not be a stranger to the name. Where the individual sets up business in his own name because it is his own name and that is the name by which potential customers know him, it will in my judgment be more likely that the court will find that his use of his own name was in good faith and made no representation as to connection with the defendant. The name of an individual is an aspect of his personal identity and thus the courts will in my judgment exercise caution before restraining the use by an individual of his own name. I have already noted the observation of Parker J in *Mrs Pomeroy Ltd v Scalé* on this point. In any event this is a case, in my judgment, not of the own name defence alone, but also of shared goodwill and the non-exclusive right to use of the name which Newman claims to own.

The practical importance of Arden LJ's interpretation of the defence seems crucially to depend on the assumption that there is a subjective element to liability in passing-off. If so, it would indeed be self-evidently likely that the court would find that 'his use of his own name . . . made no representation as to connection with the defendant'. As a matter of law, however, and subject to whatever may be said about the own name defence itself, the defendant's state of mind is wholly irrelevant to liability for passing-off, and this has been affirmed in cases of unimpeachable authority for at least a century, not least in *Parker-Knoll* itself. There is indeed an evidential presumption against fraudulent defendants, but it has no counterpart in favour of honest ones. The presence or absence of a misrepresentation is decided objectively, and if the public are deceived in fact, then it cannot matter that the defendant deceived them innocently, nor that he may have expected and intended his representation to be understood in some accurate or innocuous sense.

---

[20] [1962] RPC 265 (HL).
[21] Para. 98.

This objective standard is even accepted by Arden LJ in the passage immediately following that quoted, rendering much of her previous paragraph of dubious legal relevance. And if innocence is no defence, then it cannot matter whether an inference of innocence is drawn (rightly or wrongly) from the fact that the defendant was using his own name, or from some equally plausible set of circumstances, such as his ignorance of the claimant's business, or his honest and genuine belief that he had done enough to distinguish his own. We may be right as a matter of fact to draw the inference of innocence in any of these cases, but we should be wrong in law if we let it affect the final result. The own-name defence must stand as an exception to the general rule, or it cannot stand at all.

4. ARDEN AND JACOB LJJ ON THE IMPORTANCE OF GOOD FAITH

There is one sense in which Arden LJ's third sentence might be read in an entirely orthodox manner, which is to suppose that the customers of the defendant's business corresponded so closely to the circle of his friends and acquaintances that each and every one of the former knew for a fact that he was dealing with the defendant, and not with the claimant, despite the identity of names. If so, then there would indeed be no misrepresentation, and no passing-off, regardless of the defendant's own motives and state of mind. But the argument stretches one's credulity even on the facts of a highly localized case such as *Newman*, and could hardly be relevant on any wider scale. It also fails to support the value judgment implicit in the sentence which follows.

Considered from this more philosophical point of view, Arden LJ might be thought to have identified a line of reasoning which would have allowed the defendant in *Newman* to enjoy the unrestricted use of his name as an 'aspect of his personal identity' without interference from the claimant. But where Arden LJ would have accepted the defendant's good faith as a strong reason for withholding an injunction in an own-name case, Jacob LJ would have gone almost so far as to turn the argument against him. Jacob LJ's view, most clearly stated in *Reed*, is that the defendant's status as an innocent party will be lost as soon as he realizes that his use of his own name is actually causing deception:[22] 'Because the test is honesty, I do not see how any man who is in fact causing deception and knows that to be so, can possibly have a defence to passing off.'

---

[22] *Reed Executive plc v Reed Business Information Ltd* (CA – cited above) at para. 112, *per* Jacob LJ.

It follows that on Jacob LJ's analysis there is no room for any *'prima facie* entitlement' to carry on business under one's own name. The so-called defence can, in practice, only be a defence to damages or profits (and perhaps costs), since once the defendant is put on notice of the deceptiveness of his conduct, he forfeits his innocent status. It would follow that the use of one's own name could never in practice provide a defence against a final injunction, since by the time of the grant of the injunction deception and damage (or, in a *quia timet* action, the imminent prospect of both) would be *res judicata* against the defendant.[23]

Since the disagreement between Jacob and Arden LJJ ultimately turns on the relative importance of two incommensurable values, its eventual resolution is impossible unless one can agree on some kind of calculus by which Arden LJ's assertion of every honest citizen's right to use his name in trade as an aspect of his personality, can properly be weighed against Jacob LJ's affirmation of the first-comer's right to unqualified economic exclusivity in his.

5. CONCLUSION: DOES THE DEFENCE EXIST AT ALL?

In the first of the three cases under consideration, it did at one time seem as if Jacob J (as he then was) was inclined to follow his own argument to its logical conclusion.[24]

> Mr Thorley [counsel for the claimant], who was not interested in a detailed discussion of the limits or otherwise of the own-name defence, simply put his case on the crude and, to my mind, correct basis that once the defendant is shown to be causing deception, then the balance between the right of the trader to use his name and the right of the public and of the owner of the goodwill to stop that use of name tips in favour of the latter.

Perhaps encouraged by this, Pumfrey J, the first instance judge in *Reed*, was expressly prepared to hold that the defence did not exist at all: '. . . the only defence is "no passing off". . .'.[25] This conclusion makes a great deal of sense. Not only has the so-called defence never been known to have succeeded

---

[23] Jacob LJ in fact goes even further, to the point of concluding that there are no circumstances in which the supposed defence can exempt an innocent defendant even from liability to accrued damages, but space does not permit that argument to be followed here.

[24] *Asprey & Goddard v WRA (Guns) Ltd* (Ch. – cited above), para. 22, *per* Jacob J.

[25] *Reed Executive plc v Reed Business Information Ltd* (Ch. – cited above) at para. 139, *per* Pumfrey J.

in fact, but the logic of decisions following *Rodgers* (at least as that case has been interpreted by Jacob LJ in *Asprey*, *Reed* and *Newman v Adlem*) is inconsistent with its having any real existence. Quite apart from issue of good faith, what Jacob LJ says in those cases minimizes the importance of the defence to the point where it supposedly depends on the defendant's conduct falling precisely on the cusp between mere 'confusion' and actionable 'deception' – since on the confusing side of the cusp there is no passing off, and on the deceptive side of the cusp there is no defence:

> Thus in this case if RBI had been causing significant deception, the fact that it was using its own name would have afforded no defence to the passing off claim, even though it had no intention to deceive. That is the admitted position as regards version 1. But in relation to later versions there is at best no more than some minimal degree of confusion – significant deception is not shown and so, narrow though it is, I think RBI comes within Romer J's exception.[26]

If this is to be the conclusion, then far better to say expressly that the defence does not exist, and have done with it, as Pumfrey J was prepared to do at first instance in *Reed*.

But after pointing that way in *Asprey*, Jacob LJ seems to have become too attached to the lingering ghost of the defence to be prepared to give it its quietus either in *Reed*, where he could almost certainly have spoken for the whole Court of Appeal, or even in *Newman v Adlem*, where he was in fundamental disagreement with Arden LJ. At first sight, the judgment of the latter might be said to have granted the defence a stay of execution, in so far as the Court of Appeal was evenly split (with one abstention) over whether it existed or not. But this may be an over-simplification of the result: both Jacob and Arden LJJ seem to have proceeded on the basis that the law of passing-off is a seamless web, in which the existence (Arden LJ) or non-existence (Jacob LJ) of the defence can be deduced from the application of its acknowledged first principles to a particular set of facts. What both overlook is that the defence, if it exists at all, only deserves the name if it is not just exceptional in a purely factual sense, but anomalous as well: the result of some wholly extrinsic factor from history or policy intruding itself into the regular operation of the classical trinity of goodwill, misrepresentation and damage.

Unless the so-called defence possesses this exceptional and anomalous character then it is not properly a defence at all, and if it does possess that character then the normal working out of the principles of the tort cannot tell us

---

[26] *Reed Executive plc v Reed Business Information Ltd* (CA – cited above) at para. 113, *per* Jacob LJ. Whether Jacob LJ has correctly understood what Romer J said in *Rodgers* is another issue on which much more could be said.

whether any such defence exists or not, any more than the same exercise can tell us whether a defence arises under such disparate rules as acquiescence, human rights law, or free movement of goods. Arden LJ comes closest to this realization, but in the last resort it is not entirely clear whether she is content to let the defence arise from the regular working out of uncontested principles concerning what amounts to an actionable misrepresentation; or whether she would allow it to prevail over the latter in order to protect the rights the defendant supposedly has in his name as an aspect of his personality.

This is not to say that the foregoing exercise is unimportant or uninformative, but its value lies in the fact that decisions ritually attributed to the operation of the own-name defence may turn out, on closer examination, either to be ones in which there was never any cause of action at all, or to be ones in which the requirements of the defence were not fully met, so that in either case the defendant's use of his own name in supposed good faith never conclusively determined the final result. It is on this basis that it can be said with confidence that there is no known example in a reported case of the defence ever succeeding on the facts. A statutory defence presumably has some claim to present existence by virtue of its enactment in the statute, even if it has never been invoked successfully; but a common law defence which has never been known to succeed in fact, and which cannot be deduced from some incontrovertible common law principle, is easily and perhaps rightly dismissed as irrelevant at best, or imaginary at worst. For the time being, at least, there seems to be no place for the own-name defence in the common law of passing-off. If it exists, then it must be sought somewhere else entirely, somewhere on the plane of legal ideas which have yet to find their application in this real world.

9. The own-name defence in relation to registered trade mark law

Ashley Roughton

1. INTRODUCTION

There is much case law and some statute law relating to whether a person can use their own name or address in the course of trade as identifying their goods or services in circumstances where the use of that term could otherwise be restrained. Before looking at the detail of the law, we may want to consider a question of principle, *viz*, why should any legal system provide a sanction in relation to the use of an individual's name or address on the grounds that trade is being interfered with? Those things are, after all, labels which are given to that individual by society or by others or sometimes chosen or adopted by the individual or company concerned. Of course there are always cases where individuals deliberately choose names or addresses which are intended to confuse and deceive, but such persons are not deserving of sympathy, and consideration of their position can be left to one side when considering the more difficult policy aspects of the law. Moreover, one need not take into account situations where the use of one's own name and address is neither used, nor intended to be used, for trade or where it is intended to be used for trade but fails in that respect. Conversely one cannot leave out of the account situations where one's name or address is not intended to be used for the purposes of trade but ends up being recognized as a badge of trade.

The situation in which a person uses his or her own name and address where he or she intends it to be understood as a trading name of some sort is of most concern. In such situations there are conflicting policy issues. On the one hand there is the right of a person to describe him or herself by means of the name which he or she was given by his or her parents, or which he or she has chosen. Put in its most pithy terms, it is a matter of freedom of expression, which is guaranteed by Article 10 of the European Convention on Human Rights and Fundamental Freedoms. One must be able to say who one is and where one comes from. On the other hand, it could be said that there ought not to be such a right to use such indicia as a means of trading if the effect is to damage others. What emerges from this, though perhaps not clearly, is that so far as registered trade marks are concerned policy dictates that innocent use ought to be excused whereas deliberate use should not. Finally, as always, the crucial question must be: what is meant by innocence and does it have any relevance in relation to legal wrongs which themselves require as part of the cause of action no state of mind? The answer of the law, though perhaps pragmatic and a little inconsistent, is, as we will see, clear: if it is passing off then it is passing off and the state of mind of the putative antagonist is irrelevant, whereas in the case of trade mark infringement then a state of mind of sorts or perhaps, more properly, a state of affairs is necessary.

2. TRADE MARK INFRINGEMENT

The question of whether the use of one's own name or address amounts to trade mark infringement may be divided into two issues: (i) whether the use in question is trade mark use and (ii) whether the use falls within the exceptions to trade mark infringement. If the use made is not trade mark use, in the sense of not being a sign used in the course of trade in relation to goods (or services), then for the purposes of registered trade marks, that is the end of the line for the claimant as there is no *prima facie* infringement. The question is always: is the alleged infringement trade mark use? Thence the enquiry moves to whether an exception applies. If it does then, again, that is the end of the line for the claimant.

3. TRADE MARK USE

The rules relating to trade mark use are tolerably clear. In policy terms, trade mark use is any use where, as a result of that use, the customer has an easier task in relation to his or her purchasing decision and, as a result, search costs are decreased.[1] By search costs what is meant are the costs associated with finding something – things are easier to identify and thus find if they have distinctive markings on them. It is a mistake to say that the purpose of trade marks is to encourage products to be of better and better quality so that the incentive to produce such products is to get a stronger and stronger trade mark. The evidence for this is weak or non-existent and indeed there are some notable examples where increased trade mark recognition has led to decreasing product quality or decreasing interest in improving quality.

---

[1] See W. Landes and R. Posner *The Economic Structure of Intellectual Property Law* (The Belknap Press of Harvard University Press, Cambridge, MA and London, 2003), Chapter 7.

More fundamentally, a further mistake is frequently made, including by the courts. It is often claimed that the purpose of a trade mark is to act as a badge of origin.[2] This is in spite of the fact that there is no legislative basis for this statement. To be sure, in the majority of circumstances where damage is said to be done, untruths are told about origin, or there is confusion about origin. However, this does not mean that a trade mark *has* to be a badge of origin in all circumstances of trade. Again, once the policy objectives of trade marks are considered, it is the reduction of search costs which is important and nothing else – although in many if not the vast majority of cases the effect of a trade mark is to indicate origin, there is no reason why this necessarily has to be so; a trade mark is serving its proper function if it reduces search costs. An important caveat must be added though, which is that the objective of reducing search costs cannot be an impediment to free competition. Since uninformed choice can lead to increased search costs, it would not be appropriate to regulate every increase in search costs. Further, for reasons which are unclear, there is no sanction where search costs are increased by deception or confusion but are not actionable in a private suit between individuals.

Seen from this perspective, the person who uses personal identification information in a way that increases search costs for others should be an outlaw. The policy of the law of trade marks when transposed into law is different. As our law currently stands, certain representations which are used are unlawful *unless* the use of the representation is specifically excepted or unless the representation does not interfere with the customer's or consumer's perception of product identity (in the sense of the trade marks product you buy today being the same in terms of quality as the same you bought yesterday) and not origin.

Thus, where consumer and customer are distinct then the influence on the consumer will only be germane where that consumer is likely to become a customer at some future time or, possibly, where the influence on the consumer has some influence on the future purchasing decisions of other customers. In legal terms the law is muddled although the European Court of Justice has recognized such a concept for some time. The cases, such as they are, tend to concentrate on factual situations which may or might amount to trade mark use or where trade marks are nearly descriptive or might in certain circumstances be completely descriptive. Legally the European Court of Justice is of the view that the law is settled; any use which is not an indicator of origin is not trade mark use.

---

[2] See for example *Arsenal Football Club plc v Matthew Reed* C-206/01 [2003] ETMR 73 (ECJ), paras. 48–50.

The European court of Justice first dealt with the question of trade mark use in a substantive sense in *Michael Holterhoff* v. *Ulrich Freiesleben*,[3] where it said that it was not trade mark use, and hence did not infringe, to make oral use of a word which was a registered trade mark where such use was descriptive. Thus, to describe a gem as 'sun cut', which was an accepted technical and descriptive term, was not trade mark use and so did not infringe, even though SUN CUT was a registered trade mark.

On the same day that the ECJ handed down judgment in *Holterhoff*, it heard argument in *Arsenal Football Club Plc* v. *Matthew William Reed*[4] and eventually gave a decision confining itself to the facts in issue being that affixation of a registered trade mark to goods for which that mark was registered was infringement, notwithstanding that it would not be perceived as a trade mark as such.

In *Société des Produits Nestlé Société Anonyme* v. *Mars UK Limited*[5] the European Court of Justice, in deciding whether the words 'HAVE A BREAK' were registrable, said that otherwise indistinctive marks could only be shown to be distinctive in fact (arising by reason of the use made of it) if the use was trade mark use. According to the Court

> 29. The expression 'use of the mark as a trade mark' must therefore be understood as referring solely to use of the mark for the purposes of the identification, by the relevant class of persons, of the product or service as originating from a given undertaking.

The clear implication is that the use of an own name or address with or without intention to infringe is infringing if, barring exceptions, the use is to designate trade origin. If it is not, then the potential defendant walks free.

4. EXCEPTIONS TO INFRINGEMENT

The rules relating to exceptions to infringement are set out in section 11(2)(a) of the Trade Marks Act 1994.[6] Section 11 of the Act states (in relevant respect)

---

[3] C-2/00 [2002] All ER (EC) 665; [2002] I ECR 4187; [2002] ETMR 917; [2002] FSR 802 (ECJ).

[4] C-206/01 [2003] Ch 454; [2003] 3 WLR 450; [2003] All ER (EC) 1; [2002] I ECR 10273; [2003] 1 CMLR 345; [2003] CEC 3; [2003] ETMR 227; [2003] RPC 144; (2002) 152 NLJ 1808; *The Times* 18 November 2002 (ECJ).

[5] C-353/03 [2006] All ER (EC) 348; [2005] I ECR 6135; [2005] 3 CMLR 259; [2006] CEC 3; [2005] ETMR 1128; [2006] FSR 4; *The Times* 20 July 2005 (ECJ).

[6] Henceforth, 'the Act'. Parallel provisions can be found in Article 6(1)(a) of First Directive 89/104/EEC of the Council, of the 21st of December 1988, to Approximate the Laws of the Member States Relating to Trade Marks[5] or Article 12(a) of Council Regulation (EC) 40/94 of 20 December 1993 on the Community trade mark.

Limits on effect of registered trade mark.
11.– ... (2) A registered trade mark is not infringed by – ... (*a*) the use by a person of his own name or address ... provided the use is in accordance with honest practices in industrial or commercial matters.[7]

Despite some appalling grammar, terrible and inconsistent punctuation and some legal inconsistency, the meaning of these three provisions has some unity. The Court will allow a person to use their own name *or* address in a way that would otherwise infringe, provided that such a person does so in accordance with honest practices in industrial or commercial matters.

The Directive and Regulation speak of such (potentially infringing) use being in the course of trade, whereas section 11 of the Act does not. This is not a significant difference since any use which is not in the course of trade, that is, which is not trade mark use, is not infringing. The Act, the Directive and the Regulation all apply to individuals and corporate entities since, in accordance with domestic principles of statutory interpretation, and equally in accordance with European rules of legislative interpretation, a person can be individual or corporate.

Furthermore, what is meant by being honest in industrial or commercial matters, as opposed to simply being honest, muddles a perfectly well understood factual concept of honesty. Why should industry or commerce have its own code of honest behaviour? The courts in the UK seem to have ignored the fact that the words 'industrial and commercial matters' exist; though even if the honesty standard is respected, that is not to say that one has to be as pure as the driven snow.

In *Barclays Bank Plc* v. *RBS Advanta*[8] (the first case under the Trade Marks Act 1994 to consider the point) Laddie J suggested that honesty is to be

---

[7] Likewise, Article 6 of the Directive states

Article 6: Limitation of the effects of a trade mark
The trade mark shall not entitle the proprietor to prohibit a third party from using, in the course of trade . . . (1) his own name or address . . . provided he uses them in accordance with honest practices in industrial or commercial matters.

Article 12(a) of the Regulation states

Article 12: Limitation of the effects of a Community trade mark
A Community trade mark shall not entitle the proprietor to prohibit a third party from using in the course of trade . . . (a) his own name or address . . . provided he uses them in accordance with honest practices in industrial or commercial matters.

[8] [1997] ETMR 199; [1996] RPC 307; (1996) 15 Tr LR 262; *The Times* 8 February 1996, Laddie J.

considered in the light of what the audience public might consider as honest, given (perhaps) that they do not always expect complete accuracy and can expect some hyperbole.[9] In other words, the test was, according to Laddie J, an objective one measured by a notional candidate public·

About two years later in *Cable & Wireless Plc* v. *British Telecommunications Plc*,[10] Jacob J said that the test was to be measured by a different class of audience being the national reasonable trader; this test is likely to be a more subjective one – would a reasonably minded trader, possessed of the information which he had, think that he was behaving honestly? Jacob J had however earlier agreed with Laddie J's approach in *Barclays Bank*.[11] Obviously any person deliberately behaving dishonestly could expect little sympathy but the problem is more acute in the borderline. In the criminal field, dishonesty means conscious wrongdoing. There is a twofold test: (1) is the defendant dishonest according to the standards of reasonable and honest men (and not by reference to the defendant's own standards) and (2) did the defendant know that what he is doing was generally regarded as dishonest.[12]

In both *Scandecor Development Aktiebolag* v. *Scandecor Marketing Aktiebolag*[13] and *European Limited* v. *Economist Newspaper Limited*[14] the court simply accepted the assertion, without engaging in any analysis, that the test had to be objective from the intention of the trader, that is, the traders actual intentions were not the focus of enquiry. On the same tack, the ECJ in *Gerolsteiner Brunnen Gesellschaft mit beschränkter Haftung & Co* v. *Putsch Gesellschaft mit beschränkter Haftung*[15] said that 'It is for the national court to carry out an overall assessment of all the circumstances of the particular case in that regard.'

'[T]hat regard' in this case was to consider 'only if that use is not in accordance with honest practices in industrial or commercial matters'. However, earlier on in its judgment, the ECJ cited the *BMW* case[16] where it said that

---

[9] To which comedy and parody could be added.
[10] [1998] FSR 383, Jacob J.
[11] *Vodafone Group Plc* v. *Orange Personal Communications Services Limited* [1997] EMLR 84; [1997–98] Info TLR 8; [1997] FSR 34; *The Times* 31 August 1996, Jacob J.
[12] See generally *R v Ghosh* [1982] 1 QB 105 (CA).
[13] [1998] FSR 500; (1998) 95(12) LSG 28; *The Times* 9 March 1998, Lloyd J.
[14] [1996] EMLR 394; [1996] FSR 431, Rattee J.
[15] C-100/02 [2004] ECR I-691; [2004] ETMR 559; [2004] RPC 761 (ECJ).
[16] (1) *Bayerische Motorenwerke Aktiengesellschaft (BMW)* and (2) *BMW Nederland Besloten Vennootschap v. Ronald Karel Deenik* C-63/97 [1999] All ER (EC) 235; [1999] ECR I-905; [1999] 1 CMLR 1099; [1999] CEC 159; [1999] ETMR 339 (ECJ).

'The condition of "honest practice" constitutes in substance the expression of a duty to act fairly in relation to the legitimate interests of the trade mark owner...'

It is submitted that this is a meaningless statement, and one which the only available congruence, and even then is barely in terms of grammatical similarity, is the word 'in'. Of particular concern is the use of the term 'fairly', the meaning of which is vague. 'Fairness', on its literal meaning,[17] implies a duty to treat two people equally, but this cannot be what the ECJ intended because there are not two parties in this situation for the purposes of comparing the equality of their treatment.

Further, despite some trenchant criticism (including from the author of this chapter[18]), the ECJ continued down this course, saying in (1) *The Gillette Company and* (2) *Gillette Group Finland Osakeyhtiö* v *LA-Laboratories Limited Osakeyhtiö*[19] that *BMW* and *Gerolsteiner* were good law, and that a trader who used another's trade marks descriptively was not infringing because of the descriptive goods exception, which also carried with it the requirement of honesty in industrial and commercial matters. However, what can be extracted from the judgment of the European Court of Justice in *BMW* is that there is a duty to act fairly in relation to the legitimate rights of the trade mark owner. In the context of trade mark rights, the ECJ must have meant that fair was to mean on an equal basis as between trade mark owner and potential defendant. However, once the word is looked at from that perspective then the effect is to make a nonsense of Article 6 of the Directive since that article contains no mention of even-handedness.

In (1) *Reed Executive Plc and* (2) *Reed Solutions Plc* v. (1) *Reed Business Information Limited*, (2) *Reed Elsevier (UK) Limited* and (3) *Totaljobs.com Limited*,[20] Jacob LJ, after disclaiming what he said in *Cable & Wireless*, then said

---

[17] See for example the definition of 'Fair' *adv* offered by the *Oxford English Dictionary* (Oxford University Press, Oxford, 1989): 'Equitably, honestly, impartially, justly; according to rule'.

[18] See A. Roughton, 'Permitted Infringing Use: the Scope of Defences to an Infringement Action', in J. Phillips and I. Simon, *Trade Mark Use* (Oxford University Press, Oxford, 2005) at p.188.

[19] C-228/03 [2005] All ER (EC) 940; [2005] ECR I-2337; [2005] 2 CMLR 1540; [2005] C.E.C. 734; [2005] ETMR 825; [2005] FSR 808, E.C.J.

[20] [2004] EWCA Civ 159; [2004] ETMR 56; [2004] Info. T.L.R. 55; [2004] RPC 40; [2004] Masons C.L.R. 29; (2004) 148 S.J.L.B. 298; *The Times* 9 March 2004, CA. This case is also authority for the proposition that the own-name defence can apply to a company.

... the test is objective and one of simple causation – if the defendant in fact caused significant deception, albeit innocently, there is no defence. He must pay for the damage he unwittingly caused.

This suggests that there is no defence of being honestly mistaken, which seems odd since that is a very legitimate defence in areas of law (such as crime or civil fraud) where honesty has been a matter of discussion for centuries.[21] If it was intended that honesty should have a special meaning compared to other areas of law then perhaps another, happier, form of words should have been used. Indeed if the test is completely objective, and is measured in terms of damage via infringement, then there seems to be no point in having the exception at all. On the assumption that all trade mark use is damaging established by the objective test set out in *Reed*, the exception cannot apply because the infringer is causing damage. This is, at least in part, an unfortunate consequence of the fact that the ECJ has used the term 'legitimate interests' of the proprietor to define the scope of both infringement and the honest practices proviso. The language of the trade mark legislation sets out what is not an infringement of a trade mark.[22] It must be that such is there in the legislation since if it were not, then the activities in question would be infringing acts, and therefore would cause damage. The effect of the decision of the Court of Appeal in *Reed* is to strike out section 11 of the Act, not only for the own name defence, but also for the descriptive use and 'spare parts' defences.

Thus, the thrust of what is being said by the courts is that if the use is infringing then it is dishonest.[23] If this is so, it is submitted, there is no point in having an own-name defence. As things stand, the balance has come down firmly in favour of trade mark owners, at the expense of those who had a real need to share the marks because they contain their own names.

Having said this, the European Court of Justice has recently provided some, albeit limited, guidance on the application of the own name defence in *Celine Sarl v. Celine SA*.[24] There the Defendant was using the word Celine as its shop sign and trading title and the Claimant had a long extant registration for the

---

[21] See for example *Royal Brunei Airlines Sendirian Berhad v. Philip Tan Kok Ming* [1995] 2 AC 378, [1995] 3 WLR 64, [1995] 3 All ER 97, [1995] BCC 899, (1995) 92(27) LSG 33, (1995) 145 NLJ 888, [1995] 139 SJLB 146, (1995) 70 P & CR D12, *The Times* 29 May 1995, *The Independent*, 22 June 1995 (HL(E)).

[22] In the guises of section 11 of the Act, Article 6 of the Directive and Article 12 of the Regulation.

[23] An analogous situation can be seen under Art. 5(2) of the Directive, where the ECJ has used the precise terms which constitute infringement under that article as examples of dishonesty. See further I. Simon, 'Nominative Use and Honest Practices in Industrial and Commercial Matters – a Very European History' [2007] IPQ 117.

[24] [2007] ETMR 1320, AG and ECJ so far as the own name use is concerned.

word. The goods sold by both were not disputed to be identical and the goods sold by the Defendant were not marked with the mark in issue. The European Court of Justice divided the question down to (1) mere use as a shop sign and trading title, which was not infringement, and (2) where there appeared in the minds of the public to be a relation between the sign and the trading title and the goods sold, then there would be infringement, though the claim of the Claimant could be barred if, notwithstanding the fact that there was infringement, the honest practices exception applied.

5. PASSING OFF

In a nutshell, the law is that no person may pass off his goods (or services) as those of another. This breaks down into a requirement to prove (i) goodwill, (ii) misrepresentation and (iii) damage.[25] There may be variants on that theme,[26] but the core basis for the action for passing off lies in reputation which creates a drawing force called goodwill. It is 'the benefit and advantage of the good name, reputation and connection of a business. It is the attractive force that brings in custom.'[27]

It is sufficient (but not necessary) for the drawing force to be associated with some badge or trade dress. However, it is difficult to think of examples where a badge or trade dress is not involved. Nevertheless, neither will a badge or trade dress do *per se* – in practice they are necessary, but not always sufficient. A trickle of cases have highlighted where this is so, the most recent example of which is *SDS Biotech UK Limited* v. *Power Agrichemicals Limited*,[28] where the claimant complained that the defendant was falsely claiming to be licensed by the government to sell certain fungicides. The claimant alleged that it was the only body so licensed (by reference to a specific licence number) and so anybody else so claiming (by reference to a false licence number) was damaging the claimant's goodwill, jointly held with other traders validly licensed. The Court doubted (at the summary judgment stage) whether such behaviour amounted to passing off, despite the presence

---

[25] '... the classical trinity of (1) a reputation (or goodwill) acquired by the ... [claimant] in his goods, name, mark, etc., (2) a misrepresentation by the defendant leading to confusion (or deception), causing (3) damage to the [claimant].' *per* Nourse LJ in *Consorzio del Prosciutto di Parma* v. *Marks & Spencer Plc and Others* [1991] RPC 351, 368 (CA).

[26] Such as, for instance, in the case where associations of traders sue in relation to a commonly held mark, as has occurred with regard to Champagne.

[27] Per Lord MacNaughton in *Inland Revenue Commissioners* v. *Muller & Co's Margarine Limited* [1901] AC 217 at 233 (HL(E.)).

[28] [1995] FSR 797, Aldous J.

of all of the elements of the 'classic trinity', but let the matter proceed to trial to determine the question.

When it comes to names and addresses, the simple question is whether there has been passing off. There is no own name defence as such. The decisive issue is whether the use of a name and address amounts to what engenders any goodwill. The simple answer is if it does, there is passing off and if it does not, there will be no passing off. Ultimately this is a matter of fact.

In *Asprey & Garrard Limited* v. (1) *WRA (Guns) Limited* (*trading as William R Asprey Esquire*) and (2) *William R Asprey*[29] the Court of Appeal affirmed the proposition that own name or not, if there is passing off, then that was the end of the matter. The first defendant was passing off since a trading name had been deliberately chosen which connoted a connection with the claimant (Asprey as against Asprey). The court went on to doubt whether an individual such as the second defendant, with a name which he did not choose for himself, could be restrained from using his own name, but made no order in that respect since it was not an issue to be decided and there was no evidence that the second defendant would use his name. His only liability was joint for the acts of the first defendant. The Court of Appeal derived its authority from the case of *Joseph Rodgers & Sons Limited* v. *W. N. Rodgers & Company*:[30]

> It is the law of this land that no man is entitled to carry on his business in such a way as to represent that it is the business of another, or is in any way connected with the business of another; that is the first proposition. The second proposition is, that no man is entitled so to describe or mark his goods as to represent that the goods are the goods of another. To the first proposition there is, I myself think, an exception: a man, in my opinion, is entitled to carry on his business in his own name so long as he does not do anything more than that to cause confusion with the business of another, and so long as he does it honestly. It is an exception to the rule which has of necessity been established.
>
> To the second rule, to which I have referred, I think there is no exception at all; that is, that a man is not entitled so to describe his goods as to lend to the belief that they are the goods of somebody else. It is not necessary that there should be an exception to that. It is perfectly legitimate for a man in the cutlery business to carry on business under his own name whatever that name may be, but I can see no necessity for his marking his cutlery with a name (although it be his own name) which may have the effect of passing off those goods as the goods of the plaintiffs.

What Romer J was saying here was that while it is one thing to carry on in business, it is quite another to mark goods. In the latter situation, there is no

---

[29] [2001] EWCA Civ 1499; [2002] ETMR 933; [2002] FSR 487 (CA).
[30] (1924) 41 RPC 277, 291, Romer J.

exception. In the former situation, there is an exception, but it is limited to those acts which are not confusing.

An example of an application of this principle is to be found in *Saunders v. Sun Life Assurance Company of Canada*,[31] where the plaintiff which had traded for a significant period of time as the Sun Life Assurance Company sued the defendant, which was trading as Sun Life Assurance Company of Canada, for passing off. The action was dismissed on the basis that the defendant was using a name which incorporated the words 'of Canada', which distinguished its activities sufficiently from those of the claimant. The court accepted that a fine line was to be drawn between what is and is not actionable, which depended upon the facts of each case. Authority for the propositions which Romer and Stirling JJ expounded are to be found in what Turner LJ said in the earlier case of *Burgess v. Burgess*[32]

> No man can have any right to represent his goods as the goods of another person, but in applications of this kind it must be made out that the defendant is selling his own goods as the goods of another. Where a person is selling goods under a particular name, and another person, not having that name, is using it, it may be presumed that he so uses it to represent the goods sold by himself as the goods of the person whose name he uses; but where the defendant sells goods under his own name, and it happens that the plaintiff has the same name, it does not follow that the defendant is selling his goods as the goods of the plaintiff. It is a question of evidence in each case whether there is false representation or not.

In *Parker-Knoll Limited v. Knoll International Limited*[33] some members of the House of Lords doubted the distinction drawn by Romer J, though there was no unanimity and the majority view was that Romer J was correct in his formulation. It should be noted that, although the case of *Sir Robert McAlpine Limited v. Alfred McAlpine Plc*[34] is commonly mistaken for an own name defence case, it was not about whether there was an own name defence available, but rather whether the defendant was entitled to change its trading name from Alfred McAlpine to McAlpine or McAlpines. The parties had an agreement as to trading names and styles with field of activity demarcation – the question which arose was whether the use of an own agreed name (which was the name of one of the relations of the claimant's founder) trespassed upon the goodwill of the claimant. The court held that it did.[35]

---

[31] [1894] 1 Ch 537, Stirling J.
[32] (1853) 3 de G M & G 896; 43 ER 351 (CA).
[33] [1962] RPC 265 (HL(E)).
[34] [2004] EWHC 630; [2004] RPC 711, Mann J.
[35] The own name defence to passing off is discussed further in the previous

6. CONCLUSION

The law of registered trade marks appears to come down heavily in favour of the trade mark owner when the own name defence is relied upon. This is possibly because of the perception that any interference with trade mark rights could have the effect of scaring off investment which would inevitably stifle innovation and increase search costs. The law of passing off, however, is intended to protect investment in a different way – this is the investment associated with what members of the public think of a particular organization. Although the consumer is the touchstone, the basis for the test, the law of passing off is not about consumer protection or consumer welfare. It is possibly this difference which yields differing tests and inevitably differing results.

---

chapter, where Christopher Wadlow considers recent developments in three contemporary cases.

PART IV

Shared name transactions

10. Co-branding

Spyros Maniatis and Stefan Schwarzkopf

1. CO-BRANDING AS STRATEGIC ALLIANCE

Trade marks enable choice and competition; they allow consumers to distinguish between products and allow businesses that compete by offering rivalling products. Brands, on the other hand, are trade marks with a 'persona'. They encapsulate images, social values, and emotional attachments. Businesses use brands and branding in order to make their products and services more relevant and attractive for a number of key market stakeholder groups that include not only consumers, but also suppliers, business partners, and retailers. Strong brands help deliver superior customer value and fight off attempts by the competition to capture a firm's target market. The key to these branding activities is the successful transformation of consumers into brand loyal customers, who feel that their needs, demands, and expectations are not only met but exceeded by their favourite brand.[1] In order to make brands meaningful to a larger number of prospective customers and to capitalize on the advantages of a strong existing brand in a new market, businesses are increasingly diversifying their brand- and customer-base. Brands allow them to transfer their customer loyalty into new product markets either on their own or by exploiting synergies with other brand owners; the latter is particularly relevant for the theme of this volume.

Various techniques are known in this field and have extensively been analysed in the marketing literature.[2] Corporate brand licensing, for example, allows manufacturers to use an existing and well-recognized brand, in a particular field, to market other products to a specific target group. Toy and children's wear manufacturers are known to use brands such as DISNEY,

---

[1] See D. Aaker, *Building Strong Brands* (Simon & Schuster, London, 2002), pp. 17–24; L. de Chernatony and M. McDonald, *Creating Powerful Brands in Consumer, Service and Industrial Markets* (Elsevier, Oxford, 2003), pp. 3–19 and 447–8 and K. Keller, *Strategic Brand Management: Building, Measuring and Managing Brand Equity* (Pearson Education, Upper Saddle River, NJ, 2003), pp. 104–12.

[2] See P. Kotler et al., *Principles of Marketing* (Pearson Education, Harlow, 2005), pp. 563–7.

WINNIE THE POOH, or BARBIE to increase the recognizability and attractiveness of stationery, shoes, clothing, and accessories. Perhaps best known are techniques of (product) line extensions and brand extensions (stretching). A company can extend an existing brand by introducing new forms, sizes, or flavours of an existing product. These line extensions have taken place in various categories, most famously in the soft drink market where Coca-Cola has successfully extended its brand by introducing COKE with new flavours, in new bottle sizes, or as a diet, and most recently as a zero-sugar, variety. Coca-Cola has used these techniques mainly to revitalize its brand in the face of a very creative competitor (Pepsi Co) and in response to the challenges coming from evolving consumer behaviour and market attitudes towards its core product.[3]

Whereas line extensions often follow a pattern of organic growth, brand extensions at times resemble more aggressive, viral, and anarchic patterns of growth as existing brands are extended to entirely new product categories. Perhaps the most famous example is that of the VIRGIN brand, which has been extended by its creator, Richard Branson, to a vast array of markets, including music production, media and entertainment, internet provider, fashion, air, space and train travel, soft drinks, financial and insurance services, holidays, and most recently stem cell storage.[4] The advantages of using an already successful brand to launch a new or modified product or service in a new category have been analysed by various authors: new markets can be entered more easily with a well-recognized brand, which in turn lowers acceptance barriers in consumers and thus saves expenditure on marketing communication in mature markets.[5] Brands can transpose messages about product characteristics and raise consumer expectations in new product markets.

Another technique of increasing an existing brand's customer base and visibility in the market is co-branding. We define co-branding as a marketing communication and product strategy whereby 'two established brand names of different companies are used on the same product or service'.[6] Co-branding partners use this marketing tool to enhance each other's service or product brand through close association between two brands which are strategically capable of delivering increased customer value. Co-branding is therefore a

---

[3] A. Bahr Thompson, 'Brand positioning and brand creation', in R. Clifton and J. Simmons, *Brands and Branding* (Profile Books, London, 2003), pp. 79–95, R. Enrico, *The Other Guy Blinked and Other Dispatches from the Cola Wars* (Bantam Books, New York, 1988) and D. Yoffie, 'Cola wars continue: Coke and Pepsi in the twenty-first century'. Harvard Business School case No. 9-702-442 (January 2004).
[4] Keller, n. 1, pp. 596–7.
[5] Keller, n. 1, pp. 575–631 and D. Aaker and K. Keller, 'Consumer evaluations of brand extensions', 54 *Journal of Marketing* 27(4) (January 1990).
[6] Kotler et al., n. 2, p. 564.

major tool of the value-adding process of branding.[7] From a trade mark and intellectual property right perspective, co-branding is an exercise that allows owners of two or more brands to 'lend their intellectual property to a vehicle for their joint exploitation'.[8] Genuine co-branding must be distinguished from the coexistence of the trade marks of the manufacturer and the parallel importer, against the will of the manufacturer, in parallel import cases (see for example *Boehringer Ingelheim v Swingward*).[9]

Marketing scholars have identified various advantages to co-branding. Often, the brands that are part of the co-branding exercise are dominant players in their respective category, their combination reaches a wider consumer audience and increases brand awareness and brand equity. Because of this, co-branding allows firms to enter new markets at a much lower level of risk and investment. Also, as a result of co-branding's synergy effects, additional points of differentiation can be created for the partner-brands in consumer minds.[10]

Co-branding has a number of drawbacks that have also been exposed in the marketing literature. A company that has chosen the wrong partner will suffer from the negative impact of its choice. If a partner-brand becomes unattractive for the co-brand's target market, both parent brands will suffer from the ensuing loss of confidence. Another drawback is that co-branding relationships require complex strategic and legal skills on the side of both partners. Co-branding partners are faced with additional challenges and complexities when co-ordinating their advertising, sales promotion, and public relations efforts. This coordination needs considerable investment in terms of time and money and, often, managers have been found to underestimate the organizational capabilities needed to support and sustain this process. On top of that, co-branding relationships involve complex legal agreements (such as those discussed below) which require continuous administration after the initial

---

[7] T. Blackett and B. Boad, *Co-branding: the Science of Alliance* (St. Martin's Press, New York, 1999), Aaker, n. 1, pp. 298–300 and Keller, n. 1, pp. 360–70.

[8] J. Phillips, *Trade Mark Law: a Practical Anatomy* (Oxford University Press, Oxford, 2003), p. 533.

[9] *Boehringer Ingelheim Pharma KG and Others v Swingward Ltd and Others* and *Merck, Sharp & Dohme GmbH v Paranova Pharmazeutika Handels GmbH* C-143/00 [2002] 2 C.M.L.R. 26.

[10] A. Rao, 'Strategic brand alliances', in 5(2) *Journal of Brand Management* 111–19 (1997); J. Washburn et al., 'Co-branding: brand equity and trial effects', 117(7) *Journal of Consumer Marketing* 591–604 (2000); K. Desai and K. Keller, 'The effects of brand expansions and ingredient branding strategies on host brand extendibility', 66 *Journal of Marketing* 73–93 (January 2002) and R. Abratt and P. Motlana, 'Managing Co-branding strategies: global brands into local markets', in M. Kotabe (ed.), *International Marketing*, Sage Library of Marketing, Vol. 5 (Sage, London, 2006), pp. 355–66.

agreement is passed. The need to include clauses which regulate the co-branding partner's behaviour (moral clauses) or clauses that address the need for early termination of the licence remind both partners of the potentially severe financial consequences of such a legally binding agreement.[11] A co-branding agreement typifies the cliché that a contract becomes relevant when a relationship turns sour.

An issue that has rarely been addressed in the marketing management literature is the question of when and how a co-branding partnership can be terminated. While legal agreements can set a target and a deadline for such termination, the fact that a co-brand is taken off the market is likely to cause a perceptional rupture in the target market's social and emotional relationship with the co-brand and/or either of its parent brands. In order to avoid doubts and confusion on the side of consumers, a co-brand ideally needs to be phased out just as smoothly as any other brand's decline needs to be managed. The brand life-cycle model can help managers to communicate the 'death' of a co-brand in order to minimize the negative effects that a hasty or unplanned withdrawal might have for both parent brands' equity. Usually, the 'retirement' of brands is managed by slowly cutting back on promotional expenditure (especially advertising and sales promotion), by cutting back on the intensity of distribution (only the most profitable sales outlets will be kept) and by communicating the phasing out of a brand to partners in the distribution channel.[12] However, there may be critical instances where marketers need to convey a message instantly and widely; then, as the Disney case illustrates below, an alternative and more disruptive strategy would be to denounce the synergy publicly and abruptly and shed the burden of the co-brand.

All co-branding is part of diversification strategies of firms: two, or more, established brand owners open up new markets, seek new opportunities, and thus increase their brand's visibility and capitalize on each other's strengths (recognition, loyalty, goodwill and reputation). Co-branding makes use of brand synergy effects. These effects can also be achieved through other means, such as mergers and acquisitions. For example, the merger between Schweppes and Cadbury's and the acquisition of various car brands by Ford have been strategically undertaken so as to make maximal use of the synergies between brands in similar markets or even within the same category of products. Mergers and acquisitions however are not to be confused with co-branding (see definition above), since a co-brand requires the existence of

---

[11] Phillips, n. 8, p. 533; A. Selden and R. Toop, 'Multibranding', 24 Franchise LJ 181–205 (Winter 2005) and A. Hurwitz, 'Co-branding: managing franchise brand associations', 8 Oklahoma City University Law Review 373–93 (1995).

[12] G. Day, 'The product life cycle: analysis and applications issues', 45(4) Journal of Marketing 60–67 (1981) and Keller, n. 1, pp. 668–71.

two established and *independent* brands which *temporarily* join to lend their brand names to a *new* product or service. So, co-branding, unlike mergers and acquisitions, is viewed as a strategic and temporary *marketing* exercise which does not affect the organizational integrity of both partners as independent entities.

Figure 10.1 illustrates the links between co-branding, product and communication. Co-branding as a strategic tool is based either on a product (or service) or on marketing communication. Product-based co-branding aims to offer a new product or service in which the brand names are visible to the consumer.[13] Parallel co-branding occurs when two or more independent brands join to produce a combined brand, whereas ingredient co-branding is found when a supplier explicitly chooses to position its brand as an ingredient of another product. Communication-based co-branding is a tool to strategically link two or more different and independent brands for purposes of joint communication.

2. CO-BRANDING IN ACTION

2.1 Parallel Co-branding

Typical examples of product-based parallel co-branding are the McVitie's brownie sprinkled with M&Ms or Häagen-Daz's ice cream and Baileys liqueur combining to form Baileys flavour ice cream. Nike and Lego Bionicle

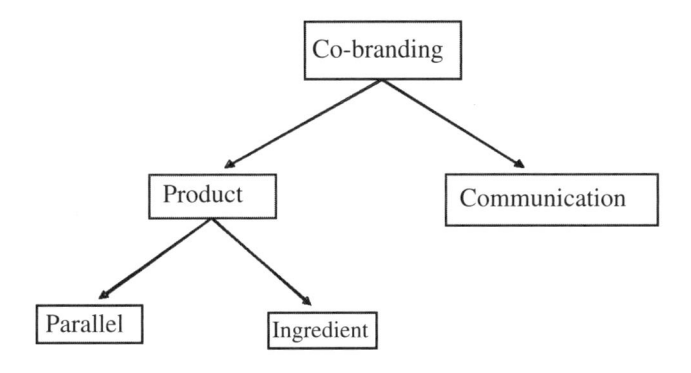

Figure 10.1   Co-branding, product and communication links

---

[13]   D. Jobber, *Principles and Practice of Marketing* (McGraw Hill, Maidenhead, 2007), pp. 353–7.

produced the 'Bionicle by Nike' trainer[14] and Ford joined the women's magazine 'Elle' in producing the 'Ford Focus Elle' car.[15]

A case of potential parallel co-branding which has recently caused debate within marketing circles is the dispute between the Ethiopian Coffee Growers' Association (ECGA) and Starbucks on whether the names of coffee varieties could be protected under registered trade mark law in the US. If the Ethiopian coffee producers had obtained a US trade mark registration, this could have forced Starbucks into compulsory co-branding.[16] However, in December 2007 Starbucks and the Ethiopian government reached an agreement, with Starbucks agreeing to pay a premium for supporting the sustainable production of Ethiopian coffee.[17]

Another example of product-based co-branding is the use of the Fairtrade logo on products directly sourced by supermarkets. When in the early 2000s more and more British supermarkets found that demand for fairly traded goods among their target markets increased steadily, organizations such as the Co-op supermarket chain, Marks & Spencer, Tesco, Sainsbury's, and Waitrose began to buy tea, coffee, chocolate, fruit and vegetables directly from fair-trade certified producers in developing countries. The Fairtrade Foundation acknowledged that the trade agreements between these supermarket chains and local producers met their requirements and so agreed for the Fairtrade logo to be displayed on, for example, Sainsbury's own-label coffee and tea. These products display two brands and are thus the product of a co-operation between two independent organizations who lend the intellectual property rights – in this case the trade marks FAIRTRADE and SAINSBURY'S – to a vehicle for their joint exploitation.[18]

The advantages for the certifier brand, the retailer brand, and the consumer are clear: through the co-branding initiative, the Fairtrade foundation ensures a wider take-up of ethically produced products; the retailer is able to offer an

---

[14] A training shoe for children linked to a range of Lego action figures which form part of the fictional Bionicle 'saga' – see R. Chandiramani, 'Lego strikes deal with Nike for kids' "Bionicle" trainers', *Marketing*, 11 July 2002, p. 1 and A. Grala, 'Building blocks', *License*, June 2004, pp. 34–6.

[15] P. Brech, 'Ford Focus targets women with "Elle" tie', *Marketing*, 8 August 2002, p. 7.

[16] 'Starbuck's vs. Ethiopia', *The Economist*, 12 February 2006 (Issue 8506), pp. 66–7; D. Holt, 'Brand Hypocrisy at Starbucks' (http://www.sbs.ox.ac.uk/starbucks.htm – accessed 10 January 2008).

[17] See http://seattletrademarklawyer.com/blog/2007/12/4/starbucks-chairman-marks-trademark-settlement-with-trip-to-a.html – accessed 10 January 2008.

[18] A. Nicholls and C. Opal, *Fair Trade: Market-driven Ethical Consumption* (Sage, London, 2005) and R. Harrison et al., *The Ethical Consumer* (Sage, London, 2005).

ethically oriented market segment its own ethically sourced products; and consumers see the FAIRTRADE sign on the Sainsbury's tea package as a sign reassuring them that they are buying independently certified, ethically produced products. There is a synergy between the brands that allows the effective communication of complex messages between all the parties involved. This win-win-win situation for the co-brands and the consumer is often described as strategic 'fit'.[19] This 'fit' ensures that the relationship between the co-brands is relevant, consistent, and mutually reinforces the brands' image and position in the mind of the consumer. Both partners have to monitor each other's activities closely: if Sainsbury's were to be accused of exploiting their trade partners, the Fairtrade brand would be accused of colluding in exploitative business practices and suffer accordingly.

2.2 Ingredient Co-branding

Perhaps the best-known example of ingredient co-branding is the chip-maker Intel, which markets and positions its products as key components of other branded products, such as Sony or Dell computers. Unlike parallel co-branding, ingredient co-branding requires a brand which is positioned on the market purely as an ingredient of another manufacturer's product. It has been pointed out by various studies that Intel's superior co-branding – not its actual product superiority – has allowed it to overtake its main rival AMD, which offers chips of the same, and sometimes even better, quality but whose brand is perceived by consumers to signify inferior quality.[20]

The case of Intel also raises a number of issues linked with market and business moral values which are often ignored by mainstream marketing scholars and specialist lawyers. Intel's practices have repeatedly been found in breach of US and EU law by putting undue pressure on computer hardware

---

[19] C. Whan Park et al., 'Evaluation of brand extensions: the role of product feature similarity and brand concept consistency', 18(2) *Journal of Consumer Research* 185–93 (1991); B. Simonin and J. Ruth, 'Is a company known by the company it keeps? Assessing the spill-over effects of brand alliances on consumer brand attitudes', 35 *Journal of Marketing Research* 30–42 (1998); C. Baumgarth, 'Effects of brand- and product-fit on the evaluation of co-branding', Proceedings of the 29th European Marketing Academy (EMAC) Conference (CD-ROM-Version, Rotterdam 2000) and R. Pruppers et al., 'Survival of the fittest: the multi-faceted role of fit in co-branding', 32(1) *Advances in Consumer Research* 245 (2005).

[20] D. Norris, 'Ingredient branding: a strategy option with multiple beneficiaries', 9 *Journal of Consumer Marketing* 19–31 (1992); D. Norris, '"Intel Inside": branding a component in a business market', 8(1) *Journal of Business & Industrial Marketing* 14 (1993).

manufacturers not to deal with its main rival AMD and to include only Intel chips in computers.[21]

2.3 Communication-based Co-branding

Communication-based co-branding can take different forms. The maker of dishwashers and washing machines for example can join a producer of detergents so that both brands recommend each other to consumers. Sponsorship often results in co-branding, too, whereby the sponsor's brand name appears on the product being sponsored. Sports events and football clubs are increasingly using this kind of co-branding. For decades Disney has used the McDonald's brand (and vice versa) to extend the brand's outreach over its target group: children, young teenagers, and families. Children received Disney figures in their 'Happy Meals', Disney opened up its theme parks to McDonald's, allowing McDonald's to open branches in the parks, and McDonald's benefited from the increased promotional activities it could offer its customers. The mutual reinforcement of the Disney and the McDonald's brand is a prime example of communication-based co-branding.[22]

Recently, however, Disney cut its ties to McDonald's, with which it had joined on various co-branding initiatives. The reasons for this widely discussed move are to be found in the negative publicity which had ravaged McDonald's in the previous years, such as that arising from *Supersize Me*[23] and *McLibel*.[24] This had begun to negatively affect the Disney brand in consumer surveys. Both brands dominate different categories (fast food and entertainment) but targeted similar segments of the population: families and consumers of low income and low education. These reasons had brought both brands together in highly successful and targeted co-branding exercises. Yet the very reasons which brought these brands together – their focus on the child

---

[21] See 'Intel investigation', 10 *Corporate Legal Times* 96 (March 2000) and 'Korea Fair Trade Commission investigating "Intel"' 51(33) *Electronic News*, 15 May 2005.

[22] R. Grossman, 'Co-branding in advertising: developing effective associations', 6(3) *Journal of Product & Brand Management* 191–201 (1997).

[23] A film in which the independent film maker Morgan Spurlock eats only food purchased from McDonald's for 30 days. Spurlock gained 24.5lb and experienced various health problems as a result. See E. Cottone and C. Byrd-Bredbenner, 'Knowledge and Psychosocial Effects of the Film Super Size Me on Young Adults', *Journal of the American Dietetic Association*, 107(7), 1197–1203,

[24] The libel trial conducted by McDonald's against two environmental campaigners. The trial exposed embarrassing facts about McDonald's business practices and was the subject of a film documentary. See John Vidal (1997), 'McLibel: Burger Culture on Trial' (New Press, New York, 1997).

and the family as consumer decision-making units – became the reason for Disney's withdrawal, as children and their families began to see McDonald's in a negative light. In October 2006, Disney therefore decided to disassociate itself from all brands that could be perceived as 'junk food', such as Kellogg's and McDonald's. This decision included all communication- and product-based activities of the Disney brand: menus at their theme park would be revised, Disney-themed biscuits would be removed from supermarket shelves, and the promotion of Disney-figures at McDonald's restaurants would be stopped.[25]

Often, communication-based co-branding is used as a positioning tool. The Sony 'Play Station Portable' (PSP) used to be produced in black or dark silver only and was introduced into the market at a very high price. As a result of this, the Sony brand suffered from a lack of recognition and take-up among female teenagers and young women. The product was perceived by this target market as a 'boys' thing'. Sony made the decision to produce the PSP in pink and to adopt the female pop-singer 'Pink' – who had built a successful brand around the concept of 'pink' – as a brand endorser. Both brands, Sony and the pop-singer, capitalized on the obvious strategic 'fit' and the consistency between the Sony PSP brand and the 'Pink' brand, which essentially try to reach the same target groups. 'Pink' is seen by her target group as an independent, 'non-girly' young woman who has her own mind and who causes controversy with her calls to end the fur trade, for example. Sony used these perceptions to surround its product with ideas of independence, open-mindedness, and urban culture in the mind of a target group that would not have seen the original PSP as attractive.[26] The use of 'Pink' in this case goes further than pure celebrity product endorsement: there is a new product that only makes sense to its target segment because of the mental connection to the values that the performer represents rather than its actual colour.

3. ISSUES OF CONTROL AND MANAGEMENT OF CO-BRANDS

The examples mentioned above point clearly at the advantages as well as disadvantages of co-branding. On the one hand, co-branding is able to tap various sources of brand equity and thus adds value to the brand. It provides

---

[25] M. Garrahan, 'Disney orders healthier food rules for children', *Financial Times*, 17 October 2006, p. 19.
[26] S. Boxer, 'The Gameboy girls', *Financial Times*, 25 May 2004, p. 13 and 'Snapshot Pink', *Musicweek*, 2 September 2006, p. 4.

brands with unique points of differentiation which in crowded markets populated by similar products are often the most important sources of competitive advantage of one brand over another. Co-branding aids the positioning of brands in the minds of consumers. By providing endorsement and promotional opportunities for each other, co-brands provide resources for their partners which lower the overall marketing communications costs for the brands involved as a co-brand carries greater brand equity than the sum of its parts. Communication-based co-branding enhances awareness and interest while product-based co-branding can reduce the overall costs associated with the introduction of a new product in a market that partners are unfamiliar with.[27]

On the other hand, co-branding is a field only to be entered if managers are confident about the consequences of the inevitable loss of control which any brand alliance brings with it. As each company loses a certain degree of control over its own brand, there is potential for disagreement, misunderstanding and conflict. All four main areas of marketing strategic decision-making – Product, Price, Place, Promotion (the '4 Ps') – can become a source of conflict. Let us take the example of an up-market celebrity who lends his or her name (brand) to be displayed on products of a well-known fashion maker. If that manufacturer were to use the celebrity's name to produce low-quality clothing (Product) in the lowest price-bracket (Price), combined with a distasteful advertising campaign (Promotion) in order to push its goods en masse into a down-market supermarket chain (Place), then the celebrity's brand name would be tarnished. Vice versa, celebrities and pop-singers as brands often have short life-cycles and their behaviour in public is often as unpredictable as it is undesirable. Sony as the maker of the PSP therefore has to closely monitor 'Pink's' action in the public sphere.[28] The loss of control over the brand means that a badly managed co-branding partnership can easily result in overall loss of brand equity for either or both brands within the partnership. The poor performance of one brand directly impacts on the perception of the other brand in the minds of the target market.

This loss of control does not only take place under the influence of the activities of the co-branding partner but also as a result of the shifting consumer perception of the parent brands. A co-branded new chocolate product involving a famous whisky brand will not only influence the attitudes of

---

[27] See J. Motion et al., 'Equity in corporate co-branding: the case of Adidas and the All Blacks', 37 (7–8) *European Journal of Marketing* 1080–94 (2003) and L. Leuthesser et al., '2 + 2 = 5? A framework for using co-branding to leverage a brand', 11(1) *Journal of Brand Management* 35–47 (September 2003).

[28] D. Avery and J. Rosen, 'Complexity at the expense of common sense? Emerging trends in celebrity endorsement deals', 23 *Entertainment and Sports Lawyer* 23 (Summer 2005).

prospective consumers of the new product but also change the attitudes and perceptions of these consumers towards the whisky brand. Its association with a chocolate brand might render it more 'soft' or 'female' in the eyes of its target group. This reminds us of the socio-philosophical and behavioural place of brands in our world, which is not only of a management and strategic, but essentially of a communicative, nature. As much as brands are the outcome of strategic actions of utility-maximizing, rational managers they are the outcomes of communicative interactions between various actors in a market. The decisions of these actors are both based on 'tangibles', such as the physical qualities of a product, as well as 'intangibles', i.e. cultural and social perceptions of a brand. Therefore, co-branding shifts meanings within the minds of target groups and leads to new types of symbolic interactions between brands and their consumers. This can result in a temporarily increased amount of control that consumers have over the market position of a brand. This control is not necessarily exercised by consumers in a pro-active way but often resides in consumers' attitudes towards and perception of brands.[29] The disaffection and consumer confusion caused by a mismanaged co-brand, for example, will be the result of attitudinal and behavioural shifts in consumers. The powerful synergy effects that the owners of brands try to achieve through co-branding can also increase consumer resentment and disaffection if the alliance is seen as a venture to dominate markets without offering more customer value.[30] Problems may emerge from the fact that a co-brand is the result of an intellectual property being lent and, thus, the result of a property transaction.[31] The lack of relevant case law however, probably shows that the relationships between the parties are exhaustively covered in the contractual agreement or that the parties choose to resolve conflicts employing commercial criteria and do not risk protracted legal battles that would cause further negative publicity.

---

[29] D. Holt, 'Why do brands cause trouble? A dialectical theory of consumer culture and branding', 29 *Journal of Consumer Research* 70–90 (June 2002); C. Lury, *Brands: the Logos of the Global Economy* (Routledge, Abingdon, 2004); A. Arvidsson, 'Brands: a critical perspective', 5(2) *Journal of Consumer Culture* 235–58 (2005), and R. Elliot and L. Percy, *Strategic Brand Management* (Oxford University Press, Oxford, 2007), pp. 44–54.
[30] N. Klein, *No Logo* (Flamingo, London, 2000), pp. 143–64; M. Haig, *Brand Failures: the Truth About the 100 Biggest Branding Mistakes of All Time* (Kogan Page, London, 2003), pp. 40–43.
[31] Phillips, n. 8, p. 533 and A. George, 'Brand rules: when branding lore meets trade mark law', 13(3) *Journal of Brand Management* 215–32 (2006).

4. CO-BRANDS AND INTELLECTUAL PROPERTY RIGHTS

Once the prospective partners have identified the synergies that will make co-branding a mutually beneficial exercise there are a number of legal issues they need to resolve. First, they have to indicate what each one of them is contributing to this exercise and identify how the co-brand is to be protected. In a straightforward case, the brands will be registered trade marks. However, the agreement might also involve unregistered trade marks, other indicia (for instance, trade names, geographical indications, or domain names), product get-up, marketing schemes, or advertising techniques. The rights the parties possess must be identified and clearly described. For example, the get-up of a product might be protected by design rights solely or cumulatively with trade mark rights.

The next step should be to delineate ways of common exploitation. These can range from simple coexistence of two brands on a common co-branded platform (for example Dell and Intel or McDonald's restaurants in a Disney theme park), to the creation of a new co-branded logo (for example the Pink PSP), or more intricate and integrated dealings such as the creation of a new product or the adoption of common production or marketing methods (for example a liqueur flavoured ice cream). The geographical extent of the co-branding must also be settled, keeping in mind that intellectual property rights are jurisdiction specific. One should note that co-branding may facilitate market entrance in one jurisdiction but undermine the value of one of the brands in another jurisdiction. Similarly, the cultural global market is still segmented into local markets with strong traditions.

Maintaining protection of the individual brands and ensuring that any new brands or logos will obtain maximum protection should be the third step; for example, parties should seek to obtain registrations of any new signs but at the same time maintain existing registrations covering their individual brands.

Contextualizing a co-branding agreement, the parties need to take a look at the future. As we have mentioned earlier, failure in co-branding can have consequences beyond the realm of the particular agreement endangering the integrity of the individual brands. The parties should ensure that any break-up is resolved amicably and effectively. After all, from a marketing perspective, co-branding is defined as a potentially long-term relationship but is, in essence only a temporary one. This is why there must also be steps in place from the outset dealing with what happens in the case of early termination. On the other hand, success in co-branding can bring the partners even closer, and they might realize that there are further synergies to exploit. A co-branding agreement should not purport to be the vehicle for closer cooperation; the scope of the agreement is delineated by the nature of the co-branding in general and the aim of the specific co-branding exercise in particular. Accordingly, setting the limits of the agreement and providing for regular monitoring and review, in other words embedding the agreement in its commercial context, is essential. If the parties decide to cooperate on a more permanent basis they should explore the appropriate vehicles, such as establishing a joint venture. Relying on a co-branding agreement would not provide the necessary contractual checks and mechanisms.

In essence, the first two steps, identified above, aim to facilitate the parties and enable the agreement. The purpose of the third step is to strengthen the positions of the respective parties within the context of the agreement, whereas the last steps must be seen as a flexible safety mechanism. Commentators have identified a number of more specific types of clauses that should be incorporated in co-branding agreements that, for our purposes, are organized below under three steps.[32]

4.1 Facilitating the Parties and Enabling the Agreement

The critical point about co-branding exercises is that they must be seen from the start as a collaborative project where the parties are committed to contribute the use of their individual brands but also to build a mechanism that will allow their common exploitation. Indeed collaboration is what is lacking in parallel importation cases where two trade marks may coexist on the same product.

So, first, the parties must indicate contractually what they will contribute to the agreement: the brands that will enable the co-branding exercise. Secondly, they must indicate how these brands are protected, realizing, once again, that intellectual property rights are territorial. Thirdly, each party must acknowledge the other party's brands and rights.

The next step is to describe how these brands will be exploited and build a structure for their relationship. For example, the parties might opt for dual branding and the grant of reciprocal licences or the creation of a new brand that incorporates or refers to their individual brands. In terms of product, they must determine whether co-branding will involve existing products or the creation of a new product. Finally, they must delineate the geographical extent and the time term of the agreement.

Then they must consider the factors that will support co-branding: funding, the allocation of marketing and product development costs, and the sharing of

---

[32] See for example A.C. Shelden and R. Scott Toop, 'Multibranding' 24 WTR Franchise LJ 181 (2005) and M. M. Squyres, *Trademark Practice Throughout the World* (West, St Paul, MN, 1998 and updates), §20:11:10.

information regarding customers and product markets. From the opposite perspective they must decide how revenues will be divided and the allocation of customers and rights, in the case of new intellectual property rights that may arise.

4.2 Supporting the Parties

At this stage the approach of the parties becomes somewhat more defensive. They must be reminded of the ephemeral nature of co-branding and provide for the reinforcement of their individual rights within the framework of the agreement.

First, each one of the brands might continue to have an independent existence and, for certain, each individual brand will continue to have a value outside the co-branding context. Accordingly, the parties must agree on the use of their brands outside that context and take measures that will enable them to maintain their integrity and value. For example, they must ensure that there will be no customer confusion regarding their identity: the brands must fit together rather than one 'morph' into the other. Moreover, according to the product market, consumers must be made aware of each party's contribution towards a new product. In principle, the weaker party – in terms of size and market positioning – must ensure that its brand or even its own separate persona will not be engulfed by the stronger brand; the NutraSweets and Gore-Texs of this world should try and maintain their own identity and stand out from the shadow of Coca-Cola and Nike. They need to communicate to their partners, but also to ultimate consumers of their products, that they are distinct entities and brands. From the opposite perspective the stronger brand must be protected from self-inflicted dilution; there is a fine balancing exercise between retaining the exclusivity attributes of a particular brand and entering new product or geographical markets. This is particularly relevant for luxury brands that can be debased by their own proliferation.[33]

The parties must undertake to maintain the validity both of their individual and common rights and seek their enforcement. In the case of a new co-brand the parties must indicate who is responsible for obtaining protection. The same applies to all other intellectual property rights that might cover new products, manufacturing processes, and marketing methods. On the other hand, confidentiality clauses will assist the parties in providing an environment that will encourage them to share information.

---

[33] See S. Stadler Nelson, 'The Wages of Ubiquity in Trademark Law', 88 Iowa L Rev. 731 (2003).

The next issue to be considered is the allocation of liability if, for example, the product is dangerous or defective. Potential liability is critical as such in any agreement involving consumer products. In co-branding, harming consumers can also affect the value of the brands. This is another fine balancing exercise the parties must attempt between achieving their common goal and protecting their own individual interests.

A tool for securing some of the goals mentioned above is the inclusion in the agreement of quality control provisions combined with the appointment of personnel that carry the responsibility of monitoring and maintaining product quality and responding to quality crises. However as the McDonald's–Disney crisis demonstrates, consumer perceptions change over time. This advocates in favour of the conclusion of medium-, rather than long-term, but renewable agreements.

4.3 Looking to the Future

Setting tangible goals that can be monitored and regularly reviewed is the main way for assessing the effectiveness of co-branding. The agreement should provide a monitoring mechanism and introduce some flexibility by allowing the parties to reconsider and negotiate their strategies at regular intervals. In addition, the parties must be prepared to resolve disputes that they are unable to foresee in the co-branding agreement. The agreement must provide a dispute resolution mechanism that will reassure the parties that co-branding will successfully overcome minor squabbles. In the case of failure the agreement must also provide for exit strategies that will at least attempt to safeguard the integrity of the parties' individual brands.

5. CONCLUSION

In this chapter we have defined co-branding, identified its variations, discussed its advantages and disadvantages, and attempted to outline its legal context.

Co-branding is a valuable communicational fiat; its scope, though, is limited in terms of product and market audiences. What underpins and characterizes, and at the same time potentially limits, co-branding is the dynamism of consumer perceptions and attitudes. And, from a theoretical perspective we have proposed the adoption of a three-step model for enabling, monitoring, and evaluating a co-branding exercise that embeds legal analysis in its commercial context. Sharing names by way of co-branding has great advantages provided there is trust and transparency between the parties; but since the partners are commercial entities a kind of 'pre-nuptial' agreement is always required.

The next issue to be considered is the allocation of liability if, for example, the product is dangerous or defective. Potential liability is critical as such in any agreement involving consumer products. In co-branding, harming consumers can also affect the value of the brands. This is another fine balancing exercise the parties must attempt between achieving their common goal and protecting their own individual interests.

A tool for securing some of the goals mentioned above is the inclusion in the agreement of quality control provisions combined with the appointment of personnel that carry the responsibility of monitoring and maintaining product quality and responding to quality crises. However as the McDonald's–Disney crisis demonstrates, consumer perceptions change over time. This advocates in favour of the conclusion of medium-, rather than long-term, but renewable agreements.

4.3 Looking to the Future

Setting tangible goals that can be monitored and regularly reviewed is the main way for assessing the effectiveness of co-branding. The agreement should provide a monitoring mechanism and introduce some flexibility by allowing the parties to reconsider and negotiate their strategies at regular intervals. In addition, the parties must be prepared to resolve disputes that they are unable to foresee in the co-branding agreement. The agreement must provide a dispute resolution mechanism that will reassure the parties that co-branding will successfully overcome minor squabbles. In the case of failure the agreement must also provide for exit strategies that will at least attempt to safeguard the integrity of the parties' individual brands.

5. CONCLUSION

In this chapter we have defined co-branding, identified its variations, discussed its advantages and disadvantages, and attempted to outline its legal context.

Co-branding is a valuable communicational fiat; its scope, though, is limited in terms of product and market audiences. What underpins and characterizes, and at the same time potentially limits, co-branding is the dynamism of consumer perceptions and attitudes. And, from a theoretical perspective we have proposed the adoption of a three-step model for enabling, monitoring, and evaluating a co-branding exercise that embeds legal analysis in its commercial context. Sharing names by way of co-branding has great advantages provided there is trust and transparency between the parties; but since the partners are commercial entities a kind of 'pre-nuptial' agreement is always required.

11. Splitting trade marks and the competition laws

Thomas Hays

1. INTRODUCTION

Intellectual property rights are, by definition, legal monopolies. Their value is in their monopolistic qualities, allowing the owners to prevent others from exploiting the same inventions, creations and brands. This is to say that the value of intellectual property rights lies in the ability they give their owners to minimize competition and, therefore, to extract higher prices for the goods and services protected by those rights. Monopolies, in general, are counter-competitive. This places intellectual property rights potentially in conflict with the competition law provisions of the Treaty of Rome,[1] specifically with Articles 81 and 82,[2] and with the national laws of the Member States derived from those articles.[3]

The European Court of Justice has developed related doctrines that apply to the general conflict between the monopolistic legal nature of trade mark rights and the policy of protecting competition as a means of promoting internal market integration, such as the distinction between the existence and the exercise of rights formulated in the *Consten and Grundig* case.[4] The precedential value of the decisions giving rise to the doctrines is complicated by the cases having been considered in extreme situations, where commercial monopolies were enforced through trade mark rights. In such circumstances the court has shown itself willing to override brand interests to the extent of ensuring the future growth of competition in downstream markets.

---

[1] Consolidated Versions of the Treaty on European Union and of the Treaty Establishing the European Community (2002), [2002] O.J. C 325/1, hereafter, 'the EC Treaty'.
[2] That is, Art. 81 (formerly Art. 85) and Art. 82 (formerly Art. 86).
[3] E.g., United Kingdom Competition Act 1998 (c.41) Chapters I and II.
[4] *Consten and Grundig-Verkaufs v. EEC Commission* 56, 58/64 [1966] ECR 299, [1966] CMLR 418.

2. THE CONFLICT BETWEEN COMPETITION AND BRAND PROTECTION

On one side of the conflict is the goal of encouraging competition by legally penalizing monopolistic concentrations of economic power. On the other side is the purpose of encouraging inventiveness, creativity and brand recognition[5] through grants of proprietary interests in intellectual property. This conflict is complicated by the nature of intellectual property, which is generally protected as part of a Member State's system of property ownership under Article 295 of the EC Treaty. This article assures 'This Treaty shall in no way prejudice the rules in Member States governing the system of property ownership.'[6] Since trade mark rights are forms of personal property granted by the 'rules', or laws, of the Member States, the EC Treaty cannot, even through the competition laws, prejudice those national rules which guarantee the existence of property.

The Commission[7] has a couple of ways avoiding this conflict. One is to define new rights, such as the *sui generis* right in databases, as not being property and therefore not subject to Article 295. Another more successful method is to create new, Community-wide intellectual property rights, such as the Community trade mark[8] and Community design rights.[9]

Articles 28 and 29 of the EC Treaty seek to facilitate and integrate the EU market by eliminating national law barriers to trade. This goal is in conflict with the national territorial nature of intellectual property rights. The multitude of conflicts generated by intra-market parallel trade (the importation of protected goods from one national territory of the EEA market into another) point to subtle principles about the reach of national intellectual property rights.[10]

---

[5] Brand recognition requires marketing of branded products, which often involves inventiveness and creativity, in the commonly understood usages of those words. Legally speaking, brand recognition fulfils a quality control and consumer protection function of assuring the consumer of the source of the branded goods.

[6] EC Treaty, Art. 295.

[7] The European Commission is the executive arm of the European Union government. It issues directives, based on the power granted it under the EC Treaty, to the Member States, requiring them to bring their laws into conformity with general Community principles.

[8] Council Regulation (EC) No. 40/94 of 20 December 1993 on the Community trade mark, [1994] O.J. L-11/1, 14 January 1994.

[9] Council Regulation 6/2002/EC of 12 December 2001 on Community designs, [2002] O.J. L3/1, 5 January 2002.

[10] For detailed explanations of these conflicts see C. Stothers, *Parallel Trade in Europe* (Hart, Oxford, 2007), pp. 40–44; T. Hays, *Parallel Importation under European Union Law* (Sweet & Maxwell, London, 2003), pp. 12–14.

The first principle derived from this conflict is that the interpretation by the European Court of Justice of the specific subject matter of intellectual property as having an affirmative portion, the right to put protected goods onto the market for the first time, is one of three policy-based interpretational choices confusing causes with effects. If intellectual property rights are defined in the negative, as the right to exclude all others from using the intellectual property to place goods into the stream of commerce, then being the first to commercialize protected goods is an effect, rather than a right in and of itself. This distinction is important because the negative exclusionary right would be exercised and, as a consequence, exhausted when an intellectual property owner or his licensee places protected goods into any level of commerce anywhere. The exhaustion of rights can occur without the intellectual property owner being afforded the opportunity to be the first to sell the goods in every market in which the goods are traded. The present definition of the specific subject matter of intellectual property rights, including a first-to-market component, allows intellectual property owners to disrupt intra-market trade at any level of commercialization, and it calls into question the legitimacy of every sale of potentially protected products except for those sales coming directly from the intellectual property owner. This has the effect of generally restricting the movement of goods within the market.

It is also confuses the issue to link the needs of market integration with the reach of intellectual property rights. As a matter of policy, it may be necessary, in order to integrate the EEA market, that intellectual property rights cease after a volitional first sale anywhere within that market. But this is a policy decision based on considerations other than determining the appropriate reach of exclusive rights.[11] It does not define that reach.

3. THE EXISTENCE AND EXERCISE OF RIGHTS

To minimize conflict in the most difficult cases where the practical exploitation of trade marks appear contrary to the purposes of the competition laws, the Court of Justice has created a legal conceptual distinction between the

---

[11] The market integration policy considerations advanced here have alternatively been described as an undercurrent of judicial concern for discrimination against imports in national intellectual property laws. G. Marenco and K. Banks, 'Intellectual Property and the Community Rules on Free Movement', (1990) 15 EL Rev 224–56. The fact that policy considerations override the development of intellectual property law is the same under either description, though the practical results of the Marenco and Banks interpretation are different in that it would allow for the partitioning of the internal market by non-discriminatory national intellectual property laws.

protected existence of intellectual property rights and the competition stifling exercise of those rights, expressed in *Consten and Grundig*. The court extended the distinction in its judgment in *Parke, Davis & Co. v. Probel, Reese, Beintema-Interpharm* and *Centrafarm*[12] to include patent licences, and in *Deutsche Grammophon v. Metro-SB-Grossmarkte*[13] the court extended it further to include prohibited territorial restrictions supported by national copyrights and to implicate the free movement of goods provisions of Article 28.[14]

The obvious question arises as to what would be the value of having an intellectual property right if it cannot be exercised in the market place. A practical basis for supplying an answer is to recognize that few, if any, intellectual property based monopolies are complete in respect of the markets in which they are exploited. There may be alternative substitute goods available to consumers based on different but acceptable technologies, designs, packaging or brands.[15] The interplay between competition law and intellectual property monopolies can be understood as the relationship between the totality of the intellectual property monopoly in the market and the disfavour with which the relevant courts view it.[16] This is to say that the less of a choice a particular intellectual property right leaves for the consumer, the less strenuously the European courts are likely to allow the intellectual property owner to enforce the legal monopoly. It is not the exclusivity of the intellectual property based interest in the products, but the exclusivity in the market for the protected products themselves, that offends the competition laws.[17]

---

[12] 24/67 [1968] ECR 55, [1968] CMLR 47.
[13] 78/70 [1971] ECR 487, [1971] CMLR 631. See also *IMA, AG and others v. Windsurfing International, Inc. and others* Decision 83/400/EEC [1983] OJ L-229/1, [1984] 1 CMLR 1, upheld in *Windsurfing International, Inc. v. EC Commission* 193/83 [1986] ECR 611, [1986] 3 CMLR 489.
[14] EC Treaty, Art. 28. The distinction between the existence and the exercise of intellectual property rights has often been criticized.
[15] A simple, well-known example of this is that of the plethora of brands of similar beers. While a particular consumer may prefer one brand to others, the other brands are still available and extreme price differences may influence the customer's choice in favour of a less preferred, but less costly brand.
[16] See generally T. Booer, 'The Economic Aspects of the Single European Market in Pharmaceuticals', (1999) 20(5) ECLR 256–64; P. Dixon and C. Mueller, 'Antitrust in the Common Market: Marx, Monopoly and the "Chill Winds of Competition"', 27 *Antitrust Law and Economic Review* 41 (1996); J. Flynn, 'Intellectual Property and Anti-trust: EC Attitudes', [1992] EIPR 49–54.
[17] See e.g., *Tetra Pak Int'l, SA v. EC Commission* T-83/91 [1994] ECR II-755; *United Brands Co. and United Brands Continental, BV v. EC Commission*, 27/76, [1978] ECR 207, [1978] 1 CMLR 429.

4. THE RELATIONSHIP BETWEEN MARKET STRENGTH AND ENFORCEABILITY

There is an inverse relationship between the totality or exclusiveness of a trade mark monopoly in the market and the trade mark owner's ability to fully exercise that monopoly. This relationship is interesting at its extremes. On the one hand is the case where a brand owner with an infinitesimally small market share would be able to ceaselessly exercise his monopoly because the *de minimis* nature of his market share would not support a distortion of the trade between Member States or within a substantial portion of one Member State. This would be true even if the anticompetitive intention of the owner was considered to be the sole determinate of culpability.

On the other hand is the situation where the trade mark based monopoly is approximately total. In such a position the brand owner would have to use the utmost delicacy and finesse in exercising his trade mark rights in order to avoid being penalized under the competition laws.

Taken together with the approximately static enforcement of the competition laws, the exercise of trade mark rights[18] in the Community results in an equilibrium where trade mark owners maximize the profitability of the exercise of their rights within their commercial context without overstepping the bounds of competition and, as a result, incurring substantial penalties. These penalties represent one of a brand owner's greatest potential costs.[19] If the enforcement of trade mark rights is allowed at all, their owners will adjust the enforcement of their rights in relation to their commercial position over time in order to achieve the greatest profitability while avoiding a competition violation. Because the determination of what is and is not a violation of the competition laws cannot be made with precision as the exploitation of intellectual property rights approaches a prohibited level in a given commercial context, the possibility of penalties takes on a cost value of its own, causing most brand owners to achieve an equilibrium position below, rather than at or above the highest level of enforcement. The efficiency of determining a competition violation is itself an economic factor borne in alternate parts by the market as a whole and by commercial undertakings within the market.[20]

---

[18] One of the 'incompatible uses' described in R. Posner, *Economic Analysis of Law* (Aspen, New York, NY, 2007), pp. 52–61.

[19] *Ibid*. A limiting transaction cost in Posner's analysis, based in part on the work of Ronald Coase. See pp. 41–43, citing R. Coase 'The Problem of Social Cost', (1960) 3 *Journal of Law & Economics* 1–44.

[20] The economics of competition policy and enforcement, beyond the scope of the present discussion except in general terms, is explained in detail in S. Bishop and M. Walker, *The Economics of EC Competition Law* (Sweet & Maxwell, London,

5. SPLIT MARKS WITH A COMMON ORIGIN

The common origin doctrine stood for the principle that subdivisions of trade mark ownership would not be allowed to divide the internal market when the mark in question, as a whole, had a common owner at some time in the past. It was reasonable to say that a brand owner could not frustrate the goal of market integration by dividing up the ownership of its various national rights, with each of them able to repel imports into their particular national markets of goods made by the other owners of essentially identical trade marks in other Member States. The court had applied this principle in a case of licenses of intellectual property,[21] and it seemed sensible to do the same in the case of an assignment of rights.[22] Owners of national trade marks could not object to the importation of goods embodying a similar right and put into circulation in another Member State under similar marks, if the various trade mark rights had at one time a common owner. Apart from protecting the integrity of the Common Market, the doctrine could be justified by the theory that the reward for the unified brand owner, who would eventually lose sales to similar goods embodying the relevant trade mark from another Member State, was received at the time of the division of the rights. Second-generation brand owners could not use their marks to stop trade in the goods from other second-generation brand owners because that diminution in the enforcement effectiveness and resultant value of the trade mark right had already been paid for, in some manner, at the time the original trade mark ownership was divided between different national markets.

The first of the *Hag* cases[23] could not have presented a worse factual basis for an application of the doctrine. There the HAG trade mark had a single owner in both Germany and the Benelux nations.[24] After the Second World War the allied powers sequestered the Belgian version of the mark as enemy property to pay war damages. In this way different ownership of the same mark was established in Belgium and Germany. When the German coffee makers began selling their product in the Benelux countries under the HAG brand, the Belgians sued for infringement. On referral, the Court of Justice held that because the HAG brand had at one time been owned by the same company (had a common origin) the Belgians could not stop importation of the legitimate German product.[25]

2002). See also S. Anderman, *EC Competition Law and Intellectual Property Rights: The Regulation of Innovation* (Oxford University Press, Oxford, 1998).

[21] *IMA, AG v. Windsurfing International, Inc.*, n. 13 above, paras. 73, 97; affirmed in *Windsurfing v. Commission*, n. 13 above, para. 36.

[22] See *Sirena, SrL v. EDA, SrL* 40/70 [1971] ECR 69, [1971] CMLR 260.

[23] Ibid.

[24] Ibid., n. 22, para. 3.

[25] Ibid., para. 14.

The decision in *Hag I* generated a great deal of criticism,[26] not least because it seemed incompatible with the origin function of marks. If similar goods, bearing the same mark but made by different companies, could circulate freely within the market, how could the mark indicate to consumers the origin of the goods? It could not, but from 1978 to 1990, after which the common origin doctrine was discarded in *Hag II*,[27] the doctrine coexisted with the essential function doctrine, a judicial attempt at defining the core, protected role trade marks play in the market place, which focuses on the mark's ability to distinguish the goods of its owner from those produced by other undertakings.[28]

During that time the common origin doctrine was affirmed in *Terrapin v. Terranova*.[29] There the Court of Justice said that any subdivision of Community-based intellectual property rights would bar an objection to the parallel importation of legitimate products.[30] It was not until the *Hag II* decision in 1990, when the essential function doctrine was well established, that the court stopped trying to reconcile the doctrines. The court held:

> The decisive fact is the absence of any element of consent, on the part of the owner of the trade mark right protected by national legislation, to the marketing in another Member-State, under a mark which is identical or may cause confusion, of a similar product manufactured and marketed by an enterprise which has no tie of legal or economic dependence with that owner.[31]

The fact that the splitting of the ownership of the mark was involuntary made it impossible to say that the original owner of the mark had consented to the division or that the recipients of the reduced, fractional marks had received their reward for the loss of rights. In establishing the supremacy of the essential function doctrine, the court said:

---

[26] See for example, W. Rothnie, 'Hag II: Putting the Common Origin Doctrine to Sleep', [1991] EIPR 24–31.

[27] *CNL-Sucal v. Hag* C-10/89 [1990] ECR I-3711, [1990] 3 CMLR 571, hereafter '*Hag II*'. Hag II was, factually, the reverse of *Hag I*. When the Belgians exported their version of HAG coffee to Germany, the German trade mark owner sued, claiming infringement of the German mark, and won.

[28] *Centrafarm v. American Home Products* 3/78 [1978] ECR 1823, [1979] 1 CMLR 326, paras. 10–13.

[29] *Terrapin (Overseas) Ltd v. Terranova Industrie C.A. Kapferer & Co.* 119/75 [1976] ECR 1039, [1976] 2 CMLR 482, para. 6.

[30] *Ibid*. But see *Pharmon v. Hoechst AG* 19/84 [1985] ECR 2281, [1985] 3 CMLR 775, a 1985 decision involving compulsory licences, where the Court of Justice took a contrary position, one that it would later affirm in *Hag II*.

[31] *Hag II*, n. 27 above, para. 15.

The essential function of the mark would be compromised if the owner of the right could not exercise his option under national law to prevent the importation of the similar product under a name likely to be confused with his own mark because, in this situation, consumers would no longer be able to identify with certainty the origin of the marked product and the bad quality of a product for which he is in no way responsible could be attributed to the owner of the right.[32]

The idea of prohibiting trade mark based opposition to the sale of branded goods after control has been voluntarily relinquished reflects a negative definition of intellectual property rights generally: intellectual property rights are not affirmative entitlements to do things but rather create causes of action to stop others from doing those things. The doctrine could be revived and developed further as a basis for determining whether or not a brand owner has voluntarily relinquished control, and therefore exhausted his rights, which is to determine whether or not the present brand owner, his affiliates or his predecessors in ownership of the brand have received some bargained-for reward for that relinquishing of control. Such a construction is not dependent on territoriality and would resolve questions concerning the trade in fractionalized brands.

6. THE END OF THE COMMON ORIGIN DOCTRINE

Any prospect for the survival of the common origin doctrine in cases where the division of the ownership of national rights was voluntary was negated in *Ideal Standard*.[33] The Court of Justice said that the protection of the essential function of trade marks required that even the divided ownership resultant from a contractual assignment of marks be allowed to stop the importation of goods, where the free movement of the goods would result in confusion as to their origin.

Though the common origin doctrine was incompatible with the development of the Court of Justice's jurisprudence on intellectual property, it had a characteristic to commend it. It placed the consent-to-market decision with the original brand owner. That decision was relative to the trade mark itself at one moment in time (whether to divide the ownership or not, and to accept the consequences of whatever may happen in the future) rather than making the legal effect of past decisions about trade marks dependent on future commercial events. If a brand owner decided to split his mark, then he and all who

---

[32] *Ibid.*, para. 16.
[33] *IHT International Heiztechnik, GmbH, Uwe Danziger v. Ideal Standard GmbH* C-9/93 [1994] ECR I-2789, [1994] 3 CMLR 857.

took title from him accepted at the time of the split, or of a purchase of fractured share in the once-unitary mark all future implications of that split, including the likelihood that each fractional owner would have to exist in the market with other owners of identical marks.

Between *Hag II* and *Ideal Standard*, there may have been an opportunity for the growth of a useful legal doctrine. That opportunity is gone now, unless the doctrine could be restated in a way that focuses less on the genealogy of ownership and more on a history of compensation for the loss of a brand owner's right to exclude goods from the market. A consensual division of a mark along national lines presumes that the owner of the original unified right received some reward from the division. The same is true of a sale of protected goods by a subsidiary or a licensee.

7. ARTICLE 81: RELATIONS BETWEEN UNDERTAKINGS

EC Treaty Article 81 provides, in relevant part:

1. The following shall be prohibited as incompatible with the common market: all agreements between undertakings, decisions by associations of undertakings and concerted practices which may affect trade between Member States and which have as their object or effect the prevention, restriction or distortion of competition within the common market, and in particular those which:
    (a) directly or indirectly fix purchase or selling prices or any other trading conditions;
    (b) limit or control production, markets, technical development, or investment;
    (c) share markets or sources of supply;
    (d) apply dissimilar conditions to equivalent transactions with other trading parties, thereby placing them at a competitive disadvantage;
    (e) make the conclusion of contracts subject to acceptance by the other parties of supplementary obligations that, by their nature or according to commercial usage, have no connection with the subject of such contracts.
2. Any agreement or decision prohibited pursuant to this Article shall be automatically void.

From a competition law point of view the great danger in allowing a mark to be divided along national or territorial lines is that the practice readily lends itself to market sharing cartels, a 'hardcore' competition violation under the UK Competition Act.[34] Cartels of this sort restrict competition by giving

---

[34] See these publications from the UK Office of Fair Trading: 'Agreements and

undertakings a degree of territorial protection. From the Community's perspective, these arrangements affront the goals of both unfettered competition and an integrated market.[35]

This is particularly true where trade mark rights are concerned, which are by nature territorial, existing only within the political jurisdiction of the government that creates them. It stands to reason then that one of the main ways market sharing arrangements diminish competition is through a reduction in intrabrand competition. Competitors could come together and agree to divide contested territories between them – 'This is my patch; that is yours' – further agreeing not to sell goods or services in each other's territory. Such an agreement, whether expressed or implied from other dealings between competitors, is prohibited under Article 81(1) of the Treaty and would be a serious cartel offence, subjecting the parties to heavy fines and their executives to the possibility of criminal prosecution.

Trade mark enforcement can achieve the same end, a reduction in intrabrand competition, but without a specific agreement as to who gets which territory. The market partitions are implied by the nature of the marks being shared: the United Kingdom mark owner gets the United Kingdom; the owner of the French equivalent, France. For example, in an effort to compartmentalize the Common Market, a brand owner might decide to grant a licence of his United Kingdom trade mark to one distributor and a licence of his identical French mark to another distributor. Territorial restrictions are ensured because the United Kingdom licensee can repel imports into the United Kingdom from France, and vice versa, the French licensee can repel imports from the United Kingdom.[36]

The Commission considers divisions of trade mark rights intended to partition the market to be Article 81(1) violations.[37] Intent to partition is implied from a lack of justification for the division of rights used or from other aspects of the agreement used to divide rights, such as additional anticompetitive promises not required by the parties' legitimate interests. On the other hand, if the parties can justify splitting a mark between them, then competition regulators may allow the split, even though there is a potential for a decrease in intrabrand competition. This might be the case where undertakings use a trade

---

Concerted Practices' OFT 401, 'The Cartel Offence' OFT 513, 'Cartels and the Competition Act 1998' OFT 435. See also The United Kingdom Enterprise Act 2002 (c.40) s. 188.

[35] See *Consten and Grundig*, n. 4 above.

[36] A France–Germany arrangement of this sort formed the basis of *Deutsche Grammophon, GmbH v. Metro-SB-Grossmärkte, GmbH & Co. KG* 78/70 [1971] ECR 487, [1971] CMLR 631, holding there was an Art. 81 violation.

[37] *BAT Cigaretten-Fabriken GmbH v. Commission* 35/83 [1985] ECR 363, [1985] 2 CMLR 470.

mark delimitation agreement to end litigation and the agreement does not go any further than absolutely necessary.[38]

8. DOMINANCE AND ABUSE BY UNILATERAL ACTORS

EC Treaty Article 82 provides:

> Any abuse by one or more undertakings of a dominant position within the common market or in a substantial part of it shall be prohibited as incompatible with the common market insofar as it may affect trade between Member States.
> Such abuse may, in particular, consist in:
> (a) directly or indirectly imposing unfair purchase or selling prices or other unfair trading conditions;
> (b) limiting production, markets or technical development to the prejudice of consumers;
> (c) applying dissimilar conditions to equivalent transactions with other trading parties, thereby placing them at a competitive disadvantage;
> (d) making the conclusion of contracts subject to acceptance by the other parties of supplementary obligations which, by their nature or according to commercial usage, have no connection with the subject of such contracts.[39]

Whether or not one is dominant in a particular product market is determined in large part by how broadly the market is defined, the bigger, more inclusive the market, the less likely one is to have a dominant share of it. The reverse is also true, the smaller the market, the more likely one is to be dominant.[40] It is often said that substitute products make up a single market, such that while the products in the market may differ from each other to a degree, they are equivalents in their important aspects.[41] According to the Commission, it is the consumer's perception of a product's characteristics that determines its substitutability in respect of other products.[42] Thus, if the public

---

[38] *Pennys* 78/193/EEC [1978] OJ L60/19, [1978] 2 CMLR 100. In this case, the Commission allowed an agreement between the American and Irish owners of identical trade marks for retail selling, wherein the Irish brand owner promised not to use the mark outside Ireland and the US brand owner promised not to use the brand inside Ireland.
[39] EC Treaty, Art. 82.
[40] *British Leyland v. EC Commission* 226/84 [1986] ECR 3263, [1987] 1 CMLR 185.
[41] *TetraPak Int'l, SA v. EC Commission* T-83/91 [1994] ECR II-755.
[42] 'All those products and/or services which are regarded as interchangeable or substitutable by the consumer, by reason of the products' characteristics, price and their intended use.' Form A.B, s. 6, Regulation 3385/94, [1994] OJ L377/28; Form CO, s. 6, Regulation 447/98, [1998] OJ L61/1.

perceived the allure of a branded product to be unique, such that no other product, branded or unbranded, was substitutable for it, then it could be the case that the brand acts to define the product market.[43] The product market for Article 82 purposes would be the market for products bearing the brand. Products that did not carry the relevant brand would not be substitutes. The brand owner would be in a dominant position in that market.

In general trade marks are the least exclusive of intellectual property rights as to the types of products that brand owners can exclude from a market. The Court of Justice recognized this in *EMI Records v. CBS United Kingdom*[44] when it held that while a trade mark right confers upon its owner a special position within a market, that position does not imply the existence of a dominant position within the meaning of Article 82, in particular where several undertakings of comparable economic strength to that of the holder of a mark operate in the market for the products in question and are in a position to compete with the trade mark owner.[45] This is to say that a trade mark gives its proprietor the exclusive right to the use of the mark, but it does not give the proprietor an exclusive right to market the types of goods to which the mark may be affixed.

Other brand owners may market equivalent goods under other brands. This fact was recognized in the *Sirena* case,[46] where the mere ownership of a trade mark was considered to be insufficient to create a dominant position.[47] The brand owner would also have to be able to prevent intrabrand competition, using some other anticompetitive mechanism in addition to the mark. In the fickle ever-changing marketplace for branded goods, such a mechanism would have to be separate from the appeal of the relevant mark to be effective, such as a superior distribution system, greater access to retail sales points or the like.

The Court of Justice has indicated that commercial advantages other than the appeal of brands act to accentuate market position. In *Nederlandsche Banden-Industrie Michelin v. E.C. Commission*,[48] the court held that the national subsidiary of an international group could be in a dominant position, even though it faced strong competition on the national market, because of the

---

[43] See the *Hag* cases discussed above and the failed attempt to introduce a substitute brand, DECOFA, recounted in W. Rothnie, *Parallel Imports* (Sweet & Maxwell, London, 1993) pp. 335–6.
[44] 51/75, [1976] ECR 811, [1976] 2 CMLR 235.
[45] *Ibid.*, para. 36.
[46] *Sirena, SrL v. EDA, SrL* 40/70 [1971] ECR 69, [1971] CMLR 260.
[47] *Ibid.*, para. 16.
[48] 322/81, [1983] ECR 3461, [1985] 1 CMLR 282.

commercial advantages it received from its parent group.[49] Thus, a trade mark may be only the more visible portion of a larger commercial presence that gives rise to a dominant position.

Unlike the case with Article 81, splitting a mark can alleviate market dominance. If it were the case that a brand was so popular that, in the opinions of consumers, there were no substitutes for it, market dominance could be found based on a definition of the relevant product market as being comprised solely of goods bearing the mark. Splitting a brand between undertakings that could then compete with each other would effectively eliminate dominance, allowing both to compete more aggressively with third parties while minimizing the risk of that aggressiveness being found to be abusive. The prime consideration here is that the owners of the divided brand can compete with each other. Otherwise while the division of a brand might alleviate an Article 82 violation, it might create one under Article 81.

9. CONCLUSION

It is possible to divide trade marks without violating the competitions laws, either of the Community as a whole or of the Member States. However the territorial nature of marks must be taken into consideration when doing so and particular sensitivity should be shown to the overarching goal of market integration. Any division of trade mark ownership that partitions the internal market is suspect. Any division that results in territorial exclusivity is a competition law violation unless the parties can show that some greater common benefit is achieved, such as putting an end to costly litigation, expanding distribution or promoting consumer welfare.

When marks are divided the parts of the competition laws come into conflict. The division of a powerful mark may diminish allegations of the abuse of a dominant position under EC Treaty Article 82 but may create a market sharing cartel under Article 81, unless the parties are allowed to compete across territorial lines. The potentialities should be weighed carefully, together with the potential for brand dilution, before a mark is divided.

---

[49] *Ibid.*, paras. 55–8. There have not been, as yet, other instances of this type of situation coming before the European Union courts.

12. Aspects of sublicensing
Neil Wilkof

The prevalence of sublicensing as a means for exploiting intellectual property rights cannot be gainsaid. Whether by way of patent, trade mark or copyright, the simple two-tier licensing arrangement between licensor and licensee often gives way to multi-tier arrangements by which the sublicensee plays a central role in the commercialization of the licensed intellectual property rights. However, the treatment of sublicensing in the professional literature has not proved commensurate with the commercial importance that sublicensing arrangements command in the commercial world.

The starting point for this chapter is that the sublicensing of intellectual property rights cannot be understood as a simple extension of the two-tier licensing arrangement between the licensor and licensee. That does not mean that no connection exists between licensing and sublicensing. The very fact that the sublicence can be said to derive from the main licence ensures that there is a nexus between the two. What it does mean, however, is that the principles that drive the licensor–licensee relationship do not necessarily apply to the sublicensee as well.

Against this backdrop of intellectual property sublicensing, the focus of this chapter will be on the sublicensing of trade mark rights. The sharing of trade mark rights with respect to the use of the mark under a sublicensing relationship gives rise to a series of unique problems. In order to understand them, it will be necessary to consider both the principles of sublicensing generally as well as the particular issues that are found when use of a mark is shared in a sublicensing relationship. In particular, we will consider four issues: (i) the conceptual foundations of sublicensing; (ii) purposes for entering into a trade mark sublicense; (iii) sublicensing, quality control, and trade mark licensing; and (iv) sublicencing, the 'have made' right, and trade mark licensing.

1. THE CONCEPTUAL FOUNDATIONS OF SUBLICENSING

One is hard-pressed to find a statutory definition for 'sublicensing'. Having regard to custom and practice, sublicensing can be described as the grant by the licensee to a third party of certain rights of use in intellectual property, based on rights of use that the licensee enjoys under the main licence.[1] This means that the scope of rights that may be granted to the sublicensee is circumscribed by the terms of the main licence. The scope of the rights of use under the sublicence may be coterminous with, or more limited than, the scope of the main licence. If more limited, the limitations themselves must nevertheless be consistent with the terms of the main licence.

It is unlikely any of the foregoing is controvertible. Nevertheless, the case law is extremely sparse in setting out exactly what is the legal basis for sublicensing. Generally speaking, courts called upon to render judgment in a dispute involving a sublicence do so without engaging in any substantial inquiry about its underlying legal nature. The sublicence is usually presumed to be valid unless challenged, and even when challenged, such disputes do not tend to reach the question of what is the underlying basis for the sublicence.

Nevertheless, from time to time, courts have endeavoured to offer a conceptual justification for sublicensing. One explanation that has been pursued with particular force is that the right to grant a sublicence is to be likened to the appointment of an agent.[2] Under such a view, the licensee becomes the agent of the licensor with respect to the appointment of additional licensees (that is, sublicensees), which are authorized to practise the licensed intellectual property right under the terms of the sublicence.

Following this approach, with respect to patent licensing, it has been observed, without extensive elaboration, that 'the law of agency nicely explains many of the principles applied to sublicensing'.[3] However, neither commentators nor case law have provided a comprehensive explanation of the application of the law of agency to a sublicense, nor whether the law of agency applies equally to the common law and civil law legal traditions.

Indeed, with respect to trade marks, the proposition that a trade mark licence creates an agency relationship has been rejected by at least two US courts, including one court of appeal.[4] For example, the *Oberlin* court rejected the argument that the requirement that the licensee must exercise quality

---

[1] See, e.g., L. Bryer, 'Sublicensing Terms Must Be Clear, Complete', *LES Nouvelles*, vol. 24, no. 1 (focusing on sublicensing of trade mark rights); J. Schwartz, 'Antitrust Issues Can Arise When Sublicensing', *LES Nouvelles*, vol. 32, no. 3. Judicial definitions of sublicensing tend to arise in disputes over whether or not a certain third-party use is a sublicence. See, *infra*, text at pp. 195–7.

[2] B. Brunsvold and D. O'Reilly, *Patent Licensing* (5th edn, BNA, Washington, 2004), at para. 3.03.

[3] *Ibid.*

[4] *Oberlin v. Marlin Am. Corp.*, 596 F 2d 1322, 1327 (7th Cir 1979); *L.A. Gear, Inc. v. E.S. Originals, Inc.*, 859 F Supp 1294, 1299–1300 (CD Cal 1994) and the cases cited therein.

control over the use of the mark by the licensee created an agency relationship that imposed liability on the licensor for the actions of the licensee. The court made it clear the nature of the required control is for the 'narrow purpose' of ensuring that there is no public deception by virtue of the licensee's use of the mark, not to confer on the licensor 'control over the day-by-day operations of a licensee'.[5]

While in principle, one might argue that the licensee is being granted a limited right of agency simply to appoint a sublicensee, the inclination of the courts not to impose an agency relationship with respect to the trade mark licensee for other purposes makes such a construction difficult. It makes little practical or conceptual sense to argue that only the act of appointment of a sublicence derives from a grant of agency, while the other facets of the licensee relationship are not so deemed. The autonomy of the trade mark licensee was graphically underscored by the House of Lords in the *Scandecor* decision, where the Court recognized under English trade mark law that the licensee, and not the licensor, could properly be identified as the source of the goods for the duration of the licence.[6] Thus, while the licensor and licensee are bound together by a complex relationship of correlative rights and duties, this relationship is not well explained by the law of agency.[7]

Further arguing against the view that a sublicence can be likened to an agency relationship is that the main licence agreement, including a trade mark licence, frequently contains a clause that explicitly provides that no agency relationship is being created by the parties.[8] While it is possible to argue that such a contractual provision need not necessarily be determinative of whether or not an agency relationship has been created, the likelihood of a court overruling the validity of such a provision must be viewed as low. Accordingly, the position that a sublicence can be likened to an agency relationship is often inconsistent with contractual practice. The upshot is that the legal basis for sublicensing must still be considered as unresolved in the law.

As well, in the main, courts have resisted giving recognition of a fiduciary duty between the licensor and licensee, and by extension, to a sublicensee as

---

[5] *Oberlin, ibid.* See text, *infra*, at pp. 192–4, for discussion of quality control requirement with respect to trade mark licensing.

[6] See text, *infra*, at pp. 193–4, for discussion of this case. See also *World Wide Fund for Nature (formerly World Wildlife Fund) v. World Wrestling Federation Entertainment Inc.* [2004] FSR 161 (CA), where the Court of Appeal distinguished between the conduct of an agent and licence (or sublicensee) with respect to the degree of the licensor's responsibility over each.

[7] This chapter does not consider whether a patent or copyright sublicence might lead to a different result, based on the different nature of each of these intellectual property rights.

[8] See also, Brunsvold and O'Reilly, *supra*, n. 2.

well. The most notable exception is the US decision in the *Original Appalachian Artworks* case, where the court of appeal recognized a fiduciary duty in favour of the licensee with respect to the right to receive a portion of the proceeds received by the licensor from a settlement agreement with the alleged infringer.[9] The court emphasized the misappropriation of the rights of the exclusive licensee by virtue of the infringer's activities. This decision has been criticized and it can be seen as a judicial solution to a special set of facts rather than a decision setting out any broad principle of law.[10] The inappropriateness of this result to a sublicence is even stronger, given the remoteness of the sublicensee to the licensor. Indeed, other courts in both England and the US have rejected a claim that a trade mark licence creates a fiduciary relationship.[11]

Given the unresolved legal basis for sublicensing, it is not surprising that the interrelationship between and among the licensor, licensee, and sublicensee is equally unresolved. Three crucial issues in this respect can be identified, namely (1) the right of the licensor to enforce a sublicence; (2) the liability of the licensee towards the licensor for the failure of the sublicensee to perform under the sublicence; and (3) the subsistence of the sublicence in the event that of early termination of the main licence.[12] No single legal position emerges.

With respect to the right of the licensor to directly seek enforcement against the sublicensee, there is scant case law in the US that appears to countenance such a possibility.[13] Similarly, there is no clear legal position on whether a licensee can be held to be responsible for the failure of the sublicensee to perform under the sublicence.[14] The parties can presumably seek to address these two issues by contractual agreement. But whether such provisions will be given effect is an open question.

---

[9] *Original Appalachian Artworks, Inc. v. S. Diamond Associates, Inc.*, 911 F 2d 1548 (11th Cir 1990).

[10] See N. Wilkof and D. Burkitt, *Trade Mark Licensing* (2nd edn, Sweet & Maxwell, London, 2004), at paras. 10-31 to 10-32.

[11] See, e.g., *Harrods Ltd. v. Harrods (Buenos Aires) Ltd. and another* [1997] FSR 420 (ChD); [1999] FSR 187 (CA); *Weight Watchers of Quebec v. Weight Watchers International*, 188 USPQ 17, 21 (EDNY 1975).

[12] Brunsvold and O'Reilly, *supra*, n. 2.

[13] Thus, in *Hazeltine Research Corporation v. Freed-Eisenmann Radio Corporation*, 3 F 2d 172 (EDNY 1924), the court did not appear to question the right of the patentee to seek enforcement directly against the sublicensee, although, applying principles of equity, the court did not grant the patentee's request. To the contrary, the court in *Good Humor Corporation of America v. Bluebird Ice Cream Charlotte Russe, Inc.*, 1 Supp 850 (EDNY 1932), appears to rule that the sublicence could only be enforced by the licensee.

[14] Brunsvold and O'Reilly, *supra*, n. 2.

Perhaps the most intriguing issue with respect to sublicensing is what happens to the continuing validity of the sublicence, should the primary licence between the licensor and licensee be prematurely terminated. At first glance, the answer to this question might seem straightforward. If the sublicensee is assumed to take its rights from the licensee, and the scope of the sublicence is bounded by the scope of the main licence, it could be concluded that the subsistence of the sublicence is dependent upon the validity of the main licence. If so, the argument would seem to go, once the main licence is terminated, the legal basis for the grant of the sublicence no longer exists, with the result that the sublicence must be viewed as terminated as well. Under this view, if the licensee wishes to protect itself against such a potentially harsh result, it can do so only by way of a provision in the sublicence agreement.

However, this result does not appear to be unequivocally supported in either the case law or legal commentary, at least under US law. Rather, there is support for the view that the sublicence may, at least under certain circumstances, survive the early termination of the main licence. The rationale for this position has been stated variously as resting on principles of equity, or that the sublicence is in effect an agreement between the licensor and the sublicensee, which is unaffected by the validity of the sublicence agreement.[15]

---

[15] Thus, the U.S. Federal Circuit Court of Appeals, being the court of appeal for patent matters in the US, has stated in *Rhone-Polenc Agro, S.A. v. DeKalb Genetics Corporation*, 284 F 3d 1323) as follows: 'Monsanto also relies on statements from various treatises on patent licensing that a sublicence continues, even where the original license is terminated as a matter of contract law, e.g., for breach of contract' [referring to fn. 7].

Footnote 7 states as follows:

See. e. g., Ridsdale Ellis, Patent Licenses sec. 62 (3d ed. 1958) ('A Sub-license Is An Independent Contract and Therefor, It Is Not Terminated by the Termination of the Main License, Unless Specifically So Provided.'); Id. At 63 ('Where a sub-licensee has lived up to the terms of the license, it is inequitable that his license should be revoked because the main license has failed to do the same, especially where the sub-licensee has made extensive investments on the strength of his license.'); Brian G. Brunsvold and Dennis P. O'Reilly, Drafting Patent License Agreements 37 (NBA 4th edn, 1998) ('An authorized sublicense is in effect an agreement with the [original] licensor. Unless the agreement with the licensee provides otherwise, the sublicense will continue despite the early termination of the license agreement.').

It is interesting to note that in the 5th edition of the Brunsvold and O'Reilly treatise, see *supra*, n. 2, there is no reference to the argument that the sublicence is in effect an agreement between the licensor and the sublicensee. Rather, the authors simply make a reference to the *Rhone-Poulenc* case itself for the proposition.

However, this position is not free from challenge. Reliance on equity is by nature an uncertain exercise, based on the particular circumstances, and its application is limited to common law jurisdictions. Whether there are equivalent principles under civil law jurisdictions is beyond the scope of this chapter. As well, not every sublicence necessarily involves the payment of royalties, directly or indirectly, to the licensor, or otherwise gives rise to the kind of inequities described by the court. To the extent that no financial hardship is worked on the sublicensee, the basis for giving effect to the sublicence in the event of early termination, may be inappropriate.

Moreover, with respect to a trade mark sublicence, at least in those jurisdictions in which quality control is still a requirement, the termination of the main licence may also have the result of bringing to an end the quality control exercised by the licensee on the sublicensee.[16] In such a case, the hardship that results from allowing the sublicence to remain valid may well fall upon the licensor and not the licensee.

This is because the continuing use of the trade mark by the sublicensee, without quality control, can have the result of leading to a 'naked licence', with all of the potential negative consequences for the validity of the mark. In jurisdictions in which quality control is relevant, a naked licence is one in which there is no quality control with respect to the use of the trade mark by the licensee. In such a circumstance, a naked licence can lead to abandonment of the trade mark by the licensor/registrant.[17]

In light of the foregoing, the parties are advised to make clear in an agreement whether or not the termination of the main licence terminates the sublicence as well. The desired result may well depend upon the particular circumstances of the licence and the relationship between the parties, such that a 'one size fits all' approach to the question is not appropriate.

2. PURPOSE FOR ENTERING INTO A TRADE MARK SUBLICENCE

There is no single commercial or competitive purpose for entering into a sublicence agreement with respect to use of a trade mark. Nevertheless, it is helpful to consider a number of recurring circumstances that have given rise to such a grant. It must be appreciated that there are additional reasons, which

---

[16] See text *infra*, at pp. 192–4, for discussion of quality control and trade mark licensing.
[17] See text *infra*, at pp. 193–4, for discussion of quality control and the implications of a naked trade mark licence. See also Wilkof and Burkitt, *supra*, n. 10, paras. 6-34 to 6-39 for further discussion about a naked licence and its consequences.

will not be discussed in this chapter, for entering into a sublicence when the focus is on a patent, copyright, or trade secret.

First, a sublicensee can provide an additional source of income for the licensor and/or the licensee. In its most simple form, the licensee may seek to charge a royalty somewhat higher than that owed to the licensor and pocket the difference between the two collected royalties.

Secondly, a sublicence may allow the licensor to set a higher level of minimum sales/royalty payments by the licensee by including royalty revenues received from the sublicensees as well as from the licensee itself. Even if there is no intention by the licensor to set a higher level of minimum royalties in this manner, the inclusion of royalty payments from the sublicensee may ease the burden on the licensee to meet the minimum requirements.

Thirdly, there may be circumstances in which the licensee itself does not directly generate any royalty income. Rather, all of the minimum requirements will have to be met by the sublicensees (subject perhaps to the licensee paying to the licensor the difference between the royalties received from the sublicensees and the amount of the minimum owing to the licensor).

Fourthly, a sublicence may enable a person to be the master licensee for a given territory, while relying on a network of sublicensees to make and distribute the branded products in the territory. This may be particularly appropriate for a brand holder who wishes to penetrate a new foreign market. This arrangement allows for the licensor to select a chosen licensee with whom to work, and then to rely on the licensee or sublicensor to manage the activities of the sublicensees within the territory.[18]

However, not all licensors have a commercial interest in allowing the licensee to grant sublicences with respect to a trade mark. Indeed, as exemplified below, circumstances may argue against granting the licensee a right to sublicence.

First, the licensor may have entered into the licence on the basis of certain characteristics of the licensee, such as its manufacturing capability, market position, or distribution channels. In each of these situations, the licensor will likely view the licence as akin to personal services agreement for which no further licensing is appropriate.

Secondly, the licensor may be concerned that the licensee not be allowed to grant a sublicence to a competitor of the licensor, or to an entity that has a commercial or similar relationship with a competitor of the licensee.

Thirdly, the conditions that gave rise to the licence may be inappropriate for sublicensing of trade mark rights. For example, if the parties have engaged in a cross-licensing arrangement to settle an infringement dispute, the parties

---

[18] In a version of this, a franchise relationship may be created.

may have no interest in contemplating further uses of their respective technologies by third parties, much less any interest to grant a trade mark licence with right of sublicence.

The upshot of the foregoing is that a variety of commercial or competitive considerations may lead the licensor to allow the licensee to enter in a sublicence under the provisions of the licence. That said, there may not be an identity of interest between the licensor and licensee in this regard, nor can it be expected that the parties will necessarily anticipate at the outset whether a right of sublicence is desirable and, if so, under what terms and conditions. This can create a certain tension in the licence relationship with respect to whether or not to explicitly include a right of sublicence in the agreement, or in the alternative, to explicitly exclude the right of sublicence.[19]

3. SUBLICENSING, QUALITY CONTROL AND TRADE MARK LICENSING

The most distinctive issue with respect to the sublicensing of trade marks centres on the matter of quality control. Traditionally, in common law jurisdictions, trade mark licensing has been subject to the quality control requirement. Valid trade mark licensing rested on the notion that if the licence is to preserve the notion of a trade mark as an indication of origin, then the licensor is obligated to ensure that the licensee exercises quality control over the licensee's use of the mark. As part of the quality control requirement, most common law jurisdictions even included a provision in their national trade mark law providing for the recording of a trade mark licensee as a registered user.[20] In the event that quality control is not maintained, that is, there is a 'naked licence', the mark no longer is deemed to indicate a single source for the goods. Under extreme circumstances, the result under such circumstances could be invalidation of the mark.[21]

---

[19] For the licensor that does not wish to grant a right of sublicence, an explicit exclusion is preferable. However, depending upon the particular circumstances, it may not be possible to obtain the licensee's agreement to the inclusion of such a provision. Even in the absence of such a provision, however, the better legal position is that there must be an explicit grant of right of sublicence in order for the sublicence to be effective.

[20] The principal exception to the recording requirement is found in the United States, where the Lanham Act never provided for the recording of a trade mark licensing.

[21] See Wilkof and Burkitt, *supra*, n. 10, at Ch. 6, for a further discussion of these points. See also Bryer, *supra*, n. 1.

Moreover, at least in some jurisdictions, the legal position of a trade mark sublicence was uncertain. Given this uncertainty, in order to enable the sublicensing of a trade mark, the solution was to provide for some form of direct agreement between the licensor and sublicensee, at least with respect to quality control, such that it could be claimed that there was a direct relationship between the licensor and the sublicensee in this regard. As a result, not infrequently, the licensor and sublicensee would execute a simple form of licence agreement between them, providing simply for a grant of right of use of the mark, but leaving the further terms and conditions for such use to be set out in the agreement between the licensee/sublicensor and sublicensee.

The wholesale reenactment of the English trade mark law in 1994 did away with the registered user provisions and gave explicit recognition of sublicensing, thereby obviating as well the need for the tripartite arrangement between the licensor, licensee and sublicensee.[22] Generally speaking, a sublicensee is now treated similarly to the licensee.[23] That said, the statutory reenactment did not on its face do away with the quality control requirement.

However, the long-standing principle of quality control under English law was overturned by the House of Lords in the *Scandecor* case,[24] at least with respect to an exclusive licence. In revisiting the quality control requirement in the context of an exclusive, albeit naked licence, the House of Lords held that the requirement no longer reflected the current state of trade mark licensing and the perceptions of the public with respect to the source of the licensed mark. In the words of Lord Nicholls, '[d]uring the licence period the goods come from only one source, namely, the licensee, and the mark is distinctive of that source.'[25]

Left unswered is the question of whether the *Scandecor* principle applies to a sublicensee. That is, can a sublicensee, as opposed to the licensor and licensee, ever be perceived by the consumer as the sole source of the goods vis-à-vis the licensor and licensee? It can be argued that the *Scandecor* principle is applicable when there are only two entities in a jurisdiction – a licensor

---

[22] The Trade Marks Act 1994, s. 28(4). It is still possible to register a licence under English law, but the effect of the registration is to provide notice to third parties and to secure a right to suit, rather than to establish quality control. A similar arrangement was legislated in Australia in the amendments to its trade mark law. By contrast, under the amended Canadian trade mark law, all registration requirements for licences were abandoned. See Wilkof and Burkitt, *supra*, n. 10, at paras. 4-01 to 4-04, for a further discussion of these points.

[23] See Wilkof and Burkitt, *supra*, n. 10, at para. 4-47. See also para. 4-03 for treatment of sublicences under the Canadian trade mark law as amended.

[24] *Scandecor Developments AB v. Scandecor Marketing AB and Others* [2001] ETMR 74.

[25] *Ibid.* at para. 42.

and exclusive licensee – and only the exclusive licensee is using the mark during the term of the licence. When, however, there are multiple parties, such as in the case of a sublicence, the traditional principle of quality control may still be more appropriate, because it forces all of the parties to the licence to act in a uniform manner with respect to the use of the mark.[26]

This is so, unless the licensee/sublicensor is in fact serving as the alter ego for the trade mark owner in the jurisdiction. For example, the foreign trade mark owner may appoint a local licensee, whose sole responsibility is to manage the manufacture and sale of the licensed product by selected sublicensees within the territory. In such a situation, the licensee itself will make no use of the mark, and it might well be that the sublicensee will be viewed by the public as the source of the goods.

The foregoing discussion on the changing law regarding quality control, and its application to sublicensing, applies only to English law and perhaps to other jurisdictions in which the *Scandecor* decision may be persuasive. In other common law countries, such as the US and Canada, the *Scandecor* rationale has not been adopted. In those jurisdictions, the quality control issues with respect to sublicensing remain relevant.

Therefore, careful attention must continue to be paid to this maintenance of quality control with respect to the use of the sublicensee, no less than that exercised with respect to the use by the licensee, under the trade mark. This is to ensure that, as a matter of law, the licensor is deemed to be the source of the goods or services emanating from the sublicensee.

Thus, in the main, it is the licensor that exercises quality control over the use of the mark by the licensee. It is not expected that the licensor will do so with respect to the use of the mark by the sublicensee, although there is nothing to prevent the licensor from doing so. More typically, it is the licensee/sublicensor that assumes responsibility, as a practical matter, for the exercise of quality control over the sublicensee. As with quality control over the use of the mark by the licensee, such exercise by the licensee/sublicensor over the sublicensee can be direct, or by means of a representative of the licensee.[27]

---

[26] Wilkof and Burkitt, *supra*, n. 10, at paras. 6-57 to 6-70. It is also noted that to the extent that there is no quality control requirement, the argument that a trade mark licence creates an agency relationship would seem to be even weaker. See text, *supra*, at pp. 185–7 for discussion of agency and quality control.

[27] See generally, Bryer, n. 1.

4. SUBLICENSING, THE 'HAVE MADE' RIGHT, AND TRADE MARK LICENSING

While a licence is a form of authorized third-party use of an intellectual property right, not every authorized third-party use is a licence. This observation applies in equal measure to a sublicence. The issue then arises how to distinguish a sublicence from other forms of third-party uses. The question becomes particularly important in two situations, namely (i) termination of the main licence on the ground that the licensee has violated the 'no sublicensing' clause[28] or (ii) a dispute between the parties over the extent of the royalty payments owed due to sublicensing.

Courts have in the main resisted the attempt to find a sublicence when the third-party use is a resale or supply agreement.[29] Courts have greater difficulty in making the distinction between the rights conferred to a sublicensee and to a contract manufacturer, respectively. The *Carey* court in the US expressed the distinction in a way that has been oft-quoted, as follows:

> A licensee having the right to produce, use or sell might be interested only in using the article or in selling it; in order to use it or sell it, the article must be produced; to have it produced, his license permits him to engage others to do all the work connected with the production of the article for him. Production of the article for the use of the licensee is production under the license.
>
> Not so under a sublicense, unless the sublicense is producing for the original licensee. To produce for his own use or for the use of someone else, the sublicensee may do so only under a sublicense. So the test is, whether the production is by or for the use of the original licensee or for the sublicense himself or for someone else.[30]

---

[28] A variant of this occurs when the licensor sues the third party for infringement, alleging that the third party was not authorized to use the intellectual property right.

[29] *Lisle v. Edwards* 771 F 2d 693 (Fed Cir 1985) (rejecting the argument that a resale relationship created a sublicence); *Novopharm Ltd. v. Eli Lilly and Co.; Apotex Inc. v. Eli Lilly and Co.* 80 CPR (3d) 321, 1998 CPR LEXIS 95 (SC Canada 1998) (rejecting the argument that an agreement reached between two parties, whereby one party would supply the other with a product, after the expiry of the compulsory licence scheme under Canadian law, was an impermissible sublicence). Of particular note is the *Lisle* court's reasoning in ruling that resale does not create a sublicence. The court observed that if a resale relationship did create a sublicence, the result would be that, as an alternative to termination for unauthorized sublicensing, the licensor could claim entitlement to a royalty for each resale of the product.

[30] *Carey v. the United States,* 326 F 2d 975 (Ct Cl 1964).

The difficulty in applying the distinction set out by the *Carey* court can be seen by considering two leading US cases, *DuPont v. Shell Oil*[31] and *Cyrix Corp v. Intel Corp.*[32] The focus of the dispute in the *DuPont* case was how to understand the legal effect of two separate agreements, both executed on the same day. In the first agreement, Shell Oil granted Union Carbide the right to make a certain chemical product under 'have made' rights. In the second, Shell Oil undertook to sell back to Union Carbide the identical minimum quantity of the product. The ultimate result of these two agreements was that Union Carbide received all the methomyl that it desired by effectively manufacturing the product for itself.

In considering whether a prohibited sublicence had been created, the lower court ruled that it was not enough to look at the end result. Rather, it focused on what it termed 'the relevant indicia', namely a consideration of matters relating to custody, control and title of the products.[33] Based on this approach, the trial court found that no sublicence had been created. The Delaware Supreme Court, in overturning the decision, took the opposite tack. Relying on the *Carey* test, the Supreme Court looked at the end result of the two agreements taken together. In so doing, it ruled that Carbide produced the product solely for itself. Accordingly, 'neatly tailored drafting' could not change the fact that a prohibited sublicence had been created.[34]

This result should be compared with the decision in the *Cyrix* case. There, the plaintiff, which designed and sold microprocessors, turned to ST to manufacture the microprocessors in accordance with designs provided by the plaintiff. ST in turn requested an Italian affiliate, ST-Italy, to carry out the manufacture. Intel argued that the arrangement between ST and ST-Italy was not permitted under the terms of the licence agreement with Intel, since it was a prohibited sublicence. Relying on the reasoning of the *DuPont* case, Intel asserted that the arrangement between and among Cyrix, ST and ST-Italy was a mere sham. The court rejected the claim, reasoning that ST-Italy properly acted as contractor under the 'have made' grant.[35]

The *DuPont* and *Cyrix* cases underscore that there is no bright-line distinction between third-party use by a sublicensee and a contract manufacturer, respectively. This uncertainty takes on a somewhat different hue when a trade

---

[31] *E.I. Du Pont de Nemours and Co. v. Shell Oil Company* 498 A 2d 1108; 227 USPQ 233 (SC Del 1985).
[32] *Cyrix Corporation v. SGS-Thomson Microelectronics, Inc. et al.* 77 F 3d 1381 (Fed Cir 1996).
[33] *E.I. DuPont & Co. v. Shell Oil Co.* Del Court of Chancery, unreported decision of 6 June 1984 ((1985) 9 Delaware Journal of Corporate Law).
[34] *DuPont, supra,* n. 31.
[35] *Cyrix, supra,* n. 32.

mark licence is concerned. Under principles of trade mark licensing, there is no requirement that the trade mark licensee itself must carry out all of the functions associated with performing its obligations under the licence. This is so, presumably, as long as the manufacture is done in such a way that ensures the quality of the product.[36] Thus, unless the licensor has a special interest in providing in the licence agreement that manufacture must be carried out only by the licensee, the licensee is free to turn to a contract manufacturer. Stated otherwise, the trade mark licensee does not require any specific grant of right to rely on a contract manufacturer.

However, the matter is not in fact so straightforward when the trade mark licence is interwoven with a patent or know-how licence. The reason is that a patent or know-how licence does not authorize the licensee to turn to a third-party contract manufacturer to make use of the licensed right unless there is an explicit grant to do so. If no such grant of right is given, the presumed right of the trade mark licensee to authorize a third party to manufacture the product under the mark may be in conflict with the provisions of the accompanying technology licence, if the latter is silent on the issue of the 'have made' right.[37]

Moreover, even if the licence contains a right of sublicence, but does not include the 'have made' right, the licensee may be in breach by authorizing a third-party contract manufacturer to produce the product.[38] This is so because the right of sublicence, and of the 'have made' right, are separate and distinct. The licensor might agree to allow a sublicence because of the potential revenue stream, but otherwise insist the licensee carry out all of manufacture of the goods on its own.

Under these circumstances, the licensee under the trade mark licence must determine whether it will wish to make use of a contract manufacturer to produce the licensed goods. If it does, and the contract manufacturer will need to make use of patent or know-how rights of the licensor, then the licence agreement must contain explicit authority for the licensee to grant the appropriate rights, irrespective of the silence in the trade mark licence on the matter.

---

[36] This statement is true whether the law of the particular jurisdiction imposes a formal requirement of quality control, such as the United States, or if no quality control is required as a legal matter, such as in England. In both circumstances, it is assumed that the licensor has a commercial interest in ensuring that the products made under the licence meet the licensor's quality standards.

[37] The licensee might claim it had an implied licence to use a contract manufacturer under such circumstances. However, reliance on the position that an implied licence has been created must be viewed as highly uncertain.

[38] This appears to have been the result in at least one English case, *Allen & Hansburys Limited's (Salbutamol) Patent* [1987] RPC 327.

5. CONCLUSION

Various legal questions arise that are specific to sublicensing, especially trade mark licensing; this chapter has discussed several of the most important such issues. However, given the absence of definitive law, together with the paucity of robust secondary literature and legal commentary on the subject, this chapter will end with a word of caution. Special attention needs to be paid to the contractual provisions of the sublicence. What compounds the difficulty in structuring a sublicence agreement is that, while the sublicence is based on the main licence, it constitutes a separate contractual undertaking. As such, the sublicence agreement will necessarily take into account the commercial needs and requirements of the parties to the sublicence.

This combination of sparsely settled law in the area, together with the special characteristics of the sublicence relationship, urges the parties to exercise particular vigilance when fashioning the terms of the trade mark sublicence agreement. This is so, whether or not the particular jurisdiction has a legal requirement of quality control, because use of the trade mark is being shared by and among the owner, licensee and sublicensee. At the end of the day, the ultimate value of a trade mark is the goodwill that it enjoys in the marketplace. To the extent that the goodwill of the mark in the sublicensing situation now depends upon the actions of at least three different entities, the potential is there for either enhancing or devaluing the mark. When one takes this into account, in addition to the various common issues that are present in all types of sublicensing relationship – be it a trade mark, copyright, or patent – awareness of the challenges in dealing with a trade mark sublicence is particularly important to all involved.

Index

Aaker, D. 155, 156
Aaker, D. and E. Joachimsthaler 23
Abratt, R. and P. Motlana 157
Ad-Lib Club v. Granville 45
Adam Opel AG v. Autec AG (OPEL BLITZ) 67
Adams, F. 33
Addley Bourne v. Swan 33
Adidas-Salomon v. Fitnessworld 26, 95, 123, 124, 125
Advocaat 108
Alchian, A. and D. Demsetz 25
Alcon Inc. v. OHIM (BSS) 68
Allen & Hansburys Patent 197
AMD, and co-branding 161, 162
American Speech-Language-Hearing Association v. National Hearing Aid Society 86–7
Andrew, J. 104
(John) Andrew v. Kuehnrich 17
Annabel v. Schlock 107
Apotex, Inc. v. Eli Lilly and Co. 195
Aristoc v. Rysta 16
Arsenal Football Club v. Matthew Reed 3, 13, 83, 143, 144
ARTHUR ET FELICIE 53, 55, 56
Arvidsson, A. 165
Asprey & Garrard v. WRA (Guns) Ltd and William Asprey 129, 130–2, 137, 138, 150
Assembled Investments (Proprietary) v. OHIM 117
association marks
    and geographical indications 96–8
    and test for confusion 89–95
    and tests for 'dilution' 95–6
Australia
    specialty, backlash against 105, 106, 108
    Trade Marks Acts 31, 44
Avery, D. and J. Rosen 164

Bactiguard Trademark 77
Bahr Thompson, A. 156
Bali Trade Mark (No.2) 45
BARBIE, and corporate brand licensing 156
Barclays Bank Plc v. RBS Advanta 145–6
BAT Cigaretten-Fabriken v. Commission 180
Baumgarth, C. 161
Baywatch Production Co. Inc. v. The Home Video Channel 122
Becker, G. and K. Murphy 23
Beebe, B. 22, 26, 94–5
Belgium, trade mark registration and coexistence 64–9
Belson, J. 79, 81
Bently, L. 33
Bently, L. and B. Sherman 33, 97
Bi-Lo App 44
Bishop, S. and M. Walker 175
Blackett, T. and B. Boad 157
Blanco White, T. and R. Jacob 113
BLUE ARC/ARC 55
BMW Nederland v. Ronald Karel Deenik 146–7
Boehringer Ingelheim v. Swingward 25–6, 157
Booer, T. 174
'Bordeaux' wine 97
Boxer, S. 163
brands
    co-branding *see* co-branding
    corporate brand licensing 14, 155–6
    and customer loyalty 155
    life-cycle model 158
    and trade mark, relationship between 16–17, 157
Brech, P. 160
Bristol-Myers Squibb v. Paranova 25
British Lead Mills Ltd's Application 73
British Leyland v. EC Commission 181

British Sugar v. Robertson 115
BROOK & CROSSFIELD/BROOKFIELD 54
Brown, R. 22
Brunsvold, B. and D. O'Reilly 186, 187, 188, 189
Bryer, L. 186, 194
BSS 68
BUD/BUD 98, 118
BUDMEN/BUD 54
BUDWEISER/BUDWEISER BUDVAR 98, 118
Burgess v. Burgess 129, 151

Cable & Wireless Plc v. British Telecommunications Plc 146, 147
Callmann, R. 82–3
CAMELO/CAMEL 58
Canada, Trade Marks Act (1985) 31
Canon Kabushiki Kaisha v. Metro-Goldwyn-Mayer Inc 90, 114, 116, 117, 118–19, 126
Carey v. United States 195–6
Carter, S. 21
Castellblanch, SA v. OHIM (CRISTAL CASTELLBLANCH) 56
CBF/CBI 91
Celine Sarl v. Celine S.A. 148–9
Centrafarm v. American Home Products 174, 177
'Champagne' 80, 111, 149
Chandiramani, R. 160
Chevy 95–6
Chocosuisse Union des Fabricants Suisse de Chocolat v. Cadbury 81
Clark v. Freeman 34
Cnl-Sucal v. Hag (*Hag II*) 16, 177, 179, 182
co-branding
   advantages and drawbacks 157–8
   and brand equity 164
   communication-based 159, 162–3, 164
   customer confusion, avoiding 168
   definition 156–7
   as diversification strategy 158–9
   and intellectual property rights 157, 166–9
   management and control 163–5
   and market pressure 161–2
   organizational and legal requirements 157–8
   parallel 159–61
   partnership termination 158, 166
   and sponsorship 162
   as strategic alliance 155–9
   and trade mark coexistence, difference between 16–17, 157
   see also brands
Coase, R. 175
Codas TM 46, 48
'Cognac' 81
COKE, and product line extensions 156
collective and certification marks 79–98
   characteristic features of certification marks 80–6, 93
   characteristic features of collective marks 80–1, 86–9
   essential function 84–5, 88
   infringement provisions 88–9
   product quality 84, 85
   scrutiny procedures 85–6
Commissioners of Inland Revenue v. Muller & Co.'s Margarine 20
common law rules
   for deceit 32–3
   and goodwill 34–5
   and honest concurrent use 32–5
   and misrepresentation 34
   passing off and own-name use *see* passing off and own-name use
   and specialty rule 102, 114
   and third party infringement 33, 34
   trade mark registration only 34–5
COMPAIR/COMPAIR 59
competition
   and brand protection, conflict between 172–3
   and common field of activity 108–9
   and dilution, effect of 120–2
   and dominant positions 182
   and split marks 171–83
   and sublicensing 191–2
   and trade mark disputes, coexistence in (EU) 53
   trade mark monopoly, market strength and enforceability relationship 175
confusion
   and co-branding, avoiding 168

and common field of activity 109
definition, European Court of Justice 114, 115–16
and passing off 104, 107, 112, 115–16
passing off and own-name use 129–39
and product differentiation 17, 118
and specialty 108, 113, 121
and trade mark disputes, coexistence in (EU) 52–6, 57–8, 59–60, 65, 66, 74–5, 93, 113
Consten and Grundig v. EEC Commission 171, 174, 180
consumers
  name sharing and possibility of misleading 25, 113–14
  protection regulation 21
  reference point, trade mark as 20, 21–3, 24–5, 84
Continental Shelf 128 Ltd v. Hebrew University of Jerusalem (Einstein Trade Mark) 71–2
Cooter, R. and T. Ulen 20, 21, 24
copyright 33, 93, 106
Cordery, B. and K. Sloper 110
Cornish, W. and D. Llewellyn 81, 83
Cottone, E. and C. Byrd Bredbenner 162
CRISTAL CASTELLBLANCH/CRISTAL 56, 63
Culatello di Zibello 91
Customer First 90
Cyrix Corp v. Intel Corp 196–7

'Darjeeling' tea 97
Davidoff v. Gofkid 26, 122, 123, 124, 125
Davis, J. 16
Dawson, N. 81
Day, G. 158
de Charnatony, L. and M. McDonald 155
DEER HEAD 61
DEF-TEC Defense Technology v. OHIM (FIRST DEFENSE AEROSOL PEPPER PROJECTOR/DEFENSE & FIRST DEFENSE) 59
Dent v. Turpin 33, 34
Desai, K. and K. Keller 157

Deutsche Grammophon v. Metro-SB-Grossmarkte 174, 180
Dewhurst & Sons' Application 40
DIN/Din-Lock 91
DISNEY 155–6, 158
Disney/McDonald's co-branding 162–3, 166
Dixon, P. and C. Mueller 174
Dogan, S. and M. Lemley 26
Drescher, T. 22
DuPont v. Shell Oil 91, 196–7
Durferrit GmbH v. OHIM (nutride/tufftride) 62

EC Treaty
  Articles 28 and 29 172, 174
  Article 81 171, 179–81, 183
  Article 82 171, 181–3
  Article 85 171
  Article 295 172
  competition and intellectual property rights 171, 172–3
  split marks, and dominance and abuse 181–3
  split marks and intellectual property 171, 179–81
ECHINAID/ECHINACIN 62
Economides, N. 20
Edelsten v. Edelsten 32
Electrix App 44
Elizabeth Emanuel 78
Elliot, R. L. Percy 165
EMI Records v. CBS United Kingdom 182
Emperor of Austria v. Day and Kossuth 34
Enrico, R. 156
ENZO FUSCO/ANTONIO FUSCO 54
Erven Warnick BV v. J Townsend & Sons(Hull) Ltd 108
Esure Insurance Ltd v. Direct Line Insurance Plc 119, 123–4
EU
  co-branding and marketing pressure 161–2
  Office for Harmonization in the Internal Market (OHIM) 51, 53, 54, 58, 59, 60, 62, 79–80, 87, 88, 90–1, 97, 117, 119, 125–7

Packaging Waste Directive 92, 93
Paris Convention 87, 102, 103
Responsible Care programme,
    chemical industry 95, 96
trade mark disputes, coexistence in
    see trade mark disputes,
    coexistence in
Trade Mark Law 13
EU Community Trade Mark Regulation
    (CTMR)
  Article 8 56, 57, 59, 90, 95–6
  Article 8(1)(b) 52–3, 57, 90, 92, 118
  Article 12 148
  Article 13(1) and 15(3) 72
  Article 51 59, 68
  Article 52(1)(a) 56
  Article 53 51, 59
  Article 64 85, 87–8
  Article 74(1) 59
  Article 98(1) 67
  association marks and test for
      confusion 89–90, 91–4
  association marks and tests for
      'dilution' 95–6
  and coexistence 51, 52–3, 54, 55, 56,
      57, 59, 60, 61, 68
  collective marks 87–8
  proprietor consent 72
  quality control 72
  specialty principle 118
EU, Court of First Instance (CFI)
  and coexistence 53, 54, 55, 56, 59,
      60, 61–3
  and similarity of goods 117–18, 119
European Convention on Human Rights
    and Fundamental Freedoms 141
European Court of Justice
  common identity of designated
      products 17
  confusion definition 114, 115–16
  essential function definition 78, 83,
      143–4, 177–8
  honesty in own name cases 146–7,
      148–9
  intellectual property rights 177–8,
      182
  proprietor consent 72
  protection scope and distinctive
      character 65–9
  quality guarantee of trade mark 16
  specialty principle 115, 116, 118,
      120, 122–3, 124–5
  trade mark function definition 3, 13,
      15
  trade mark rights, monopolistic
      nature of 171
*European Limited v. Economist
    Newspaper Limited* 146
European Norms Electrical Certification
    (ENEC) 80
European Trade Mark Directive 89/104
    65, 67, 68, 144, 145
  Article 4 90, 124
  Article 5 119, 120, 121–5, 126, 148
  Article 5(1)b 90, 114–15, 119, 120
  Article 6 148
  Article 7(3) and 10(3) 72
  effect of 45–6
  and first marketing of goods 19
  infringement scope 148
  intellectual property rights
      enforcement 66
  proprietor consent 72
  protection of earlier mark 65, 67, 68
  reputation protection 26
  and similarity to earlier mark 45–6,
      47, 90
  and 'special circumstances', cessation
      of 45
  specialty and registered trade marks
      under 112–27
  trade mark definition 13
European Trade Mark Directive 2004/48
    66

*Faber Chimica Srl v. OHIM
    (FABER/NABER)* 62–3
Fairtrade co-branding 160–1
*Fenchurch Environmental Group Ltd v.
    Ad Tech Holdings Ltd (Bactiguard
    Trademark)* 77
Fiorelli Trade Mark 74
*FIRST DEFENSE AEROSOL PEPPER
    PROJECTOR/DEFENSE &
    FIRST DEFENSE* 59
Firth, A. 81
FLEXI AIR/FLEX 61–2
Florida v. Real Juices Inc 80–1
Flynn, J. 174
Folliard-Monguiral, Arnaud 51–70

Ford mergers 158
Ford/Elle co-branding 160
Fortuna-Werke 45
franchising 24, 191

Gangjee, Dev 79–98
GARO/GIRA 55, 56
Garrahan, M. 163
GE Trade Marks 32, 33, 44
General Motors v. Yplon 26, 95, 123
geographical indications of origin 80, 81, 86, 88, 96–8
George, A. 165
Germany, trade mark registration and coexistence 59–60, 62
Gerolsteiner Brunnen mit Haftung & Co v. Putsch mit Haftung 146, 147
Geronimo Stilton/STILTON 97
Gervais, D. 103
GfK AG v. OHIM 63
Gillette Group Finland v. LA-Laboratories Limited 147
Glaeser, E. 23
Glaxo Group v. Dowelhurst 16
GOLDSHIELD/SHIELD 52, 54
Good Humor Corporation of America v. Bluebird Ice Cream Charlotte Russe 188
goodwill 18, 20, 21, 23, 24, 25, 34–5, 45, 83, 121, 149, 150
Goschen Committee and honest concurrent user 43
Grala, A. 160
Grana Biraghi/GRANA PADANO 97–8
Granada 43, 44
Green Dot 91–4
GRENFELL/GREENFIELD 54
Griffiths, Andrew 13–27
Grossmann, R. 162
GRUPO SADA/SADIA 55, 56

Häagen-Daz/Baileys co-branding 159, 166
Habib Bank Ltd v. Habib Bank AG Zurich 34
Hag I 176–7, 182
Hag II 16, 177, 179, 182
Haig, M. 165
Harrods Ltd. v. Harrods (Buenos Aires) Ltd. 188

Harrods v. Harrodian 109–10
'Havana' tobacco 97
Hays, Thomas 19, 171–83
Hazeltine Research Corporation v. Freed-Eisenmann Radio Corporation 188
HELLO/HALLO 54
Henderson v. Radio Corporation 105, 106, 108
Herschell Committee and 'three mark rule' 39
Higgins, D. 32
Hodson, Tessie and Co's TM 39
In re Hodson, Tessier and Co 36
Hoffmann-la Roche v. Centrafarm 3, 15
Holt 45
Holt, D. 160, 165
Holterhoff v. Freiesleben 144
honest concurrent use 31–49
  death of 47–9
  Goschen and Mathys Committees 43
  high point for 43–5
  introduction of 41–3
  low point and Trade Marks Bill 45–7
  and period of use 44–5
  and proof of earlier mark 44, 48
HUBERT/SAINT-HUBERT 119
Hurwitz, A. 158

Idaho Potato Commission v. M & M Produce Farm & Sales 86
IMA, AG v. Windsurfing International, Inc. 174
Inland Revenue Commissioners v. Muller & Co's Margarine Limited 149
Institut National Des Appellations d'Origine v. Brown-Forman 81
Intel 161–2, 166, 196–7
Intel v. CPM 124, 126
intellectual property rights
  and co-branding 157, 166–9
  and competition 174
  European Court of Justice 177–8, 182
  existence and exercise of rights 173–4
  split marks 171, 176–81
  and sublicensing *see* sublicensing
International Heiztechnik v. Ideal Standard 178, 179
Irvine v. Talksport 110–11

ITMA (Institute of Trade Mark Attorneys) collective mark 87

Jackson v. Napper 38
James & Sons v. Wafer Razor 34
Japan Tobacco, Inc. v.OHIM (CAMELO/CAMEL) 58
Jelly's Case 35, 38
'JIF Lemon case' 108
Jobber, D. 159
John Fitton & Co's Application 43
Johnson, Phillip 31–49
José Alejandro, SL v. OHIM (BUDMEN/BUD) 54

Keller, K. 155, 156, 157
Kerly, D. 39, 42
Kitchin, D. et al. 79
Klein, B. and K. Leffler 21
Klein, N. 17, 165
KOJAKPOPS 106
Kotler, P. 155, 156
Kur, A. 102

Ladas, S. 79, 82, 83, 87
Landes, W. and R. Posner 20, 21, 84, 142
Leather Cloth Company v. The American Leather Cloth Company 34
LEE/LEE COOPER 55
Legal Aid 85
Lego v. Lemelstrich 108, 109
Lehmann & Co's App 42
Re Leonardt 39
Leuthesser, L. et al. 164
Levi Strauss & Co v. Casucci Spa 61, 64–9
Levi Strauss v. Costco UK 19
Levi Strauss v. Tesco Stores 19
licensing 14, 24–5, 72, 92, 155–6, 188
  sub-licensing *see* sub-licensing
LIFESPASPA 126
Lisle v. Edwards 195
Lloyd Schuhfabrik Meyer & Co. GmbH v. Klijsen Handel BV 90
LORAC/LIERAC 54
L'Oréal SA v. Bellure SA 111
L'Oréal SA v. OHIM (FLEXI AIR/FLEX) 61–2
LTJ Diffusion SA v. Sadas Vertbaudet SA 90

Lury, C. 14, 165
Lyndon's TM 38
Lyngstad v. Anabas 108

McCarthy, J. 121
McCulloch v. May 104, 105, 106, 108, 110, 112
McLibel 162
McManis, C. 102
Macneil, I. 18
McVitie/M&M co-branding 159
'Madara Rock' and 'Madeira' wine 97
Madaus AG v. OHIM (ECHINAID/ECHINACIN) 62
Maeder 42
MAGIC/MAGIC BOX 54
Major Bros. v. Franklin 16
MANGO 57–8
Maniatis, Spyros 155–69
Marenco, G. and K. Banks 173
MARIE-CLAIRE/MARIE-CLAIRE 56, 126
Mast-Jägermeister AG v. OHIM (VENADO) 63
Mathys Committee and honest concurrent user 43
'Member of the Society of Financial Advisers' 87
Merck, Sharp & Dohme v. Paranova Pharmazeutika Handels 157
mergers and acquisitions, and co-branding 158–9
Mermonde/DER GRÜNE PUNKT (The Green Dot) 91–4
Michaels, A. 114
Midwest Plastic Fabricators Inc. v. Underwriters Laboratories Inc. 81
MISS ROSSI/SISSI/ROSSI 117
Re Mitchell 39
monopoly 19, 171, 175
see also split marks
Moscona, R. 134
Motion, J. et al. 164
Mrs Pomeroy Ltd v. Scalé 135
Mühlens v. OHIM; Minoronzoni intervening 117
MX HONDA/HONDA 54

Nabisco v. PF Brands Inc and Pepperidge Farm 127

name sharing
   and character merchandizing 106
   different goods and principle of specialty 101–28
   and economic role of trade marks 23–6
   involuntary, and market exploitation 26
   and 'origin', possibility of misleading consumers 25, 113–14
   similarity of goods 116–19
   and specialty *see* specialty
   and transaction costs 23
   voluntary and involuntary 14, 18–19, 20, 24, 25–6
   see also own name defence and registered trade mark law
Nederlandsche Banden-Industrie Michelin v. EC Commission 182–3
Nestlé SA's Trade Mark Application 75
New Zealand, Trade Marks Act (2002) 31
Newman v. Adlem 129, 130, 133–4, 135–6, 138
NF/MF 85, 91
Nice Classification 14
Nicholls, A. and C. Opal 160
Nicholson's Application 17
Nike/Lego Bionicle co-branding 159–60
NIKE/NIKE 51
NO LIMITS/LIMMIT 54
Nokia Corp v. Joachim Wärdell 67
Norman, H. 122
Norris, D. 161
Novopharm Ltd. v. Eli Lilly and Co. 195
nu-tride/tufftride 62

Oberlin v. Marlin Am. Corp. 186–7
Ogus, A. 20
OHM/OHM 54
OMEGA/OMEGA 60, 77
OPEL BLITZ 67
OPIUM/OPIUM 126
Original Appalachian Artworks v. S. Diamond Associates 188
Origins Natural Resources Inc v. Origin Clothing Ltd 34
own name defence and registered trade mark law 141–52
   and badge or trade dress 149–50
   company use 147
   and honesty 145–9
   infringement exceptions 144–9
   and names and addresses 150
   passing off 149–51
   and reputation 149
   search costs and trade mark recognition 142, 143
   trade mark as badge of origin 143
   trade mark use 142–4
   see also name sharing
own name use, and reputation 149

Parke, Davis & Co. v. Probel 174
Parker-Knoll v. Knoll International 129, 130, 133, 135, 151
Parkington's Application 44
passing off
   and confusion 104, 107, 112, 115–16
   and good faith 32–3, 34, 136–7, 138
   infringement exceptions 144–9
   and own-name use 129–39
   and reputation 104, 115–16
   patents 33, 36, 39, 48–9, 65, 174
   and sublicensing 186, 189, 197
Patishall, B. 102
Pebble Beach Co v. Lombard Brands Ltd 125
Peddie 44
Pennys 181
PepsiCo, Inc. v. OHIM (RUFFLES/RIFFLES) 53, 54, 55
Perry v. Truefitt 33
Pharmon v. Hoechst 177
Phillips, J. 79, 147, 157, 158, 165
Phillips, J. and A. Coleman 104, 105, 109
Pires de Carvahlo, N. 103
Pirie and Sons 42, 43
Pirie's Application 44, 73
POLO/FARTONS POLO 54
Portogram 44
Posner, R. 20, 21, 84, 142, 175
Postkantoor 75
Premier Brands v. Typhoon 125
Primark v. Lollypop Clothing 16
'Prosciutto di Parma' (Ducal Crown) 88
Prosciutto di Parma v. Marks & Spencer Plc and Others 149
Pruppers, R. et al. 161

quality control
    and co-branding 169
    and sublicensing 190, 192–4, 197
quality guarantee, trade mark as 16, 17, 20, 24–5, 143
QUICKY/QUICK, QUICKIES 63

Rao, A. 157
Reckitt & Colman Products Ltd v. Borden Inc 108
RED STAR/BLUE STAR 62
Reed Executive v. Reed Business Information 47, 73, 129, 130, 132–3, 136–7, 138, 147–8
REEF TM 42
REGENT ASSOCIATES/MASTER CARD 52–3
reputation 21, 22–3, 24–5, 26, 45, 56, 57
    and common field of activity 109–10
    and own name use 149
    and passing off 104, 115–16
    and specialty, diminishing role of 108, 120
    and transaction cost reduction 21–2
Rhone-Polenc Agro v. DeKalb Genetics Corporation 189
Road Tech v. UNISON 48
Roadrunner Case 48
'ROBERTSON'S TOFFEE TREAT' 115
Rodgers v. Rodgers 129–30, 132, 133, 138, 150–1
Rothnie, W. 177, 182
Roughton, Ashley 141–52
Royal Brunei Airlines v. Philip Tan Kok Ming 148
royalties, and sublicensing 190, 191
RUFFLES/RIFFLES 53, 54, 55

Sabatier 77–8
Sabel BV v. Puma 90, 92, 115–16, 122
Sadas SA v. OHIM (ARTHUR ET FELICIE) 53, 55, 56
Sainsbury/Fairtrade co-branding 160–1
Saunders v. Sun Life Assurance Company of Canada 151
Scandecor Development v. Scandecor Marketing 16, 17, 72, 146, 187, 193–4
Schechter, F. 33, 82, 120
Schwartz, J. 186

Schwarzkopf, Stefan 155–69
Schweppes/Cadbury merger 158
'Scottish Craft Butchers' collective mark 87
SDS Biotech UK Limited v. Power Agrichemicals Limited 149–50
Sea Island Cotton 86
search costs 20–1, 22, 142, 143
Sebastian, L. 36, 38, 39, 82
Selden, A. and R. Topp 158
Sennett, R. 22
SER/SER (FIG.MARK) 126
Sergio Rossi SpA v. OHIM; Sissi Rossi intervening 117
Shelden, A. and R. Scott Toop 167
Simon Fhima, Ilanah 3–11, 13, 95, 101–28, 148
Simonin, B. and J. Ruth 161
Singapore, Trade Marks Act (1998) 49
Singer Manufacturing v. Loog 33
Sir Robert McAlpine Plc v. Alfred McAlpine Plc 151
Sirena, SrL v. EDA 176, 182
Smith, Edward 71–8
So Young Yook 102
Société des Produits Nestlé SA v. OHIM (QUICKY/QUICK, QUICKIES) 63
Société des Produits Nestlé Société Anonyme v. Mars UK Limited 144
SOL DE AYALA/AYALA 53
Sony PSP/'Pink' co-branding 163, 164, 166
Southorn v. Reynolds 33, 34
Spa Esprit Pte v. Esprit International 49
Spain, trade mark registration and coexistence 57–8, 60
specialty
    backlash against 105–10
    and common field of activity 105–7, 112
    and common field of activity, rejection of 107–10
    and confusion 108, 113, 121
    and dilution, effect of 110–11, 112, 119–23
    diminishing role of, and reputation 108, 120
    global appreciation and interdependence 114–15

and passing off 103–12
principle and name sharing 101–28
prior to harmonization 112–14
reincarnation of 123–7
and unfair advantage 125–7
split marks
and common origin 176–9
and competition law 171–83
dominance and abuse by unilateral actors 181–3
and EC Treaty Article 81 171, 179–81, 183
intellectual property 171, 176–81
Stadler, Nelson, S. 168
Star Industries v. Yap Kwee Kor 45
Star Pads 90
Starbucks/Ethiopia coffee co-branding 160
Stilton 82, 83, 97
Stothers, C. 172
Stringfellow v. McCain 108–9
sublicensing 185–98
and competition 191–2
conceptual foundations of 185–90
definition 185–6
enforcement against, by licensor 188 and franchises 191
'have made' right and trade mark licensing 195–7
infringement settlement 188, 191–2
licensee as agent 186–7
and patent licensing 186, 189, 197
and quality control 190, 192–4, 197
and royalties 190, 191
territorial choice 191, 194
third party use, authorized 195–6
trade mark, purpose of entering into 190–2
validity, continuing 189–90
SUN CUT 144
Sutherland v. V2 Music 45
Swann, J. 23

Tadelis, S. 21
Tattinger SA v. Allbev Ltd 111
Tavener Rutledge v. Trexapalm 106
Tea Board of India v. The Republic of Tea, Inc. 91
Teletech Holdings, Inc. v. OHIM (TELETECH GLOBAL VENTURES/TELETECH INTERNATIONAL) 54, 56
Terrapin v. Terranova 177
Tetra Pak Int'l, SA v. EC Commission 174, 181
The European Ltd v. The Economist Newspaper Ltd. 74
Thomas Plant (Birmingham) Ltd v. Rousselon Freres et Cie (use of the mark Sabatier) 77–8
Thorneloe v. Hill 17
'three mark rule' 35–40, 41
TORTI/TOSTI 54
TOSCA BLU 117–18
totaljobs.com 132, 147–8
trade mark
association marks *see* association marks
and brands, relationship between 16–17, 157
collective and certification marks *see* collective and certification marks
concurrent use and exclusivity 34
as consumer reference point 20, 21–3, 24–5, 84
definition 3, 13, 15, 31, 113
differentiation of similar products 22, 26, 96, 113–14
dilution protection 95–6, 120–2
economic role of 19–26
flexibility as structuring device 18
honest concurrent use *see* honest concurrent use
monopoly, market strength and enforceability relationship 175
'origin', meaning of, in law 15–19
own name defence *see* own name defence
ownership, and commercial responsibility 15–17, 20
parallel imports of trademarked goods 19, 25
and prestige and social status 23
protection against dilution for similar and dissimilar products 120–3, 124–5
as quality guarantee 16, 17, 20, 24–5, 143
and reputation *see* reputation

208 Index

'three mark rule' 35–40, 41
and transaction cost reduction 20–1, 23, 24
use with the consent of the proprietor 71–3
trade mark disputes, coexistence in (EU) 51–70, 74–5
and ambiguity 60
and competition 53
consent to registration by owner of earlier mark 75
deception, danger of 78
and degree of distinctiveness 56
distinctive character of earlier mark and common name for product or service 68
distinctive character of earlier mark and damage or unfair advantage 57–8, 62–9, 96
distinctive character of later mark and damage or unfair advantage 63–4
equitable discretion 75–6
essential function role 77–8, 83–4
identical earlier marks 55
impact of coexistence on likelihood of confusion 52–6, 57–8, 59–60, 65, 66, 74–5, 93, 113
impact of coexistence of two conflicting marks 52–60
impact of earlier mark's scope of protection 61–9
impact of earlier mark's scope of protection, and behaviour of other providers 65
and market coexistence 54, 56, 95–6
national authorities' involvement 54, 55–6, 57
notional conflicts, avoidance of 76
private agreements 76–7
and reputation 56, 57, 96, 97
rights limitation conferred by registration 75
similarity of design and uniqueness 61–3
third party marks, impact of 61, 63, 69
trade mark filed by an agent 59
TRIPS Agreement
Articles 19(2) and 21 72

authorization and quality control 72
and Geographical Indications (GIs) 97
Paris Convention 87
and specialty rule 103
trade mark definition 13
TUDAPETROL/HandsLogo 95
Turton v. Turton 129

UK
association marks and test for confusion 90–1
Bill of Middlesex 32
certification marks 81–4
collective marks 86–9
Competition Act (1998) 171
deception, danger of 78
and EU Trade Marks Directive 45–6
Geographical Indications (GIs) 97
honest concurrent use 73–4
Intellectual Property Office (UK-IPO) and co-ownership of registered trade marks 71–8
Judicature Acts (1873 and 1875) 32
Legal Aid Board 85
licensing without quality control 72
Manchester cotton merchants and 'three mark rule' 35–6, 38
Merchandise Marks Act (1862) 31, 32, 38
passing off law 104, 106
passing off and own-name use 129–39
Patent Office consultation (2006) 48–9
Patents, Designs and Trade Marks Acts 36, 39
private agreements 76–7
Process in Courts of Law at Westminster Act (1832) 32
refusal grounds 74
Registry, equitable discretion of 75–6
Registry, essential function role before 77–8
'special circumstance' registration 45
specialty rule 103, 115, 122, 123–5
specialty rule and common field of activity 105–6, 107–8
sublicensing 187, 193

trade mark registration and
coexistence 61–2, 74–5
trade mark registration and likelihood
of confusion 52
Trade Marks Act (1905) 33, 34, 35,
38, 39, 40, 41–2, 43, 82
Trade Marks Act (1919) 35, 42, 43
Trade Marks Act (1938) 34, 38, 43,
45, 46, 73, 86, 112–14
Trade Marks Act (1994) 13, 17, 19,
40, 46, 47–8, 73–4, 75, 80, 81,
84, 85, 87, 113, 115, 129,
144–6, 193
Trade Marks (Amendment) Act
(1937) 43
Trade Marks Bill and honest
concurrent user 45–7, 48
Trade Marks Registration Act (1875)
31, 35, 39, 40
Trade Marks Registration
Amendment Act (1876) 36
Trade Marks (Relative Grounds)
Order (2007) 46, 49
'UL' (Underwriter's Laboratory)
certification mark 81, 83
Underhay, F. 42, 82
Unidoor v. Marks and Spencer 23
United Brands v. EC Commission 174
US
anti-dilution legislation 121
certification marks 80–1, 83, 86–7,
96
co-branding and marketing pressure
161–2
collective marks 86–7
Lanham Act 82, 121, 192
specialty rule 127
sublicensing 188, 189, 195–6
trade mark protection 160
Trademark Dilution Revision Act
(2006) 127
Trademark Trial and Appeal Board
(TTAB) 80

Vedial v. OHIM (HUBERT/SAINT-
HUBERT) 119

VENADO 63
Re Veregas 38
VICHY/VICHY CATALAN 60
Vidal, J. 162
Vincenzo Fusco v. OHIM (ENZO
FUSCO/ANTONIO FUSCO) 54
VIRGIN, and brand extensions 156

Wadlow, Christopher 33, 34, 80, 109,
129–39
In re Walkden Aerate Waters Co 36, 38,
39
Washburn, J. et al. 157
Waterford Wedgewood plc intervening
117
*Weight Watchers of Quebec v. Weight
Watchers International* 188
Whan Park, C. 161
Wheels 'R' Us Limited v. Geoffrey Inc.
123
White Rose 40
WiFi/WISI 90–1
Wilkof, Neil 185–98
Williamson, O. 18
*Windsurfing International, Inc. v. EC
Commission* 174
WINNIE THE POOH, and corporate
brand licensing 156
WIPO, Standing Committee on Trade
Marks 102, 118
Wombles 105–6
Wood, A. 65
'Woolmark' 81–2
*World Wide Fund for Nature v. World
Wrestling Federation
Entertainment* 187
Worthington TM 38
WTO
Geographical Indications (GIs) 97
specialty rule 103

YAGER/YAGA 59
Yoffie, D. 156

Zino Davidoff v. A & G Imports 19